Joan of Arc and the Hundred Years War

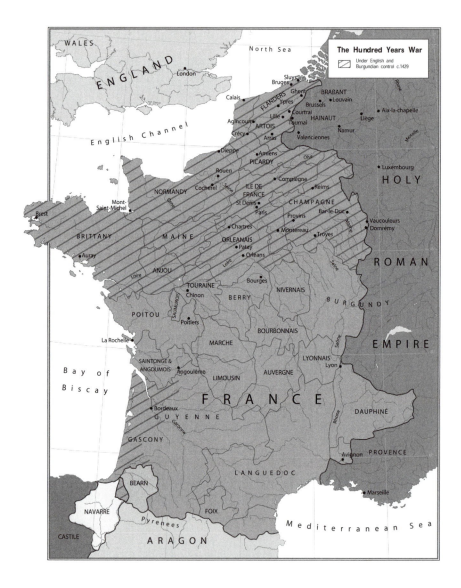

The Hundred Years War

Under English and Burgundian control c.1429

WALES

ENGLAND

London

North Sea

English Channel

Brest

Mont-Saint-Michel

BRITTANY

Auray

NORMANDY

Cocherel

Rouen

Dieppe

Calais

Sluys

Bruges

Ghent

Ypres

Lille

Agincourt

Crécy

Arras

ARTOIS

FLANDERS

Courtrai

Tournai

BRABANT

Brussels

Louvain

HAINAUT

Valenciennes

Namur

Liège

Aix-la-chapelle

Amiens

PICARDY

Oise

Compiègne

Reims

Luxembourg

HOLY

ILE DE
FRANCE

St Denis

Paris

Seine

CHAMPAGNE

Provins

Bar-le-Duc

Vaucouleurs

Domrémy

ROMAN

MAINE

Orne

Chartres

ORLEANAIS

Patay

Orléans

Montereau

Troyes

Seine

Bourges

NIVERNAIS

BURGUNDY

EMPIRE

ANJOU

Loire

TOURAINE

Chinon

BERRY

Saône

Loire

SARMUROIS

POITOU

Poitiers

MARCHE

BOURBONNAIS

AUVERGNE

LYONNAIS

Lyon

Saône

La Rochelle

SAINTONGE &
ANGOUMOIS

Angoulême

LIMOUSIN

Bay of
Biscay

Bordeaux

GUYENNE

Garonne

FRANCE

DAUPHINE

Rhône

GASCONY

LANGUEDOC

PROVENCE

Avignon

BEARN

NAVARRE

Pyrenees

FOIX

Marseille

CASTILE

ARAGON

Mediterranean Sea

Rhine

Meuse

Moselle

JOAN OF ARC AND THE HUNDRED YEARS WAR

Deborah A. Fraioli

Greenwood Guides to Historic Events of the Medieval World
Jane Chance, Series Editor

GREENWOOD PRESS
Westport, Connecticut · London

Library of Congress Cataloging-in-Publication Data

Fraioli, Deborah A., 1942–
    Joan of Arc and the Hundred Years War / Deborah A. Fraioli.
        p.   cm.—(Greenwood guides to historic events of the medieval world)
    Includes bibliographical references and index.
    ISBN 0–313–32458–1 (alk. paper)
    1. Joan, of Arc, Saint, 1412–1431.   2. Christian women saints—France—Biography.
3. Hundred Years War, 1339–1453.   4. France—History—Charles VII, 1422–1461.
I. Title.   II. Series.
    DC103.F68   2005
    944'.026'092—dc22   2004022531

British Library Cataloguing in Publication Data is available.

Library of Congress Catalog Card Number: 2004022531
ISBN: 0–313–32458–1

First published in 2005

Greenwood Press, 88 Post Road West, Westport, CT 06881
An imprint of Greenwood Publishing Group, Inc.
www.greenwood.com

Printed in the United States of America

The paper used in this book complies with the
Permanent Paper Standard issued by the National
Information Standards Organization (Z39.48–1984).

10 9 8 7 6 5 4 3 2 1

To Anthony

CONTENTS

ILLUSTRATIONS

SERIES FOREWORD

The Middle Ages are no longer considered the "Dark Ages" (as Petrarch termed them), sandwiched between the two enlightened periods of classical antiquity and the Renaissance. Often defined as a historical period lasting, roughly, from 500 to 1500 C.E., the Middle Ages span an enormous amount of time (if we consider the way other time periods have been constructed by historians) as well as an astonishing range of countries and regions very different from one another. That is, we call the "Middle" Ages the period beginning with the fall of the Roman Empire as a result of raids by northern European tribes of "barbarians" in the late antiquity of the fifth and sixth centuries and continuing until the advent of the so-called Italian and English renaissances, or rebirths of classical learning, in the fifteenth and sixteenth centuries. How this age could be termed either "Middle" or "Dark" is a mystery to those who study it. Certainly it is no longer understood as embracing merely the classical inheritance in the west or excluding eastern Europe, the Middle East, Asia, or even, as I would argue, North and Central America.

Whatever the arbitrary, archaic, and hegemonic limitations of these temporal parameters—the old-fashioned approach to them was that they were mainly not classical antiquity, and therefore not important—the Middle Ages represent a time when certain events occurred that have continued to affect modern cultures and that also, inevitably, catalyzed other medieval events. Among other important events, the Middle Ages saw the birth of Muhammad (c. 570–632) and his foundation of Islam in the seventh century as a rejection of Christianity which led to the imperial conflict between East and West in the eleventh and twelfth centuries. In western Europe in the Middle Ages the foundations for modern nationalism and modern law were laid and the concept of romantic love arose in the Middle Ages, this latter event partly one of the indirect consequences of the Crusades. With the shaping of national identity came the need to defend boundaries against invasion; so the castle emerged as a military outpost—whether in northern Africa, during the Crusades, or in Wales, in the eleventh century, to defend William of Normandy's newly acquired provinces—to satisfy that need. From Asia the invasions of Genghis Khan changed the literal and cultural shape of eastern and southern Europe.

In addition to triggering the development of the concept of chivalry and the knight, the Crusades influenced the European concepts of the lyric, music, and musical instruments; introduced to Europe an appetite for spices like cinnamon, coriander, and saffron and for dried fruits like prunes and figs as well as a desire for fabrics such as silk; and brought Aristotle to the European university through Arabic and then Latin translations. As a result of study of the "new" Aristotle, science and philosophy dramatically changed direction—and their emphasis on this material world helped to undermine the power of the Catholic Church as a monolithic institution in the thirteenth century.

By the twelfth century, with the centralization of the one (Catholic) Church, came a new architecture for the cathedral—the Gothic—to replace the older Romanesque architecture and thereby to manifest the Church's role in the community in a material way as well as in spiritual and political ways. Also from the cathedral as an institution and its need to dramatize the symbolic events of the liturgy came medieval drama—the mystery and the morality play, from which modern drama derives in large part. Out of the cathedral and its schools to train new priests (formerly handled by monasteries) emerged the medieval institution of the university. Around the same time, the community known as a town rose up in eastern and western Europe as a consequence of trade and the necessity for a new economic center to accompany the development of a bourgeoisie, or middle class. Because of the town's existence, the need for an itinerant mendicancy that could preach the teachings of the Church and beg for alms in urban centers sprang up.

Elsewhere in the world, in North America the eleventh-century settlement of Chaco Canyon by the Pueblo peoples created a social model like no other, one centered on ritual and ceremony in which the "priests" were key, but one that lasted barely two hundred years before it collapsed and its central structures were abandoned.

In addition to their influence on the development of central features of modern culture, the Middle Ages have long fascinated the modern age because of parallels that exist between the two periods. In both, terrible wars devastated whole nations and peoples; in both, incurable diseases plagued cities and killed large percentages of the world's population. In both periods, dramatic social and cultural changes took place as a result of these events: marginalized and overtaxed groups in societies rebelled against imperious governments; trade and a burgeoning middle class came to the fore; outside the privacy of the family, women began to have a greater role in Western societies and their cultures.

How different cultures of that age grappled with such historical change is the subject of the Greenwood Guides to Historic Events of the Medieval World. This series features individual volumes that illuminate key events in medieval world history. In some cases, an "event" occurred during a relatively limited time period. The troubadour lyric as a phenomenon, for example, flowered and died in the courts of Aquitaine in the twelfth century, as did the courtly romance in northern Europe a few decades later. The Hundred Years War between France and England generally took place during a precise time period, from the fourteenth to mid-fifteenth centuries.

In other cases, the event may have lasted for centuries before it played itself out: the medieval Gothic cathedral, for example, may have been first built in the twelfth century at Saint-Denis in Paris (c. 1140), but cathedrals, often of a slightly different style of Gothic architecture, were still being built in the fifteenth century all over Europe and, again, as the symbolic representation of a bishop's seat, or chair, are still being built today. And the medieval city, whatever its incarnation in the early Middle Ages, basically blossomed between the eleventh and thirteenth centuries as a result of social, economic, and cultural changes. Events— beyond a single dramatic historically limited happening—took longer to affect societies in the Middle Ages because of the lack of political and social centralization, the primarily agricultural and rural nature of most countries, difficulties in communication, and the distances between important cultural centers.

Each volume includes necessary tools for understanding such key events in the Middle Ages. Because of the postmodern critique of authority that modern societies underwent at the end of the twentieth century, students and scholars as well as general readers have come to mistrust the commentary and expertise of any one individual scholar or commentator and to identify the text as an arbiter of "history." For this reason, each book in the series can be described as a "library in a book." The intent of the series is to provide a quick, in-depth examination and current perspectives on the event to stimulate critical thinking as well as ready-reference materials, including primary documents and biographies of key individuals, for additional research.

Specifically, in addition to a narrative historical overview that places the specific event within the larger context of a contemporary perspective, five to seven developmental chapters explore related focused aspects of the event. In addition, each volume begins with a brief chronology and ends with a conclusion that discusses the consequences and impact of the event. There are also brief biographies of twelve to twenty key individuals (or places or buildings, in the book on the cathedral); primary documents from the period (for example, letters, chronicles, memoirs, diaries, and other writings) that illustrate states of mind or the turn of events at the time, whether historical, literary, scientific, or philosophical; illustrations (maps, diagrams, manuscript illuminations, portraits); a glossary of terms; and an annotated bibliography of important books, articles, films, and CD-ROMs available for additional research. An index concludes each volume.

No particular theoretical approach or historical perspective characterizes the series; authors developed their topics as they chose, generally taking into account the latest thinking on any particular event. The editors selected final topics from a list provided by an advisory board of high school teachers and public and school librarians. On the basis of nominations of scholars made by distinguished writers, the series editor also tapped internationally known scholars, both those with lifelong expertise and others with fresh new perspectives on a topic, to author the twelve books in the series. Finally, the series editor selected distinguished medievalists, art historians, and archaeologists to complete an advisory board: Gwinn Vivian, retired professor of archaeology at the University of Arizona Museum; Sharon Kinoshita, associate professor of French literature, world literature, and cultural studies at the University of California–Santa Cruz; Nancy Wu, associate museum educator at the Metropolitan Museum of Art, The Cloisters, New York City; and Christo-

pher A. Snyder, chair of the Department of History and Politics at Mary-
mount University.

In addition to examining the event and its effects on the specific cultures involved through an array of documents and an overview, each volume provides a new approach to understanding these twelve events.
Treated in the series are: the Black Death; the Crusades; Eleanor of
Aquitaine, courtly love, and the troubadours; Genghis Khan and Mongol rule; Joan of Arc and the Hundred Years War; Magna Carta; the medieval castle, from the eleventh to the sixteenth centuries; the medieval
cathedral; the medieval city, especially in the thirteenth century; medieval science and technology; Muhammad and the rise of Islam; and the
Puebloan society of Chaco Canyon.

The Black Death, by Joseph Byrne, isolates the event of the epidemic
of bubonic plague in 1347–52 as having had a signal impact on medieval
Europe. It was, however, only the first of many related such episodes involving variations of pneumonic and septicemic plague that recurred over
350 years. Taking a twofold approach to the Black Death, Byrne investigates both the modern research on bubonic plague, its origins and
spread, and also medieval documentation and illustration in diaries, artistic works, and scientific and religious accounts. The demographic, economic, and political effects of the Black Death are traced in one chapter,
the social and psychological patterns of life in another, and cultural ex-
pressions in art and ritual in a third. Finally, Byrne investigates why
bubonic plague disappeared and why we continue to be fascinated by it.
Documents included provide a variety of medieval accounts—Byzantine,
Arabic, French, German, English, and Italian—several of which are
translated for the first time.

The Crusades, by Helen Nicholson, presents a balanced account of various crusades, or military campaigns, invented by Catholic or "Latin"
Christians during the Middle Ages against those they perceived as threats
to their faith. Such expeditions included the Crusades to the Holy Land
between 1095 and 1291, expeditions to the Iberian Peninsula, the "crusade" to northeastern Europe, the Albigensian Crusades and the Hussite
crusades—both against the heretics—and the crusades against the Ottoman Turks (in the Balkans). Although Muslim rulers included the concept of jihâd (a conflict fought for God against evil or his enemies) in
their wars in the early centuries of Islam, it had become less important
in the late tenth century. It was not until the middle decades of the

twelfth century that jihâd was revived in the wars with the Latin Christian Crusaders. Most of the Crusades did not result in victory for the Latin Christians, although Nicholson concedes they slowed the advance of Islam. After Jerusalem was destroyed in 1291, Muslim rulers did permit Christian pilgrims to travel to holy sites. In the Iberian Peninsula, Christian rulers replaced Muslim rulers, but Muslims, Jews, and dissident Christians were compelled to convert to Catholicism. In northeastern Europe, the Teutonic Order's campaigns allowed German colonization that later encouraged twentieth-century German claims to land and led to two world wars. The Albigensian Crusade wiped out thirteenth-century aristocratic families in southern France who held to the Cathar heresy, but the Hussite crusades in the 1420s failed to eliminate the Hussite heresy. As a result of the wars, however, many positive changes occurred: Arab learning founded on Greek scholarship entered western Europe through the acquisition of an extensive library in Toledo, Spain, in 1085; works of western European literature were inspired by the holy wars; trade was encouraged and with it the demand for certain products; and a more favorable image of Muslim men and women was fostered by the crusaders' contact with the Middle East. Nicholson also notes that America may have been discovered because Christopher Columbus avoided a route that had been closed by Muslim conquests and that the Reformation may have been advanced because Martin Luther protested against the crusader indulgence in his Ninety-five Theses (1517).

Eleanor of Aquitaine, Courtly Love, and the Troubadours, by ffiona Swabey, singles out the twelfth century as the age of the individual, in which a queen like Eleanor of Aquitaine could influence the development of a new social and artistic culture. The wife of King Louis VII of France and later the wife of his enemy Henry of Anjou, who became king of England, she patronized some of the troubadours, whose vernacular lyrics celebrated the personal expression of emotion and a passionate declaration of service to women. Love, marriage, and the pursuit of women were also the subject of the new romance literature, which flourished in northern Europe and was the inspiration behind concepts of courtly love. However, as Swabey points out, historians in the past have misjudged Eleanor, whose independent spirit fueled their misogynist attitudes. Similarly, Eleanor's divorce and subsequent stormy marriage have colored ideas about medieval "love courts" and courtly love, interpretations of which have now been challenged by scholars. The twelfth century is set in context, with commentaries on feudalism, the tenets of Christianity, and the position of women, as well as summaries of the cultural and philosophical background, the cathedral schools and universities, the influence of Islam, the revival of classical learning, vernacular literature, and Gothic architecture. Swabey provides two biographical chapters on Eleanor and two on the emergence of the troubadours and the origin of courtly love through verse romances. Within this latter subject Swabey also details the story of Abelard and Heloise, the treatise of Andreas Capellanus (André the Chaplain) on courtly love, and Arthurian legend as a subject of courtly love.

Genghis Khan and Mongol Rule, by George Lane, identifies the rise to power of Genghis Khan and his unification of the Mongol tribes in the thirteenth century as a kind of globalization with political, cultural, economic, mercantile, and spiritual effects akin to those of modern globalization. Normally viewed as synonymous with barbarian destruction, the rise to power of Genghis Khan and the Mongol hordes is here understood as a more positive event that initiated two centuries of regeneration and creativity. Lane discusses the nature of the society of the Eurasian steppes in the twelfth and thirteenth centuries into which Genghis Khan was born; his success at reshaping the relationship between the northern pastoral and nomadic society with the southern urban, agriculturalist society; and his unification of all the Turco-Mongol tribes in 1206 before his move to conquer Tanquit Xixia, the Chin of northern China, and the lands of Islam. Conquered thereafter were the Caucasus, the Ukraine, the Crimea, Russia, Siberia, Central Asia, Afghanistan, Pakistan, and Kashmir. After his death his sons and grandsons continued, conquering Korea, Persia, Armenia, Mesopotamia, Azerbaijan, and eastern Europe—chiefly Kiev, Poland, Moravia, Silesia, and Hungary—until 1259, the end of the Mongol Empire as a unified whole. Mongol rule created a golden age in the succeeding split of the Empire into two, the Yuan dynasty of greater China and the Il-Khanate dynasty of greater Iran. Lane adds biographies of important political figures, famous names such as Marco Polo, and artists and scientists. Documents derive from universal histories, chronicles, local histories and travel accounts, official government documents, and poetry, in French, Armenian, Georgian, Chinese, Persian, Arabic, Chaghatai Turkish, Russian, and Latin.

Joan of Arc and the Hundred Years War, by Deborah Fraioli, presents the Hundred Years War between France and England in the fourteenth and fifteenth centuries within contexts whose importance has sometimes been blurred or ignored in past studies. An episode of apparently only moderate significance, a feudal lord's seizure of his vassal's land for harboring his mortal enemy, sparked the Hundred Years War, yet on the face of it the event should not have led inevitably to war. But the lord was the king of France and the vassal the king of England, who resented losing his claim to the French throne to his Valois cousin. The land in dispute, extending roughly from Bordeaux to the Pyrenees mountains, was crucial coastline for the economic interests of both kingdoms. The series of skirmishes, pitched battles, truces, stalemates, and diplomatic wrangling that resulted from the confiscation of English Aquitaine by the French form the narrative of this Anglo-French conflict, which was in fact not given the name Hundred Years War until the nineteenth century.

Fraioli emphasizes how dismissing women's inheritance and succession rights came at the high price of unleashing discontent in their male heirs, including Edward III, Robert of Artois, and Charles of Navarre. Fraioli also demonstrates the centrality of side issues, such as Flemish involvement in the war, the peasants' revolts that resulted from the costs of the war, and Joan of Arc's unusually clear understanding of French "sacred kingship." Among the primary sources provided are letters from key players such as Edward III, Etienne Marcel, and Joan of Arc; a supply list for towns about to be besieged; and a contemporary poem by the celebrated scholar and court poet Christine de Pizan in praise of Joan of Arc.

Magna Carta, by Katherine Drew, is a detailed study of the importance of the Magna Carta in comprehending England's legal and constitutional history. Providing a model for the rights of citizens found in the United States Declaration of Independence and Constitution's first ten amendments, the Magna Carta has had a role in the legal and parliamentary history of all modern states bearing some colonial or government connection with the British Empire. Constructed at a time when modern nations began to appear, in the early thirteenth century, the Magna Carta (signed in 1215) presented a formula for balancing the liberties of the people with the power of modern governmental institutions. This unique English document influenced the growth of a form of law (the English common law) and provided a vehicle for the evolution of representative (parliamentary) government. Drew demonstrates how the Magna Carta came to be—the roles of the Church, the English towns, barons, common law, and the parliament in its making—as well as how myths concerning its provisions were established. Also provided are biographies of Thomas Becket, Charlemagne, Frederick II, Henry II and his sons, Innocent III, and many other key figures, and primary documents—among them, the Magna Cartas of 1215 and 1225, and the Coronation Oath of Henry I.

Medieval Castles, by Marilyn Stokstad, traces the historical, political, and social function of the castle from the late eleventh century to the sixteenth by means of a typology of castles. This typology ranges from the early "motte and bailey"—military fortification, and government and economic center—to the palace as an expression of the castle owners' needs and purposes. An introduction defines the various contexts—military, political, economic, and social—in which the castle appeared in the Middle Ages. A concluding interpretive essay suggests the impact of the castle and its symbolic role as an idealized construct lasting until the modern day.

Medieval Cathedrals, by William Clark, examines one of the chief contributions of the Middle Ages, at least from an elitist perspective—that is, the religious architecture found in the cathedral ("chair" of the bishop) or great church, studied in terms of its architecture, sculpture, and stained glass. Clark begins with a brief contextual history of the concept of the bishop and his role within the church hierarchy, the growth of the church in the early Christian era and its affiliation with the bishop (deriving from that of the bishop of Rome), and the social history of cathedrals. Because of economic and political conflicts among the three authorities who held power in medieval towns—the king, the bishop, and the cathedral clergy—cathedral construction and maintenance always remained a vexed issue, even though the owners—the cathedral clergy— usually held the civic responsibility for the cathedral. In an interpretive essay, Clark then focuses on Reims Cathedral in France, because both it and the bishop's palace survive, as well as on contemporary information about surrounding buildings. Clark also supplies a historical overview on the social, political, and religious history of the cathedral in the Middle Ages: an essay on patrons, builders, and artists; aspects of cathedral construction (which was not always successful); and then a chapter on Romanesque and Gothic cathedrals and a "gazetteer" of twenty-five important examples.

The Medieval City, by Norman J. G. Pounds, documents the origin of the medieval city in the flight from the dangers or difficulties found in the country, whether economic, physically threatening, or cultural. Identifying the attraction of the city in its urbanitas, its "urbanity," or the way of living in a city, Pounds discusses first its origins in prehistoric and classical Greek urban revolutions. During the Middle Ages, the city grew primarily between the eleventh and thirteenth centuries, remaining essentially the same until the Industrial Revolution. Pounds provides chapters on the medieval city's planning, in terms of streets and structures; life in the medieval city; the roles of the Church and the city government in its operation; the development of crafts and trade in the city; and the issues of urban health, wealth, and welfare. Concluding with the role of the city in history, Pounds suggests that the value of the city depended upon its balance of social classes, its need for trade and profit to satisfy personal desires through the accumulation of wealth and its consequent economic power, its political power as a representative body within the kingdom, and its social role in the rise of literacy and education and in nationalism. Indeed, the concept of a middle class, a bourgeoisie, derives from the city—from the bourg, or "borough." According to Pounds, the rise of modern civilization would not have taken place without the growth of the city in the Middle Ages and its concomitant artistic and cultural contribution.

Medieval Science and Technology, by Elspeth Whitney, examines science and technology from the early Middle Ages to 1500 within the context of the classical learning that so influenced it. She looks at institutional history, both early and late, and what was taught in the medieval schools and, later, the universities (both of which were overseen by the Catholic Church). Her discussion of Aristotelian natural philosophy illustrates its impact on the medieval scientific worldview. She presents chapters on the exact sciences, meaning mathematics, astronomy, cosmology, astrology, statics, kinematics, dynamics, and optics; the biological and earth sciences, meaning chemistry and alchemy, medicine, zoology, botany, geology and meteorology, and geography; and technology. In an interpretive conclusion, Whitney demonstrates the impact of medieval science on the preconditions and structure that permitted the emergence of the modern world. Most especially, technology transformed an agricultural society into a more commercial and engine-driven society: waterpower and inventions like the blast furnace and horizontal loom turned iron working and cloth making into manufacturing operations. The invention of the mechanical clock helped to organize human activities through timetables rather than through experiential perception and thus facilitated the advent of modern life. Also influential in the establishment of a middle class were the inventions of the musket and pistol and the printing press. Technology, according to Whitney, helped advance the habits of mechanization and precise methodology. Her biographies introduce major medieval Latin and Arabic and classical natural philosophers and scientists. Extracts from various kinds of scientific treatises allow a window into the medieval concept of knowledge.

The Puebloan Society of Chaco Canyon, by Paul Reed, is unlike other volumes in this series, whose historic events boast a long-established historical record. Reed's study offers instead an original reconstruction of the Puebloan Indian society of Chaco, in what is now New Mexico, but originally extending into Colorado, Utah, and Arizona. He is primarily interested in its leaders, ritual and craft specialists, and commoners during the time of its chief flourishing, in the eleventh and twelfth centuries, as understood from archaeological data alone. To this new material he adds biographies of key Euro-American archaeologists and other individuals from the nineteenth and twentieth centuries who have made important discoveries about Chaco Canyon. Also provided are documents of archaeological description and narrative from early explorers' journals and archaeological reports, narratives, and monographs. In his overview chapters, Reed discusses the cultural and environmental setting of Chaco Canyon; its history (in terms of exploration and research); the Puebloan society and how it emerged chronologically; the Chaco society and how it appeared in 1100 c.e.; the "Outliers," or outlying communities of Chaco; Chaco as a ritual center of the eleventh-century Pueblo world; and, finally, what is and is not known about Chaco society. Reed concludes that ritual and ceremony played an important role in Chacoan society and that ritual specialists, or priests, conducted ceremonies, maintained ritual artifacts, and charted the ritual calendar. Its social organization matches no known social pattern or type: it was complicated, multiethnic, centered around ritual and ceremony, and without any overtly hierarchical political system. The Chacoans were ancestors to the later Pueblo people, part of a society that rose, fell, and evolved within a very short time period.

The Rise of Islam, by Matthew Gordon, introduces the early history of the Islamic world, beginning in the late sixth century with the career of the Prophet Muhammad (c. 570–c. 632) on the Arabian Peninsula. From Muhammad's birth in an environment of religious plurality—Christianity, Judaism, and Zoroastrianism, along with paganism, were joined by Islam—to the collapse of the Islamic empire in the early tenth century, Gordon traces the history of the Islamic community. The book covers topics that include the life of the Prophet and divine revelation (the Qur'an) to the formation of the Islamic state, urbanization in the Islamic Near East, and the extraordinary culture of Islamic letters and scholarship. In addition to a historical overview, Gordon examines the Caliphate and early Islamic Empire, urban society and economy, and the emergence, under the Abbasid Caliphs, of a "world religious tradition" up to the year 925 c.e.

As editor of this series I am grateful to have had the help of Benjamin Burford, an undergraduate Century Scholar at Rice University assigned to me in 2002–2004 for this project; Gina Weaver, a third-year graduate student in English; and Cynthia Duffy, a second-year graduate student in English, who assisted me in target-reading select chapters from some of these books in an attempt to define an audience. For this purpose I would also like to thank Gale Stokes, former dean of humanities at Rice University, for the 2003 summer research grant and portions of the 2003–2004 annual research grant from Rice University that served that end.

This series, in its mixture of traditional and new approaches to medieval history and cultures, will ensure opportunities for dialogue in the classroom in its offerings of twelve different "libraries in books." It should also propel discussion among graduate students and scholars by means of the gentle insistence throughout on the text as primal. Most especially, it invites response and further study. Given its mixture of East and West, North and South, the series symbolizes the necessity for global understanding, both of the Middle Ages and in the postmodern age.

Jane Chance, Series Editor
Houston, Texas
February 19, 2004

PREFACE

The Hundred Years War is the invention of historians living long after the time of the war itself. There is no truly compelling reason for lumping the conflicts that afflicted France and England between 1337 and 1453 together and then acting as if they constituted a single war, with an exact beginning and end, and a single character. It is a term of convenience, invented in the nineteenth century, and inaccurate at that, since the war lasted 116 years. One might even ask how *many* hundred-year wars there were and why only one is distinguished by giving it a name. Should the real starting point be considered the Norman invasion of 1066, when the contradictory roles of being simultaneously French duke and English king first arose? Or did the war begin in 1152 when Eleanor of Aquitaine retrieved her rich estates from her first husband, the king of France, and brought her inheritance to her second husband, Henry II, king of England? Could the initial salvo have been the Treaty of Paris in 1259 whereby the king of England became the liegeman of the king of France for Aquitaine? The event that in fact sparked the Hundred Years War in 1337 was the seizure of Aquitaine by the king of France, but it was already the third such seizure in recent years.

More to the point, no doubt, in defining the chronological limits of the Hundred Years War is the opinion of those people who lived through the events. We can set aside the story of the man who told his creditor, early in the war, that he would pay off his debt "six years after the war ends." Other witnesses, however, tend to confirm the modern chronology of the war. A French poet writing in 1389 spoke of desolation that had lasted fifty-two years (thus since 1337), and a secretary of Henry VI complained in 1435 (in the war's ninety-eighth year) that the Franco-

English conflict had produced irreparable harm "for one hundred years." The war cannot be defined as continuous conflict, yet the domestic crises and secondary hostilities that continued during periods of truce were sometimes as significant as the broader military contest. No fewer than a half-dozen truces were arranged, the longest one running uneasily for thirty-five years, but actual peace remained elusive and treaties of any sort were easily broken, even violated while the negotiations were still under way.

What we can be sure of, at least, is that those living toward the end of the war knew that the suffering they witnessed had gone on for generations and that the devastation to France had bled the population nearly dry. No one knew this better than Joan of Arc, who swore in the name of Jesus that the English would be booted out of *all* France. It has been said with some justice that Joan of Arc both created nationalism and arose because of it. The anonymous poet of the twelfth-century *Chanson de Roland* could speak of "sweet France" as if it were an intelligible entity. But the truth is that for centuries in France strong feudal princes prevented the monarchy from creating the centralized government or geographical unity that we now associate with the modern French state. The dukes of Burgundy held out the longest as independent rulers, but eventually that elusive blueprint for France, which Joan of Arc referred to as all the cities "that *should* belong to the holy kingdom," came into being. It is really this story that the Hundred Years War recounts.

The topics of the theme chapters in this book have been selected to cover as many different aspects as possible of a war that was in fact complex and all embracing. Chapter 1 explores the origins of the war, weighing the feudal quarrel over Aquitaine against the problem of dynastic succession. Chapter 2 describes the age of popular rebellion, stimulated by, and therefore coincident with, the Hundred Years War. Chapter 3 examines chivalry's effect on fourteenth- and fifteenth-century warfare. Chapter 4 presents an overview of the religion of the monarchy and the role of sacred kingship in building the French monarchy. Chapter 5 attempts, despite the scant evidence, to determine how Joan of Arc knew and understood the Hundred Years War in which she was a participant. The biographies of personalities and the primary documents have been selected to make people and events in this distant war seem less remote and more recognizably human (despite the brutality) for the modern reader.

I would like to express my gratitude to series editor Jane Chance, Greenwood Press editors Kevin Ohe and Michael Hermann, and my chair at Simmons College, Dolores Benítez Peláez, for their patience, help, and understanding as I tried to complete more projects at once than was reasonable. My deepest appreciation is reserved for my husband, Anthony, whose support throughout was peerless.

CHRONOLOGY

1066	William I the Conqueror, duke of Normandy, conquers Anglo-Saxon England.
1152	Annulment of marriage of Louis VII of France and Eleanor of Aquitaine.
1154	Henry II Plantagenet succeeds to throne of England. Becomes vassal of king of France for new wife Eleanor's province of Aquitaine.
1259	Treaty of Paris. Louis IX of France cedes Aquitaine to Henry III of England, but demands homage, a root cause of the Hundred Years War.
1302	Battle of the Golden Spurs. Flemish infantry, rebelling against suzerain Philip IV of France, defeats French cavalry under Robert of Artois.
1323	Maritime Flanders rebels against Flemish count Louis of Nevers, vassal of French king.
1327	Edward III ascends throne of England, beginning fifty-year reign.
1328	Philip VI succeeds to throne of France. First king of Valois dynasty. Edward III's right to French throne is denied.
	French victory against Flemish rebels at Cassel. Louis of Nevers regains control of Flanders.

1329	June 6: Edward III compelled to pay homage to Philip VI for Aquitaine, as vassal of king of France.
1336	Pope Benedict XII cancels crusade. Philip VI uses idled fleet to threaten southern England.
	English apply pressure to Flanders by initiating wool embargo against Flanders.
1337	Philip VI's confiscation of Aquitaine starts Hundred Years War.
1338	January 3: Activist Jacob van Artevelde named captain of Ghent.
	July 22: Edward III lands at Antwerp to begin war against France.
1340	February 6: Edward formally declares self king of France at Ghent.
	June 24: England reduces threat to shores by major naval victory against France at Sluys.
	September 25: Truce of Esplechin ends military stalemate between Edward III and Philip VI.
1341	Duke John III of Brittany dies. Begins two decades of struggle over Breton succession, affecting balance of power in Hundred Years War.
1345	Jacob van Artevelde murdered.
1346	Edward III inflicts major defeat on Philip VI at Crécy. Dismounted English army defeats disorganized French cavalry charge.
1347	Edward III takes Calais after inhabitants hold out nearly a year.
	Onset of epidemic known as Black Death accentuates socioeconomic impact of Hundred Years War.
1350	Philip VI dies. John II the Good succeeds to throne of France.

1351	John the Good marries daughter to Charles of Navarre. Grants county of Angoulême to Charles of Spain, which provokes lasting hostility of son-in-law.
1354	France approves preliminary peace agreement with England. Devastating terms for France are finally rejected by the French.
	January 8: Assassination of Charles of Spain, constable of France, by Charles of Navarre's men.
1356	Charles of Navarre seized and companions murdered at banquet held by dauphin Charles at Rouen. Questions raised about dauphin's loyalty. Philip of Navarre vows to carry on brother Charles' war against John II.
	September 19: English victory by Edward, the Black Prince, at Poitiers. Mounted English army defeats dismounted French. John II captured.
1358	February 22: Etienne Marcel, provost of the merchants of Paris, maneuvers murder of dauphin Charles' two closest advisers, the marshals of Champagne and Normandy, in the royal bedchambers.
	May–June: Two-week peasant uprising, known as *Jacquerie*, in region of Paris.
	Murder of Etienne Marcel.
1359	Edward III begins campaign in Northern France, seeking coronation at Reims.
1360	Failed Reims campaign ends in Treaty of Brétigny, signed at Calais on October 24. Edward III never returns to France. End of first phase of Hundred Years War.
1364	John the Good dies in English captivity. Charles V succeeds to throne.

May 16: Battle of Cocherel. Bertrand du Guesclin defeats Charles of Navarre by feigned withdrawal.

September 29: French-backed Charles of Blois killed at battle of Auray, deciding Breton succession in favor of Jean IV of Montfort. Twenty-year war of Breton succession ends. Truce concluded following year.

1367	Black Prince defeats du Guesclin at Nájera. Pedro the Cruel of Castile thus gains ascendancy over half-brother Henry of Trastamara.
1369	Charles V confiscates Aquitaine. Edward III reassumes title "king of France." War reopens.
1370	Charles V appoints Bertrand du Guesclin constable of France.
1376	Black Prince dies.
1377	Edward III dies. Richard II succeeds to throne of England.
1378	A wave of popular revolutions begins in Europe lasting four years.
1379	Rebellion begins in Flanders including Ghent, Ypres, and Bruges.
1380	Charles V dies. Son Charles VI succeeds to throne of France.
	Thirty-five-year cessation of fighting in Hundred Years War begins.
1381	Wat Tyler leads Peasants' Revolt.
1382	January 26: Philip van Artevelde, son of Jacob van Artevelde, becomes captain of Ghent.
	February: Rebellion in Rouen known as the *Harelle*.
	March: Rebellion in Paris known as the *Maillotins*.

November 27: Philip the Bold, duke of Burgundy, crushes three-year rebellion in Flanders by victory at Roosebeke.

1383	English forces under Henry Despenser launch doomed offensive to aid Ghent against Philip the Bold, taking only Flemish seacoast to Ypres.
1384	Louis II of Male, count of Flanders, dies.
1385	December 18: Peace of Tournai. Ghent finally submits to Philip the Bold, duke of Burgundy.
	Marriage of Charles VI to Isabeau of Bavaria.
1386	Philip the Bold's invasion of England is postponed.
1388	August 18: Philip the Bold drops plan to invade England, agreeing to truce.
1389	Truce of Leulinghen between France and England.
1392	August 5: Onset of Charles VI's madness near Le Mans.
1396	March 9: Richard II of England weds Isabella, the six-year-old daughter of Charles VI of France, by proxy, reducing prospect of new Anglo-French hostilities.
	Truce of Leulinghen between France and England is extended.
	Second phase of Hundred Years War ends.
	Crusade led by heir to Burgundy (future John the Fearless) is crushed by Ottoman Turks at Nicopolis in eastern Europe.
1399	Richard II deposed. Henry IV ascends English throne.
1407	Assassination of Louis, duke of Orleans, by cousin John the Fearless, duke of Burgundy. Beginning of French civil war.

1410	Charles of Orleans marries daughter of Bernard VII, count of Armagnac.
1413	Cabochian revolution in Paris. John the Fearless flees Paris, leaving capital to Armagnac faction.
	Henry IV dies. Henry V succeeds.
1414	Henry V reasserts England's claim to the French throne.
1415	Henry V renews war in France and commands great victory at Agincourt.
1416	Bernard VII, count of Armagnac, made constable of France.
1417	Henry V leads second campaign in Normandy.
	John the Fearless subdues numerous French cities and surrounds Paris.
1418	Paris falls to the Burgundians. Dauphin Charles (future Charles VII) flees capital.
1419	January 13: Rouen forced to surrender to Henry V.
	John the Fearless, duke of Burgundy, assassinated on bridge at Montereau. New duke, Philip the Good, aligns self with England.
1420	Treaty of Troyes cedes kingdom of France to England.
1422	Death in same year of English (Henry V) and French (Charles VI) monarchs.
1429	Joan of Arc's interview with dauphin Charles at Chinon.
	May 8: Victory over English at Orleans.
	June: Loire campaign successfully retakes Meung-sur-Loire, Beaugency, and Patay.

July 17: Charles VII crowned king at Reims following successful campaign through Burgundian territory.

1430   May 23: Capture of Joan of Arc at Compiègne.

1431   May 30: Joan of Arc burned at Rouen after conviction for heresy.

1435   Peace of Arras ends French civil war.

1436   Charles VII retakes Paris.

1450   Normandy retaken.

1453   Hundred Years War ends. Charles takes full possession of Aquitaine. Only Calais remains in English hands.

Chronology of French and English Kings

FRANCE

Direct Capetians

Hugh Capet	987–996
Robert II the Pious	996–1031
Henry I	1031–1059
Philip I	1059–1108
Louis VI	1108–1137
Louis VII	1137–1180
Philip II Augustus	1180–1223
Louis VIII	1223–1226
Louis IX (Saint Louis)	1226–1270
Philip III	1270–1285
Philip IV the Fair	1285–1314
Louis X	1314–1316
John I the Posthumus	1316
Philip V the Tall	1316–1322
Charles IV the Fair	1322–1328

Valois Dynasty

Philip VI of Valois	1328–1350
John II the Good	1350–1364
Charles V the Wise	1364–1380
Charles VI	1380–1422
Charles VII	1422–1461

ENGLAND

Normans

William the Conqueror	1066–1087
William II	1087–1100
Henry I	1100–1135
Stephen	1135–1154

Plantagenet Dynasty

Henry II of Anjou	1154–1189
Richard I	1189–1199
John	1199–1216
Henry III	1216–1272
Edward I	1272–1307
Edward II	1307–1327
Edward III	1327–1377
Richard II	1377–1399

House of Lancaster

Henry IV	1399–1413
Henry V	1413–1422
Henry VI	1422–1461, 1470–1471

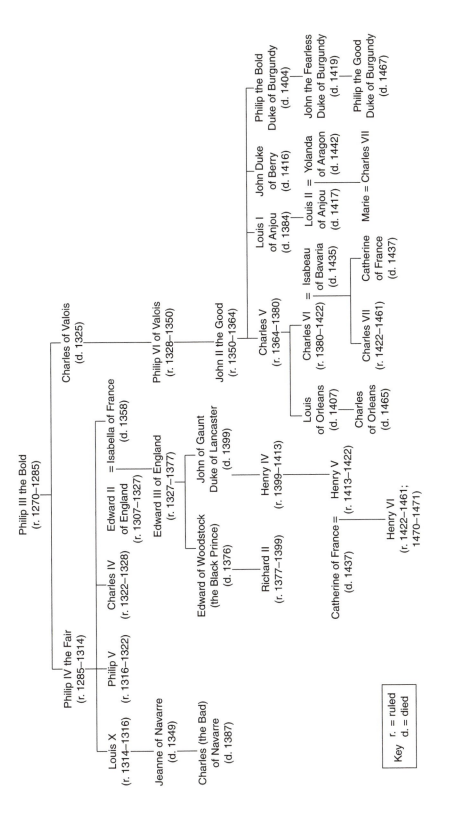

GENEALOGY OF FRENCH AND ENGLISH RULERS DURING THE PERIOD OF THE HUNDRED YEARS WAR

HISTORICAL
OVERVIEW

The Hundred Years War is the term used to refer to the many years of war (1337–1453) during which England and France clashed over England's possessions in present-day France. By the time the war ended, only Calais, a town on the English Channel, remained of the vast continental possessions once held by England. The deepest roots of the war can be found in the political situation resulting from William the Conqueror's conquest of England in 1066. William, duke of Normandy, prior to the conquest, created a perplexing situation for future kings of England. While English kings ruled their own realm as sovereign rulers, they were vassals of the king of France for the duchy of Normandy, and consequently the inferiors of their French suzerain (overlord). This was an unintended complication of medieval feudalism, which required the duke to pledge homage to his suzerain for the lands he held as fiefs. It was a weakness in the system that two kings who were otherwise equals could simultaneously be unequal as vassal and suzerain.

No serious problem developed until 1152, when Eleanor of Aquitaine, queen of France, who had inherited the family duchy of Aquitaine, was divorced by her husband Louis VII, king of France. Shortly thereafter, she married Henry, duke of Normandy and count of Anjou, who became King Henry II of England in 1154. With the newly acquired Aquitaine, which Eleanor brought to the marriage, the English monarch ruled over possessions that included over half of France and all of England. Modern historians refer to these vast territories as the Angevin Empire, the continental portion of which included western France as far south as the Pyrenees.

It was an inevitability, subject only to opportunity, that France would challenge England for its continental possessions, given France's geographical proximity to this prosperous region with its western seaports, salt, and Bordeaux vineyards. It was Philip Augustus (r. 1180–1223) who devised a pretext to allow the seizure of all England's French lands. By the end of Philip's reign, the Angevin Empire had been dissolved. Throughout the course of the Hundred Years War, however, English kings, hardly reconciled to the loss, intermittently embraced the dream of reclaiming their ancient empire.

It fell to Philip Augustus' grandson Saint Louis (Louis IX) to sign the peace agreement that officially dismantled the Angevin Empire. The rival kings, also brothers-in-law, appear to have been genuinely committed to peace, but Louis was perhaps too generous in his offer to hand over an enlarged Aquitaine to Henry III of England in return for peace and Henry's homage. When Louis was criticized for the redistribution finally approved in the Treaty of Paris (1258), he declared himself satisfied. From Louis' perspective the resolution of the Anglo-French conflict would "create affection between my children and his, who are first cousins."[1] The treaty also allowed Louis the freedom to launch a new crusade. Henry received Aquitaine but, importantly, it was converted into a French fief for which the kings of England would be required to do homage. Louis also obtained Henry's permanent renunciation of the conquered provinces of Normandy, Anjou, Maine, and Poitou.

The Treaty of Paris did not extinguish resentment between France and England. Furthermore, France and England had long been involved in matters beyond their borders affecting their attitudes to one another as well as the balance of power between them. Flanders, a French fief since the ninth century, was obedient only insofar as independent rule in the county went unthreatened. In the thirteenth century, when Philip Augustus interfered in the naming of Flemish counts, Flanders rebelled. The rebellion was brought under control at the battle of Bouvines (1214). In the following century, Philip the Fair failed to subdue a similar rebellion. The troops Philip sent into Flanders suffered a humiliating defeat at Courtrai (1302), forcing recognition of Flemish autonomy. This blow to French prestige made England more confident in its rivalry with France, but the Franco-Flemish peace signed at Athis (1305) punished the rebels with a large indemnity and the loss of the towns of Lille, Douai, and Bethune. The defeated French walked away with the spoils of a victor. Flanders' determination to recover the three towns became an integral part of the greater problems of the Hundred Years War.

France's strained relations with Flanders found its equivalent in England's strained relations with Scotland. Not as strategic geographically as Flanders, Scotland had nonetheless been a perennial rival of England, a situation aggravated after 1295 when France signed its first alliance with Scotland. England experienced a humiliation similar to that of the French at Courtrai, when Scotland defeated Edward II at Bannockburn in 1314. Since then England had been unable to repress the Scottish urge for independence.

While these problems festered in Flanders and Scotland, Aquitaine remained the real bone of contention. French kings, as suzerains, controlled their English vassals through the homage ceremony, which required renewal at the start of each new reign. This was a continual irritant to English kings, especially when the short reigns of the sons of Philip the Fair—Louis X, Philip V, and Charles IV—called for three ceremonies in twelve years. But France wanted more than control; it had an appetite for acquisition. It was as if French kings, in the general move of the monarchy toward centralization, were exploiting the feudal relationship to the point where they could extinguish it, ending England's presence in France. A second mechanism of interference was judicial in nature. France wielded control over the local Gascon inhabitants by declaring the Parlement of Paris to be the court of last resort, which gave the French courts the possibility of overturning English verdicts. Those who brought grievances against their English suzerain to French courts stood to gain a decision in their favor, disposing them favorably toward the French.

French rulers found reason to confiscate Aquitaine three times—in 1294, 1324, and 1337. The first seizure resulted from a naval dispute, but the fief was returned. The second confiscation, provoked when the Gascons burned a French *bastide* (fortified town) encroaching on Gascon territory, caused the war of Saint-Sardos (1324). The settlement was an English humiliation. The French king, Charles IV, refused to return the entire duchy to Edward II, holding back Perigord and the Agenais for damages.

When the last Capetian king, Charles IV, died in 1328, a major dynastic quarrel further damaged French and English relations. Charles IV was the third son of Philip the Fair to die without leaving a male heir in twelve years. When the eldest son, Louis X, had died in 1316, the middle son, Philip V, solved the dynastic crisis by disinheriting Louis' daughter in favor of himself. Philip displaced his niece by nonchalantly asserting that women do not succeed to the crown of France. The youngest son, Charles IV, used the precedent set by his brother Philip to ascend the throne in his turn, disinheriting Philip's four daughters. When Charles IV died, the only remaining descendent of Philip the Fair was his daughter Isabella, the widow of King Edward II of England and mother of the young Edward III. The direct male heirs of the Capetian dynasty had come to an end. The French barons quickly elected Philip VI of Valois as their king. He was a mere cousin of the deceased Capetian, but he was experienced, French, male, and on good terms with the barons. To the anger of the Plantagenets, Edward III, crowned king of England the previous year following his father's dethroning and murder, was quickly passed over. Yet the threat that Edward's blood claim posed to Philip's elective kingship—even if through a woman—must have been universally acknowledged. In England, resentment at Edward's disinheritance was made worse by France's failure to return the confiscated part of Aquitaine. In a move to recover his usurped rights, Edward signed letters on May 16, 1328, appointing two bishops to debate his rights to the kingdom "as rightful heir."[2] The response of Philip's lawyers to Edward's demands was to dismiss them. Two weeks later Philip VI was crowned at Reims, with Edward III conspicuous by his absence.

The start of the fledgling Valois dynasty was unexpectedly strong. The first victory of Philip's reign was to reinstate Louis of Nevers as count of Flanders, after a terrible rebellion had driven him to France, by winning the battle of Cassel (August 23, 1328). The second was to compel Edward III to perform simple homage for Aquitaine at Amiens (June 6, 1329), after Edward had attempted to forestall it. The following winter Edward's researchers pored over the historical record to see if Edward's homage at Amiens should have been liege homage (the most restrictive). In the spring of 1331 Edward reluctantly acknowledged liege homage to Philip. Anglo-French relations were to be frayed even further. Between 1333 and 1335, while Edward was at war with Scotland, France provocatively answered a Scottish request for aid against the English. In the meantime, Philip VI had assembled ships for a crusade, but the project was suddenly halted by the pope, who said that peace in the West must precede any crusade to the East (1336). Philip promptly redirected the fleet to Norman ports, which Edward viewed as further provocation.

In the meantime, a new problem arose. A close adviser to Philip VI, named Robert of Artois, a rare individual for the times to lose a disputed inheritance to a woman, broke ranks with Philip and fled to Edward III's court. Robert was gleefully received by the English king, whom Robert then served as enthusiastically as he had previously served Philip. France and England had now reached a point of irreconcilable differences. Philip charged Robert with crimes of *lèse-majesté* (capital offense against a sovereign) in March 1337, since a vassal (Edward) was forbidden from harboring his suzerain's mortal enemy (Robert). On May 24, 1337, Philip confiscated Aquitaine.

Edward reacted sharply. All his earlier resentment boiled to the surface, as he stepped up his search for allies and prepared for war against France. To obtain a continental base of operations that would permit attack from the north, Edward had already tried to arouse Flemish disloyalty to its French suzerain, but Count Louis of Nevers' indebtedness to Philip VI kept him at Philip's side. In August 1336, Edward resorted to tougher measures. In an economic maneuver designed to strike at the prosperous Flemish textile industry, Edward halted all English exports of wool to Flanders. By January 1338 the strategy was beginning to pay off. A popular leader named Jacob van Artevelde argued that Flanders "must make a friend of England" to survive. The Anglo-Flemish accord that followed served its purpose, but secured only Flemish neutrality, since the pope threatened to excommunicate Flanders for any betrayal of its suzerain. The Anglo-Flemish agreement ended peace negotiations between England and France. Edward began protesting to friendly as well as hostile audiences about injustices and favoritism (see Document 3). A letter from Edward to Pope Benedict XII in July 1339 complained that Philip sought to make Edward "disappear from the world of the living" and could not stand for him to "see the light of day."[3] But there was something in Edward's war chest—other than money—that he had yet to use. When Flanders finally agreed to acknowledge him as the true king of France, Edward unveiled his diplomatic weapon publicly. It was the case of his wrongful disinheritance. In a manifesto of February 8, 1340 (see Document 4), Edward III staked his claim on the title "king of France" and made a play for the hearts of the French people. His appeal drew attention to his French blood by promising to continue the ancient traditions of his great-great-grandfather, Louis IX, and he called on the populace to swear an oath of fidelity before Easter.

The war, which had now begun in earnest, did not immediately live up to the tall talk that had directly preceded it. The English annihilated the French fleet at Sluys in June 1340 (see Figure 1), but failed to defeat even the isolated northern French town of Tournai. The result was a two-year truce signed at Esplechin—to run from September 1340 to June 1341—between two already war-weary kingdoms. In the spring of 1341, Edward drew another disgruntled and luckless heir into his camp. When Duke John III of Brittany died in April, John of Montfort lost the succession dispute that followed to Philip VI's niece. Edward's condition for helping Montfort was to be acknowledged as the king of France, to which Montfort agreed. In October 1342, Edward entered the war of Breton succession on the side of Montfort, but within six months a military stalemate led to the truce of Malestroit (January 1343). A papal peace conference took place at Avignon in 1344, but Edward, then in the ascendancy, simply reiterated the proofs of his right to the French throne. War began again in 1345.

By 1346 a new fugitive had sought partnership with Edward. This time it was the Norman Geoffrey of Harcourt. Using Harcourt as an adviser, Edward attacked Normandy. One of the four most memorable battles of the war was fought at Crécy on this campaign. The French attack began in a light rain near nightfall on August 26, 1346. Edward III fought from a defensive position, with longbowmen, primitive gunpowder artillery, and dismounted soldiers—a tactic England learned from the wars with Scotland. Philip VI used Genoese crossbowmen, a pedigreed mounted cavalry, and an incomplete contingent of infantrymen. The French were badly beaten. A combination of tactical errors, miscommunications—the French cavalry had even ridden down its own Italian crossbowmen—and senseless bravery hastened the English victory. Such a momentous victory for England was not to be repeated, however, for ten years. An English attack on Calais followed. It lasted eleven months (September 1346–August 1347) and became famous for the six burghers who, according to chronicler Jean Froissart, threw themselves on the mercy of Edward III and his wife in order to save the city. In September 1347, Edward signed a truce at Calais and returned to England. The Black Death, or bubonic (and pneumonic) plague, broke out in December 1347, first

Figure 1. English naval victory at Sluys. *Courtesy Bibliothèque nationale de France, Paris.*

arriving in France at Mediterranean seaports. Despite the difficulty of assessing the number of dead, it appears that about one-third of the western European population died. In 1345, disillusionment with Jacob van Artevelde led to his assassination; Flanders returned to the authority of Count Louis of Male in 1349. Van Artevelde's blunder had been to propose turning Flanders over to Edward III's son, the Black Prince, an inadmissible strike against Flemish independence. On August 26, 1350, Philip VI died, leaving his son John II as his successor.

Between 1350 and 1355, there were no direct confrontations between the English and the French, but war continued indirectly in Brittany where the English (in 1352) and the French (in 1354) each gained a victory. Mindful of the disaster at Crécy, in 1351, John II, who practically defined himself by the chivalric principles of honor and bravery, established the chivalric Order of the Star. Its purpose, unlike Edward III's Order of the Garter (1348) which celebrated the English victory at Crécy, was to raise standards among John's elite knights to better withstand the English enemy. But John II would have to reckon with an enemy of a different sort—the resentful and unscrupulous Charles of Navarre who was a prince of the royal blood. He was called Charles the Bad (*el Malo*) by the Navarrese but the term also described his career in France. His mother, the royal princesse Jeanne, daughter of Louis X, had been cast aside when her uncle seized the crown as Philip V (1316). In 1349, after John II gave lands owed Charles' mother to his favorite, Constable Charles of Spain, Charles of Navarre arranged for the constable's murder (January 8, 1354). John himself had ordered the execution of the previous constable, Raoul de Brienne, for obscure reasons. Although peace was arranged by the dowager queens (April 1354), this did not prevent an English-Navarrese coalition in 1355. John II now believed that Charles of Navarre was capable of plotting with his son Charles, the duke of Normandy (future Charles V), against him. In April 1356, as the duke of Normandy hosted a banquet in Rouen, with Charles of Navarre and the count of Harcourt among the guests, John made a surprise attack on the dinner party, took the prince of Navarre captive, and ordered Harcourt and others to be executed (see Figure 2). Next came the event that would abruptly alter John II's reign—the second major battle of the Hundred Years War, the battle of Poitiers. King John's opponent at Poitiers was Edward of Woodstock, Prince of Wales, known today as the Black Prince. The French king, with forces significantly outnumbering those of Edward,

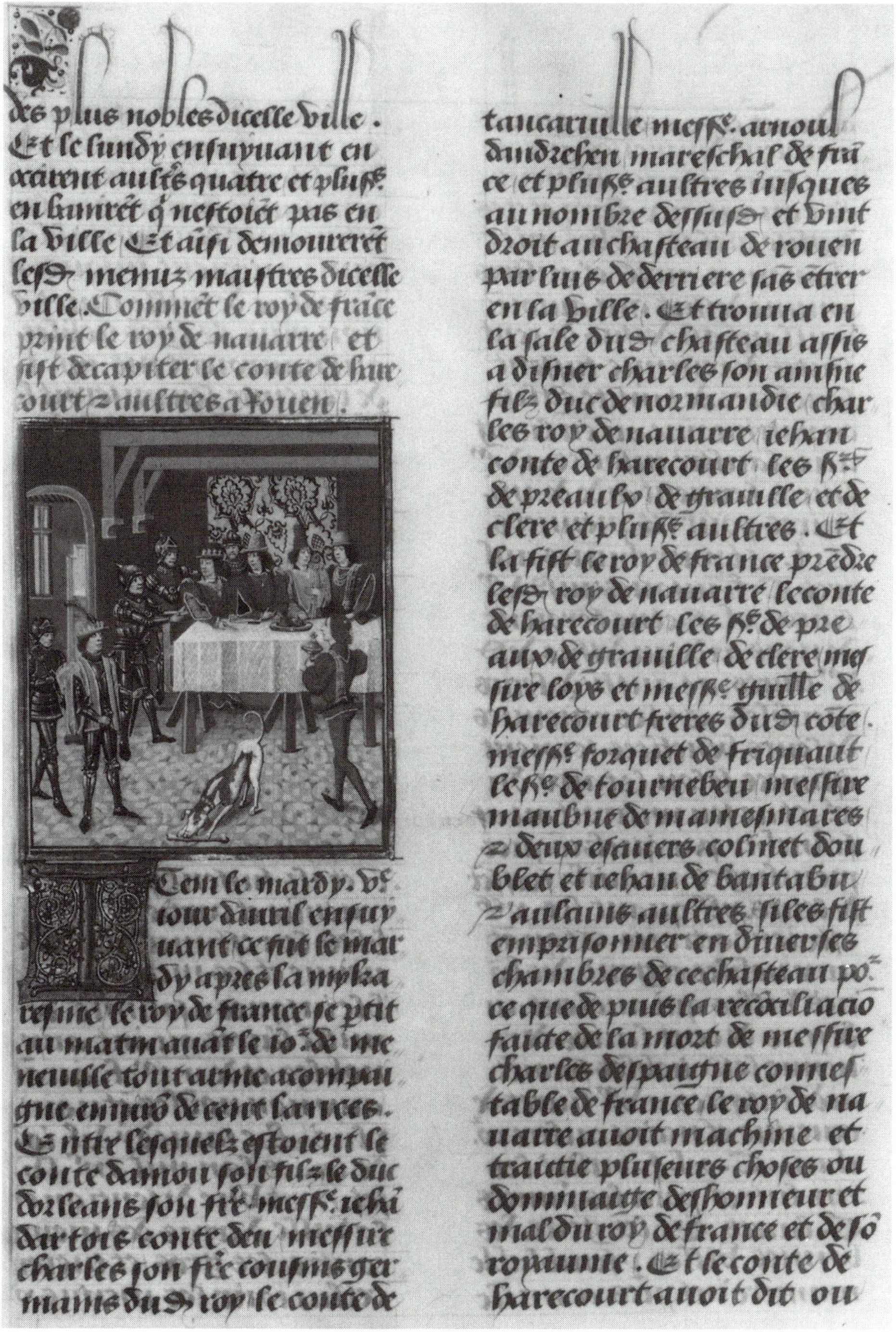

des plus nobles dicelle ville .
Et le lundy ensuyuant en
oxient aultres quatre et pluss
en laurent q nestoiet pas en
la ville Et ainsi demoureret
less menuz maistres dicelle
ville Comment le roy de frace
print le roy de nauarre et
fist decapiter le conte de har
court z aultres a rouen.

Item le mardy vie
tour dauril ensuy
uant ce fut le mar
dy apres la myka
resme le roy de france se prit
au matin auat le io de mie
nenille tout arme acompai
gne enuiz de cent lances.
Entre lesquelz estoient le
conte damou son filz le duc
dorleans son fre messs iehan
dartois conte deu messire
charles son fre cousins ger
mains dus roy le conte de

tancaruille messs arnoul
dandrehen mareschal de fra
ce et pluss aultres iusques
au nombre dessuss et vint
droit au chasteau de rouen
par luis de derriere sas etre
en la ville. Et trouua en
la sale dus chasteau assis
a disner charles son amsne
filz duc de normandie char
les roy de nauarre iehan
conte de harecourt les fs
de preaulx de graulle et de
clere et pluss aultres. Et
la fist le roy de france predre
less roy de nauarre le conte
de harecourt les fs de pre
aulx de graulle de clere mg
sire loys et messe guille de
harecourt freres dus cote.
messs forquet de friquaut
le fs de tournebeu messire
maubue de mamesnares
z deux escuiers colinet dou
blet et iehan de bantabu
z aulains aultres sy les fist
emprisonner en diuerses
chambres de cechasteau po
ce que depuis la reconciliacio
faicte de la mort de messire
charles despaigne connes
table de france le roy de na
uarre auoit machine et
traictie plusieurs choses ou
dommaige deshonneur et
mal du roy de france et deso
royaume. Et le conte de
harecourt auoit dit ou

Figure 2. Seizure of Charles of Navarre. *Courtesy Bibliothèque nationale de France, Paris.*

provoked the battle. An initial French cavalry charge was met by English longbowmen, who created chaos by killing or wounding the French knights' horses. This was followed by brutal hand-to-hand combat. In the final phase of battle, the English remounted and made a surprise charge against the still-dismounted French forces. By the end of the day, John found himself a captive of the English, and his futile bravery, marked by an unwillingness to retreat, had made him the prized booty of the Black Prince in a decisive French defeat (September 19, 1356). Additional booty from the king's tent included expensive books, a crown, a silver centerpiece for his table, and ironically, a jeweled emblem of the Order of the Star.

After the humiliation of the king's capture and the defeat of the chivalric nobility, the non-nobles condemned the nobility, but they spared the king. They readily believed the nobility's flight from the battlefield equaled treason, and some wondered whether the French knights had actually sold themselves to the English. In the *Grievances concerning the battle of Poitiers*, an anonymous poem that was clearly not written by a knight, all blame falls on the nobility, whereas the king is called "the absolutely noblest of all creatures."[4] The poet even recommends that *Jacques Bonhomme* (symbolic name for the peasantry) "ought to replace the nobility, if the dauphin obtains good counsel."[5]

Who was advising the dauphin Charles was in fact very much the issue, so much so that a meeting of the Estates General in Paris in October 1356 ended with an ordinance for reform drafted by eighty of the more than eight hundred delegates. The general agreement of the assembly was to approve finances for an army that could emancipate France from its enemies. Brittany had come under attack in September, Paris was unprotected, the army had been decimated, and bands of plunderers—idled men-at-arms, mercenaries, and adventurers—were on the loose everywhere. There was no interest in truces that would prolong the war. Furthermore, in the view of the delegates, who included Etienne Marcel—the provost of the merchants, or mayor—then on the brink of becoming a major political force, the decision-making power of the monarchy had to be taken from a coterie of corrupt royal advisers and placed with the Estates. In December 1356, John II wrote to Marcel from Bordeaux, where the king remained in comfortable but frustrating captivity under the guardianship of the Black Prince, urging Marcel that negotiating, not making war, was the only way "to get me back." The winter brought raids in Brittany by the joint forces of the English and Navarrese. The warrior Bertrand du Guesclin, who would make his fortune under Charles V, was already leading retaliatory guerilla raids. The strength of the Anglo-Navarrese coalition, however, depended on the peaceful coexistence of Edward III and Philip of Navarre, then fighting for Philip's imprisoned brother Charles. There were tensions on both sides.

Trouble broke out in January between Marcel and the dauphin Charles over the devaluation of coinage. On January 20, 1357, the dauphin responded by first bravely asserting his right to devalue money in the kingdom, but then wisely backing down. When the Estates met again between February 5 and March 3, the Great Ordinance they drew up, which called for more representation, supervision, and control, was duly signed by the dauphin. In late March a truce was concluded at Bordeaux between King John and the English, but in Paris the news was not well received. John instructed everyone to observe the truce and refuse to pay the war taxes voted by the Estates. But the dauphin, who was then completely under the power of the Paris war party, announced on April 10 that the levying of taxes would proceed. To add to the general turmoil, Charles of Navarre escaped from prison in November and made straight for Paris. On November 30, at Pré-aux-Clercs on the left bank of Paris, the faithless king of Navarre made a propaganda speech to the Parisians asking for their full trust, and declaring, according to the chronicler Jean le Bel, that he "wanted to live and die while defending the kingdom."[6] Charles also let it be known that his right to the crown was stronger than that of either Edward III or the king who was currently a prisoner in England. While these events were taking place in Paris, a provisional agreement was reached in England between Edward III and his captive John II. It called for an extravagant ransom and the full surrender of an expanse of territory equal to at least a quarter of France. The treaty drawn up by the two kings, ratified in May 1358, was later known as the first Treaty of London. The treaty made no mention of Edward III's having to relinquish his claim to the French throne. In Paris, the university and clergy declared themselves against the treaty but the Estates General left no record of an opinion. In Normandy, English and Navarrese forces launched a new offensive.

On January 11, 1358, the dauphin Charles retaliated against Charles of Navarre with a propaganda speech at the market at les Halles, but Marcel and the Paris revolutionaries were already out of hand. The early weeks of January also saw English and Navarrese troops close in on Paris. On February 22, 1358, while the dauphin was meeting in his bedchambers with his advisers, a mob broke in and murdered the marshals of Champagne and Normandy, leaving the dauphin splattered with their blood and a red and blue revolutionary cap on his head (see Figure 3). In March the dauphin began to call himself regent of France rather than John II's lieutenant. The dauphin, who could do nothing in Paris, left the city at the end of March. His next move was to call a meeting of the Estates of Champagne in the town of Provins on April 9, where he warned his audience that France was in great danger. Days later the dauphin seized a fortress near Paris and ordered artillery to be brought from Paris. Marcel countered this move by seizing the Louvre as well as the artillery within. Marcel wrote to the dauphin on April 18, 1358, politely pointing out that Charles had mistaken loyal Parisians for the enemy, while the real enemy—the English and Navarrese armies—was ravaging the countryside south of Paris (see Document 5). As Marcel sent letters looking for allies outside Paris, a bloody peasant rebellion broke out north of Paris in late May. Known as the *Jacquerie*, it added an additional burden to the kingdom, as civil war raged between the dauphin and Marcel. Charles of Navarre, sensing the precariousness of his position with the nobility, suppressed the peasant revolt and won favor with the nobility. As support for the dauphin increased, Marcel's Paris revolution lost ground. The sign that it was over came at the end of July when Marcel was murdered in the street. The crowds welcomed the dauphin back to Paris with as much enthusiasm as they had previously shunned him. On August 21, 1359, the dauphin agreed to the peace of Pontoise, which returned the unruly Charles of Navarre, who now proclaimed himself a "good Frenchman," to favor.

Two notable events took place in 1359. Edward III, thinking he could squeeze better peace terms from John II, raised the stakes in March 1359 with the second Treaty of London. For the additional territory demanded, however, Edward agreed to renounce his claim to the French crown. To the prospect of suffering more losses so that Edward would merely drop "king of France" from his title, the French replied with an emphatic "neither tolerable nor feasible." Therefore, on November 1, Edward set out from Calais to decide the question by force. He was accompanied by four of his sons, a large army, and mercenaries fighting at their own risk for booty. Edward had offered to divest himself of the French royal title, but

Figure 3. Murder of the marshals. *Courtesy Bibliothèque nationale de France, Paris.*

when his treaty of March was scorned, he must have decided to turn the as-yet hollow words "king of France" into something tangible—a Reims coronation. As his army pillaged and burned its way across northern France, it eventually reached the sacred city where the kings of France received confirmation of their kingship from God. But the people of Reims had laid in a strong supply of provisions, and they held off the English. The chronicler and friar Jean de Venette reported that for all Edward's efforts "he accomplished nothing."[7] Although Edward made a march on Paris, the march never led to an attack. Then, in a minor episode in March 1359, a small French fleet spread terror on the coast of England. The crew sailed to Winchelsea, sacked the city, and left.

In the first week of May 1360, the English and the French agreed to meet at Brétigny, near Chartres, to discuss terms for peace. John was to be released for 500,000 pounds sterling, a portion of which was due immediately. Edward got Aquitaine in full sovereignty, as well as other counties and towns, but much less than the previous draft had awarded him. The truce was to extend for eighteen months. On October 24, at Calais, the final peace was ratified. It was not airtight, because it left Edward's renounced title and John's renounced sovereignty over Aquitaine to be sworn to only after all territories were ceded. The peace of Calais nevertheless ended the first phase of the Hundred Years War.

On May 19, 1364, the young man who had served a tumultuous apprenticeship in politics in the absence of his father, John II, ascended the throne of France as Charles V. King John had died with honor in 1364 after returning to captivity in England when his son Louis, a hostage until the remaining ransom was paid, took flight. But John's legacy to France was a crushing debt, immense devastation, and vastly shrunken territory. In a secret act of September 1363, John left his mark on the kingdom in another way. On his son Philip, who had remained at his side at Poitiers, he bestowed the rich duchy of Burgundy. This would later enrage an heir with a closer right to Burgundy than Philip—none other than Charles of Navarre.

The slant that Charles V would put on his kingship was already revealed in a personally supervised manuscript containing a coronation ritual, or *ordo*, produced within two years of his May 1364 coronation and believed to reflect quite accurately his actual ceremony. The liturgy insists on the divine nature of French kings and includes new prayers asking God to fortify Charles' army and allow him to overcome his enemies, making this, in the words of one historian, "more warlike than any previous French ordo."⁸ This suggests that Charles V saw the treaty of Brétigny as in no way permanent. In fact, bloodshed could still be found in the kingdom. In addition to the war of succession in Brittany, which was exempt from the peace treaty, bands of soldiers known as *routiers* who had been dismissed when the fighting stopped were continuing to make their fortunes in brigand bands called companies. The worst was called the Great Company. A Breton guerilla fighter named Bertrand du Guesclin was already active on the side of Charles of Blois, the French-backed claimant in the war of succession in Brittany. Du Guesclin was the obvious person to play a three-fold role in Charles V's reign. Du Guesclin's assets were his practical skill and stealth tactics in executing raids, an uncontested ability to recruit and control the rising generation of lawless non-noble warriors, and his value as a substitute general for Charles himself, who had no taste for the battlefield. Du Guesclin quickly brought glory to the king in the early days of Charles' reign by winning a victory at Cocherel over a Navarrese army, three days before the dauphin's coronation in 1364. Charles of Navarre would make peace the following year. Du Guesclin was defeated at Auray that September, where Charles of Blois was killed. With the installation of the English-backed Montfort, duke of Brittany after the treaty of Guérande in 1365, the long conflict at last came to an end.

The contemporary writer Christine de Pizan, in her biography of Charles V, cautiously lets it be known that Charles V needed a military cause to rid France of the harmful companies. He found it in Spain, where the wife of Pedro of Castile, who was Charles' sister-in-law, had been murdered. Therefore, the French king backed Henry of Trastamara, the murder suspect Pedro's bastard half-brother, in an effort to take Castile. Du Guesclin drew the companies out of France and led them into Spain. The French won the first battle and placed Henry on the throne. Pedro hastened to the usual place for support—the English—where Edward, the Black Prince, answered the call. Edward led an English force at the battle of Nájera in 1367, where the French were badly defeated and Pedro regained his crown. Henry remained a friend of France, however, and signed an alliance in November 1368 promising to put the Castilian fleet at the disposal of the French.

The formal renunciations required by the treaty of Brétigny had never taken place. In 1368 Charles V used this legal point to his advantage. As the Black Prince, now duke of Aquitaine, increasingly burdened his subjects with taxes, his subjects became resistant. At the end of the year, claiming that he still held jurisdiction over the duchy, Charles insisted that he therefore retained the right to hear appeals. In January, Charles called on the Black Prince to appear in Paris for a hearing at Parlement. The prince replied that he would be happy to appear in Paris on the assigned day, but it would happen with a helmet on his head and a company of sixty thousand soldiers at his side. Quite naturally, when Charles V declared the Black Prince forfeit (in neglect of duty), Edward III quickly reassumed the title of king of France (May–June 1369). The same year an important marriage took place between Margaret of Flanders and Philip the Bold of Burgundy. By arranging this marriage for his brother, Charles V managed to sabotage Flemish plans for Margaret to marry Edward III's son, Edmund. No one could have foreseen then the dangers for the future posed by this expansion of Burgundian territory and power. In November 1369, after soliciting tax appeals that undermined Edward III's jurisdiction in Aquitaine, Charles officially confiscated the duchy for the fourth time since 1294. War had in fact already resumed some months before.

The years from 1369 to 1375 tell the story of the French reconquest of lands lost by the Treaty of Brétigny. In these years, French strategy reflected the lessons learned at Crécy and Poitiers. Charles V forbade pitched battle unless the numerical odds were extravagantly in his favor. What Edward III had won from the saddle between 1340 and 1360, Charles V took back without ever going to war. Charles relied on his commander in chief, Bertrand du Guesclin, who recaptured fortresses one by one, in a dogged piecemeal strategy. As towns and castles changed hands in the war zone, inhabitants faced a considerable dilemma. Should they surrender to the French armies only to find themselves subsequently retaken by the English? The English, in any event, were not everywhere considered to be unjust occupiers. Sometimes, as at Poitiers in August 1372, the inhabitants were of divided loyalties, but du Guesclin's promise to restore ancient privileges and his appeals to their French origins carried the day. Although several English campaigns swept through vast stretches of France during the period, French fortresses withstood the English assault. In the meantime, French plans for a naval attack against England in 1369 never bore fruit. The commander of the proposed invasion, Philip the Bold, was forced to divert his men in order to contain a land attack launched from Calais.

As usual, Charles of Navarre, the eternal trouble-maker, presented a special challenge. He negotiated deceitfully with both the English and the French, finally making peace with Charles V in 1371. In 1372 Henry of Trastamara's Castilian fleet won a naval battle for the French at La Rochelle, limiting England's ability to resupply its army on the Continent and diminishing English control of the seas. An English campaign, unable to make headway, ended in a local truce with du Guesclin in early 1374. A general peace followed in 1375, which would run for two years, but talks seeking a permanent peace at Bruges drew the delegates into the old quarrel—what to do about Aquitaine? Several proposals to divide Aquitaine resulted in a deadlock because neither king would relinquish his claims to sovereignty. The Black Prince, laid low by illness, died in 1376. War began again in May of the following year, and then, on June 21, 1377, Edward III followed his son to the grave, after a fifty-year reign.

For a brief period, France appeared to hold a great advantage in the war. In England, a ten-year-old boy, Richard II, now ascended the English throne, while political intrigue swirled around him. But du Guesclin died on July 13, 1380, and Charles V died two months later on September 16, 1380. Charles VI took the French throne on November 4, 1380, just before turning twelve. Both rulers now held the legal status of minor. In the meantime, an event called the Great Schism, which would last forty years, produced a papal split in 1378, resulting in two popes, one pro-English, the other pro-French.

Among the last acts of Charles V were provisions for his son's minority and the abolition—in a remorseful moment before dying—of the hearth tax. Immediately, the boy's four uncles, Louis of Anjou, John of Berry, Philip of Burgundy, and Louis of Bourbon, decided to rule the kingdom jointly, ignoring the deceased king's wishes while furthering their own interests. The taxes that had financed Charles V's army soon had to be reinstated, and rebellions broke out in response. At this time (1378–1382), a general period of rebellion and unrest swept over western Europe. Disturbances occurred in Italy, Flanders, and England, as well as France. The Flemish revolt, led by Philip van Artevelde, son of the earlier agitator, worried France the most given the potential for an Anglo-Flemish alliance. So when van Artevelde sought aid from England, the French, under the command of Philip the Bold, duke of Burgundy, helped Philip's father-in-law Count Louis of Male defeat the rebels at Roosebeke in 1382. By this maneuver, Philip the Bold not only managed to safeguard his Flemish inheritance but also received handsome payment for his military expenses from both the young Charles VI and Louis of Male. In 1383, an English bishop, Henry Despenser, invaded Flanders under the appearance of a crusade against the supporters of Pope Clement VII. Despenser's real purpose was to open the blockade of the English wool route through Flanders, but the venture failed. A short truce followed, which remained in effect from January 1384 until May 1385. France then planned a two-pronged naval attack on England, but it was not ready until November 1386, when it was called off due to the lateness of the season. When the Flemish rebellion ended once and for all with the peace of Tournai in December 1385, Philip the Bold confidently accepted his Flemish inheritance, Louis of Male having died in 1384.

A period of uneasy but prolonged peace began in 1389. The previous year Charles VI had declared that henceforth he would manage his own affairs. At that time, he had recalled his father's counsellors, derisively termed Marmousets, or "little boys," for their questionable pedigrees. The looting of the royal treasury by the four princes ended, and a more frugal era began. When a series of short truces were set to expire in 1398, a twenty-eight-year truce was announced. As so often happened, however, an event not directly related to the war between France and England had an unexpected effect on its course. On a hot August day in 1392, Charles VI, then only twenty-four, suffered an attack of insanity while riding to battle against the duke of Brittany. The repercussions for French fortunes were devastating. Although still lucid during long intervals, Charles now fell under the control of Philip the Bold. The bureaucrats whom Charles VI had called to his side in 1388 were expelled. Since Philip's economic interests in Flanders were served by peaceful relations between France and England, Philip arranged a marriage between Charles VI's daughter, Isabella, and King Richard II of England. The marriage agreement in 1396 coincided with the twenty-eight-year extension of the truce of Leulinghen. In formalizing the agreement, Charles called his five-year-old daughter "the guarantee of perpetual peace," and Richard removed the title "king of France and England" from the coins of his realm. For Philip, the seas were now safe for Flemish trade with England. The English war party, however, balked at the reconciliation.

As Froissart related, many complained of Richard II that "his heart is so French that he cannot hide it." Richard's uncle, the duke of Gloucester, had to remind him of the sacrifices already made by his father and grandfather "in sweat and toil" to conquer France. The conflict was settled in 1399, when Henry IV of Lancaster, who had been banished and deprived of his estates by Richard II, usurped the English throne and did away with Richard.

The course of events was no more charitable to France, even though the truce of Leulinghen had ended another phase of the Hundred Years War. The young heir to the duchy of Burgundy, the future John the Fearless, saw his crusading army decimated at Nicopolis in 1396. After Charles VI's madness struck in 1392, discord grew between Philip of Burgundy and his nephew Louis of Orleans. When Philip died in April 1404 and the duchy passed to John, the bitterness increased. The years 1404 and 1405 were supposed to mark the beginning of a great campaign, a concerted effort on three fronts to expel the English from France. But the ships of Jacques of Bourbon were beaten back to shore by foul weather (1405), little came of Louis of Orleans' attempt to take Aquitaine (1406–1407), and John the Fearless failed to take Calais. Great opportunities did not present themselves very often, but this one had been lost. Whatever the cause of the campaign's failure, the venture had been initiated by Louis of Orleans and John the Fearless had resisted. Rival politics already seemed to be prolonging the war.

On November 23, 1407, returning home from the palace of Queen Isabeau of Bavaria, Louis of Orleans was ambushed, his hand cut off, and his head split open. The gloves were now off and civil war had begun in France. John the Fearless, who soon confessed to his uncles Berry and Anjou, had the absolute arrogance to defend the murder. A master from the University of Paris named Jean Petit justified the brutality to the royal court on the grounds that it was permissible to kill a tyrant. The political opponents of Louis of Orleans rallied to the Bugundian cause. There were now two factions dividing France in a struggle that far overshadowed the war with England. In fact, it occurred to each side—the Armagnacs (named after Bernard of Armagnac, father-in-law of Louis of Orleans' son Charles) and Burgundians—that England was the ideal ally in its cause against the other. In 1411 the duke of Burgundy approached England. The Armagnacs imitated him in January 1412 offering a better bargain—nothing less than the French territorial gains of 1369 to 1375.

In this pact, authorized by the dukes of Berry, Orleans, and Bourbon and the count of Alençon, the counts of Armagnac and Albret would aid Henry IV in recovering "*his* duchy" of Aquitaine. The dukes of Berry and Orleans asked only to keep their possessions in Aquitaine for life, as fiefs of England. For his part, Henry IV agreed to send eight thousand troops and to warn Flanders not to become involved. But the agreement was intercepted in Normandy and soon read aloud to the king's council in Paris. Charles VI begged for advice and his council insisted on vengeance. All these maneuvers did nothing but persuade the English to invade France on their own behalf. A new phase of the war started after more than two decades of relative peace.

In March 1413, when Henry IV died and his son Henry V took the English throne as the second Lancaster monarch, Henry V vigorously reopened the question of England's rights on the continent. One immediate priority, however, was practical. The English had always been terrified of coastal attacks by the French, and wished to end French harassment of the English navy. Therefore, when Henry V set sail in 1415, he headed straight for the port of Harfleur on the Norman coast. But after seizing Harfleur, as he turned north toward Calais, Henry was met by French forces—the rival factions of Armagnac and Burgundy having settled their differences to confront the greater threat they now faced. A battle ensued at Agincourt on October 25, 1415, between two armies facing very different odds. The French army outnumbered the English by at least four to one. According to a French contemporary "all the lords wished to be in the first battalion, for each was so jealous of the others that they could not in any way be reconciled."[9] English archers targeted the French mounts, and crazed horses trampled the French foot soldiers as they galloped directly into an English "funnel" formation and certain disaster. The day went to the English without their ever sustaining a frontal attack. Henry promptly departed for England.

As early as 1413–1414, the French had engaged in negotiations to satisfy Henry V's ambitions. These included reopening the question of King John's unpaid ransom, offering the French princess Catherine to Henry as his bride, and, of course, Aquitaine, which Henry demanded be reinstated as defined in the treaty of Calais of 1360. Henry made it increasingly clear, however, that he would only settle for the ancient Angevin Empire. As a first step, Henry launched a campaign in 1417 into Normandy, a province lost by the English in the time of Philip Augustus and duly acknowledged as having been lost by Henry III in the Treaty of Paris (1259). Taking Rouen in January 1419, Henry next headed for Paris. But fifty miles southeast of Paris, at Montereau, another shocking murder took place on September 10, 1419. This time, a meeting between the dauphin Charles (future Charles VII) and John the Fearless, intended to end the civil war, reignited it. Charles' men cut down the duke of Burgundy in retaliation for the murder of Louis of Orleans. John the Fearless had in fact signed an alliance with Henry V on October 6, 1416, but it was his son and successor, Philip the Good, who now turned to the English for revenge. The immediate result was an agreement that English and Burgundian forces would join together to fight against the dauphin and his partisans. More important, on May 21, 1420, a treaty was signed at Troyes, accepted by King Charles VI and Queen Isabeau. The main provisions of the treaty included the disinheritance of the "so-called" dauphin Charles for his crime at Montereau, the marriage of Princess Catherine of France to Henry V, and the granting of the kingdom of France to Henry and his heirs, as their inheritance, forever (see Document 10).

In the meantime, John the Fearless had seized Paris from the Armagnacs on May 29, 1418. Bernard of Armagnac was among those killed in the attack. The dauphin was rescued from bed and quickly fled Paris. On August 31, 1422, Henry V died, leaving his infant son, Henry VI, with the responsibility of conquering France, of which he was now, at least on parchment, the reigning monarch. Charles VI died two months later, on October 21, after a forty-two-year reign, leaving a divided realm. There was little that the dauphinist (or French) party—renamed after the death of the count of Armagnac—could do, other than retreat south of the Loire river. But Charles' party still held roughly half of France. Although the dauphin's diplomatic correspondence shows that he took serious and sensible actions during the 1420s, and was therefore far from the dim-witted slacker of some literary portraits, a number of contemporaries—even Joan of Arc herself—implied that his determination to win back his inheritance needed reinforcement. It was this task that the young girl from Domrémy took upon herself "at God's command."

At Vaucouleurs, the local seat of government, Joan of Arc convinced Captain Robert of Baudricourt to provide her with a small escort, men's clothes and shoes, and a horse so that she could travel to Chinon to deliver a secret message to the dauphin Charles regarding his kingdom. In this she declared herself to be God's envoy. Once interviewed by the dauphin, she was sent to Poitiers for further scrutiny by his theologians. She promised that she would produce a miraculous victory at Orleans, then under siege. When the victory was quickly achieved on May 8, 1429, the dauphin granted permission to extend the campaign to the Loire valley. French forces succeeded in taking Jargeau, Meung-sur-Loire, Beaugency, and Patay during the early weeks of June. The next campaign began in late June, its object the city of Reims. There, the dauphin, who had been denied his crown by the Treaty of Troyes, sought to confirm his right to the throne by a proper anointing and coronation. The coronation took place on July 17, 1429. Of the twelve peers of France—the kingdom's most noble princes and churchmen—the most noticeable absence was that of Philip the Good, duke of Burgundy.

Joan of Arc believed that Charles' army should now head for Paris, a strategic destination that had been set aside in favor of the coronation campaign. But Philip the Good was currently engaged in shifty politics reminiscent of Charles of Navarre. At the time of the coronation, Philip was being entertained in Paris by the duke of Bedford, brother of the deceased Henry V. For Philip, however, dealing with the duke of Bedford proved to be a delicate operation. In pursuing his own self-interest, Philip always risked manipulation by the English. From the day of the coronation, the duke had also been in negotiations with Charles VII for a reconciliation. On August 28, 1429, two days after Joan and her army arrived at Saint-Denis on the outskirts of Paris in preparation for an attack to regain the capital, Charles agreed to a truce with the Burgundians, which would cover a large part of France but exclude Paris. While an embassy of Burgundians was shuttling between Arras and Compiègne arranging the truce, other Burgundians, under Louis of Luxembourg, were preparing to fight the French army, then at the walls of Paris. Arthur of Richmond, a Breton prince and French supporter since 1424, had recently threatened the borders of English-occupied Normandy, and Bedford had moved many English troops to Rouen in response. This left a largely Burgundian contingent to defend Paris. On September 8 an attack on Paris failed. The French army returned toward the Loire. As Charles continued to seek reconciliation with Philip the Good, he practically halted military activity. Joan of Arc, convinced that France must be won by the sword, was all but immobilized. For Joan only one encounter remained. On May 23, 1430, as she rode out of Compiègne in the rearguard after an unsuccessful attack on the town, she was pulled from her horse and captured. Régine Pernoud observed that she was captured because "she had always been in the vanguard when it was a question of making an attack; and in the rearguard when [it was] a retreat."[10] It is possible, however, that she was betrayed.

The influence of Joan of Arc can be seen in the immoderate response that her capture produced. According to a chronicler, the man to whom she surrendered claimed to be "more joyful than if he had had a king in his hands." Philip the Good went to speak to her after learning of her capture. Unfortunately, what he said is not known. The very day of her capture, Philip sent out letters announcing that she had been taken. Moved from castle to castle during her year in captivity, Joan was tried in Rouen between January 9 and May 29, 1431. Then, condemned as a relapsed heretic—technically for reassuming male clothing (prohibited by the Bible) after renouncing it—she was burned at the stake in Rouen on May 30, 1431.

Despite Joan of Arc's failure to win France for Charles VII, there is general agreement that she turned the tide of the war in favor of the French. Some would argue that efforts by Charles and Philip the Good to end the civil war were more important, but there seems little doubt that Joan's chain of successes helped to convince Philip, in his indecision about where to cast his lot, which side would be the winning side.

On December 16, 1431, the nine-year-old Henry VI was crowned king of France in Paris. Reims, which was in French hands, had seemed too risky a goal to attempt. After preliminary negotiations in 1434, Philip the Good finally decided to pardon Charles, who agreed to make numerous amends for the crime at Montereau, more than a decade before. Peace was restored between the princes on September 21, 1435, at Arras. Nicholas Rolin, the Burgundian chancellor, built a clever but inconsistent argument allowing Philip to break his pact with the English. Since Henry V, in line to receive the French crown, had died before Charles VI, Rolin argued that England had lost the opportunity to inherit the kingdom. The English were infuriated at Philip's betrayal of the Treaty of Troyes and all subsequent confirmations of the Anglo-Burgundian alliance. Among the details sparking their anger was Philip's recognition of Charles VII as king of France, a title to which the English still laid claim. But Bedford had died one week before the Treaty of Arras was signed, and England, in his absence, was divided over whether to pursue the path of war or peace against France. Eventually, the war faction, led by Humphrey, duke of Gloucester (brother of Henry V), prevailed over the peace party of Henry Beaufort. Gloucester embarked on a military challenge to Philip the Good's sovereignty in the Low Countries, ultimately without success. Paris returned to French obedience on April 13, 1436. A blockade, which prevented food from reaching the capital helped the Parisians make up their minds.

At Gravelines, in July 1439, peace talks between France and England, under the sponsorship of Philip the Good and assisted by his wife Isabel of Portugal, failed to advance past the old question of whether Henry VI would renounce the title "king of France." The answer was that he would not. An event called the *Praguerie*—named after a rebellion in Bohemia—furnished one of those periodic and alarming distractions to the war. Numerous French princes, on whom Charles VII should have been able to rely, plotted the removal of unpopular royal administrators. Included in the list of agitators were names linked to the campaigns of Joan of Arc—the duke of Alençon, Dunois, the bastard of Orleans—as well as the king's own son, the future Louis XI. Charles VII responded by rekindling war against England. When the English proved incapable of a successful battlefield response, peace talks opened again in 1444 at Tours. In place of a general peace, the negotiators managed a two-year truce and a noteworthy marriage agreement between Henry VI and Charles VII's niece, Margaret of Anjou. The duke of Gloucester died in prison in 1447. The count of Suffolk, William de la Pole, now took charge, advocating peace. Provoked by an incursion into Brittany, Charles VII broke the truce with England in August 1449 and advanced into Normandy. The campaign lasted an entire year. Finally, Rouen, the town where Joan of Arc's trial had taken place behind enemy lines, fell in November 1450. In England, the count of Suffolk, blamed for his failed attempts at peace, was banished, then killed. Fighting continued in Aquitaine between 1451 and 1453. The old general John Talbot, now eighty, whom Joan had challenged, along with Suffolk, in her *Letter to the English* of 1429, died on the battlefield at Castillon in Aquitaine, on July 17, 1453. The French army's advanced use of artillery under the leadership of two brothers named Bureau helped ensure the French victory at Castillon. Bordeaux, so long an English stronghold, fell on October 19, 1453, completing France's achievement of its three military objectives since Arras: Paris, Normandy, and Aquitaine. Only Calais remained of England's continental possessions.

No one could be quite sure that the war, which by then had lasted 116 years, was over. There was no signed accord, and French watches continued to survey the horizon for the English. England retained Calais until 1553 and continued to use the title "king of France" until the early nineteenth century. As if history were to repeat itself, in 1453 on the other side of the channel, Henry VI lost his mind and a civil war in England soon followed.

NOTES

1. *Historiens et chroniqueurs du moyen age: Robert de Clari, Villehardouin, Joinville, Froissart, Commynes*, ed. Albert Pauphilet (Bibliothèque de la Pléiade) (Paris: Gallimard, 1952), p. 353.

2. Eugène Déprez, *Les préliminaires de la guerre de cent ans: La papauté, la France et l'Angleterre (1328–1342)* (Paris: Fontemoing, 1902), p. 36.

3. Déprez, *Préliminaires*, p. 219.

4. Charles de Beaurepaire, "Complainte sur la bataille de Poitiers," *Bibliothèque de l'Ecole des Chartes*, sér. 2, 12 (1851), p. 259.

5. Ibid., p. 260.

6. *Chronique de Jean le Bel*, ed. Jules Viard and Eugène Déprez, vol. 2 (Paris: Champion, 1977), p. 253.

7. *The Chronicle of Jean de Venette*, trans. Jean Birdsall, ed. Richard A. Newhall (New York: Columbia University Press, 1953), p. 96.

8. Richard A. Jackson, ed., *Ordines Coronationis Franciae: Tests and Ordines for the Coronation of Frankish and French Kings and Queens in the Middle Ages* (Philadelphia: University of Pennsylvania, 2000), p. 455.

9. Jean Juvenal des Ursins cited by Ian Heath, *Armies of the Middle Ages: Organisation, Tactics, Dress and Weapons*, vol. 1 (Goring-by-Sea: Wargames Research Group, 1982), p. 71.

10. Régine Pernoud, *Joan of Arc: By Herself and Her Witnesses*, trans. Edward Hyams (New York: Stein & Day, 1966), p. 151.

CHAPTER 1

BACKGROUND CAUSES OF THE HUNDRED YEARS WAR

THE CONFISCATION OF AQUITAINE

The Hundred Years War began in the early fourteenth century, when there was as yet nothing inevitable about the boundaries of present-day England and France. In fact, the war itself can be seen as the gradually unfolding history of establishing frontiers. Astonishingly, the map of France in the late twelfth century shows that almost half of modern France belonged to England. These vast continental holdings of England, known as the Angevin Empire, extended from the English Channel to the Pyrenees mountains. The possession by English kings of inheritances in France originated with William the Conqueror, a Frenchman and duke of Normandy, whose successful conquest of England (Hastings, 1066) made him at once an English king and a French duke. When Henry II Plantagenet, also French by birth, ascended the English throne in 1154, further inheritances and acquisitions brought Plantagenet lands in France to their greatest extent. With the origins of the Plantagenet dynasty solidly French, the principal issue of the Hundred Years War was to determine how the continental lands claimed by England would ultimately be distributed. The French challenge to English rule on the Continent took more than a century of bloodshed to resolve.

No single event can be held responsible for causing the Hundred Years War. The ingredients which together form the deep-seated causes of war were the result of evolving political, economic, social, and ideological circumstances. It is more or less by convention that historians date the beginning of the Hundred Years War to 1337. In that year Philip VI, king of France, confiscated the duchy of Aquitaine (also Guyenne) from its English duke, Edward III, king of England. That a contested Aquitaine was the spark that started the war is not surprising. By 1337 Aquitaine was the main remnant of England's possessions in France. The disintegration of the ancient Angevin Empire had come about through the centralizing tendencies of the French king Philip II Augustus (1165–1223). Land losses by Henry II's heirs culminated in the signing of the Treaty of Paris in 1259. The agreement forced Henry III, who desired peace but also acknowledged the current balance of power, to concede those provinces over which he had effectively lost control, that is, the bulk of the family heritage, or Angevin Empire. Thus, the English king Henry III, when he acknowledged Louis IX's sovereignty over Normandy, Anjou, Maine, Touraine, and Poitou, signed away his claims to these lands. Henry retained Aquitaine but the price paid was an oath of liege homage. This meant that Henry swore fealty in an agreement of "exclusive personal loyalty" to his brother-in-law, the king of France, and the duchy became a French fief. For the sake of convenience, this relationship can be called feudal, although the term *feudalism* refers to a jurisdictional relationship (relating to spheres of authority) characterized by much variety, and not to a pervasive social system as has frequently been believed. At the time, Louis IX seemed fully conscious of his victory in the negotations over Aquitaine. His biographer Joinville in the *History of Saint Louis* captures his reaction: "It seems to me that what I give him I do well, for he was not my man and now he enters in my homage." In technical terms, Henry III became the vassal of Louis IX, who was his suzerain (overlord). An important source of revenue with a strategic maritime location, Aquitaine had slipped in and out of the control of the Franks and Carolingians, but it was still coveted by the French. It was rightly seen by historian Edouard Perroy as "the eternal apple of discord between the two dynasties."

In the mid-twelfth century, the French monarchy had come tantalizingly close to permanently joining Aquitaine to the royal domain. The marriage of Eleanor of Aquitaine to Louis VII (1137) had brought the duchy to the royal kingdom of France. The failure of the royal couple to produce a male heir, however, resulted in the dissolution of the marriage in 1152. Eleanor left with the family heritage intact, the same year marrying Henry II, count of Anjou and duke of Normandy. With Henry's accession to the English throne in 1154, Eleanor's lands passed into English possession, and the die was cast for three centuries of dispute over Aquitaine. As this territory, so geographically French, passed into English control across the channel and out of French jurisdiction, there must have been those in France who murmured disapprovingly about the perils of allowing females to inherit.

The seizure of Aquitaine that took place in 1337, based on a quarrel over the English king's protection of a mortal enemy of the king of France, though it marks the starting point for the war, was not a unique or defining moment in history. Two earlier incidents, a skirmish between Gascon and Norman sailors at Bayonne and La Rochelle in 1294 and the destruction of a French *bastide* (fortified city) at Saint-Sardos in 1323, had led to similar confiscations. Whether or not these seizures were initiated to apply temporary pressure on the English vassal by his French overlord or, more seriously, to permanently annex the duchy to France is difficult to determine. In each case, resolution, with at least partial restitution of the confiscated territory, took place within a few years. By 1337, however, the incident that ignited the new confiscation directly involved a case of feudal disobedience and was augmented in scale by the identities of the parties involved—Edward III, king of England, and Philip VI, king of France—a pair of powerful antagonists and both claimants to the French throne in 1328. The incident set a French king intent on maintaining control through an aging system of medieval allegiances against an English king who was increasingly able, and thus inclined, to break free of the chafing feudal mantle. Disobedience was necessary for Edward's future independence. His pursuance of full sovereignty over his French inheritance has been seen as a root cause of the Hundred Years War. As Malcolm Vale has fittingly asked, how could sovereigns with equal authority play the old game of lord and vassal? The result of this feudal unravelling was eventually to foster the creation of modern nation-states.

When Philip VI ascended the French throne in 1328, Edward III was disinclined to pledge homage to his new overlord. English kings had arched their backs at the insult to their dignity and independence entailed in the homage ceremony, and they were traditionally slow to perform this ritual of subservience. However, Edward owed homage to a cousin who had outmaneuvered him to the throne of France. Edward dodged several efforts to bring him to heel, but he was finally forced to perform homage in 1329 in person at Amiens. Liege homage, which would have required that in the future Edward violate his own interests or alliances when they conflicted with those of the king of France, had not been performed. Philip VI's lawyers must have sized up the potential threat of the young English monarch, and in 1331 Edward was obliged to concede that the force of his earlier homage was liege. This was a particularly bitter concession for Edward, given his status as rival claimant to the French throne, for it would be used to argue that he fully recognized Philip VI as king of France.

DYNASTIC QUESTIONS

Historians have argued that there was nothing about the confiscation of Aquitaine in 1337, which occurred as Philip's retaliatory act for Edward's harboring of his mortal enemy, Robert of Artois, that should have led inevitably to war. Some historians, in fact, are inclined to see war as becoming inevitable only gradually between 1337 and 1340. During this time Edward decided to renounce his homage, break off negotiations for peace with France, and eventually, from a strategic location at Ghent in Flanders, formally stake his claim on the throne of France.

Presenting his case to the English people in a manifesto of August 28, 1337 (see Document 3), Edward did not yet mention his right to the French throne. Had Edward already planned to engage in full-scale war? If so, was his objective full sovereignty of Aquitaine, or did he seek nothing less than the kingdom of France? The consensus today is that when Edward assumed the title of king of France, he was posturing, hoping to get less (Aquitaine) by asking for more (France). Since a dynastic claim to the French crown served his immediate strategic purpose of negotiating an alliance with Flanders, experts question Edward's sincerity. All historians, however, admit some measure of justice to Edward's claim, and some have concluded that Edward believed in his claim and genuinely felt that its attainment was not illusory. Edward III was, in fact, through his mother, Isabella, the nearest male heir to the French throne. The grounds for debate centered on the question of female succession. Therefore, it will be necessary, in the next section, to explain the case for and against females succeeding to the French throne, as determined by custom and as argued by contemporaries. But the persistence with which Edward insisted on his title, openly displaying his sense of injury and injustice, also suggests a still deeper problem with regard to medieval inheritance patterns: the risk of rebellion by males who felt unjustly compensated for their station in life.[1] An immeasurable amount of strife during the Hundred Years War was to be caused by three improperly compensated heirs: Edward III, Robert of Artois, and Charles of Navarre (Charles the Bad). In the end, society would pay dearly for the oversight.[2]

FEMALE SUCCESSION

The Capetian dynasty, from Hugh Capet (d. 996) to Philip IV the Fair (d. 1314), had produced an unprecedented eleven generations of male heirs in unbroken line. The result was a tradition of male succession without theoretical basis. It was also without provision for the opposite prospect, which was near at hand—an unbroken line of female heirs. No one had bothered to fix a problem that had not yet manifested itself. But in three successive reigns from 1316 to 1328, no son of Philip the Fair produced a living male heir, forcing upon the ingenuity of nobles, magnates, and the claimants themselves decisions regarding the future course of the monarchy, without the benefit of legal precedent. In theory, nothing prevented a female from ruling the kingdom of France, although no female ever had. There was ample precedent for women to rule and to inherit land, and the royal domain might be thought of in the same terms as any other fief. A recent example in the neighboring county of Artois proved that a daughter of the deceased count, Mahaut of Artois, could hold off two bitter challenges by a grandson, Robert of Artois, and could rule as countess. Even a third attempt, bolstered by forged documents, failed to deliver to the grandson the county granted to his aunt. But known examples of female inheritance and the absence of explicit legislation excluding women from the throne were weak counterparts to a deeply entrenched preference for male kings. For Louis VII, the same king whose marriage to Eleanor of Aquitaine had been annulled, it took three wives and the birth of five daughters before he produced the desired son. A charter written at the time of Philip Augustus' birth in 1165 reads like a fairy tale celebration of the masculine principle. "For a long time," the charter states, "it was the unique and irremediable longing of the whole kingdom, that God, in his kindness and mercy, grant us a child, someone who after us would wield the scepter and rule the kingdom. We were also inflamed by the ardent desire that God grant us progeny of the better sex, we who had been terrified by a multitude of daughters."[3] On a theoretical level, only some time in the 1320s did a commentary on Augustine's *City of God* by François de Meyronnes first suggest in writing that although private inheritances could devolve to women, this was not true of the kingdom, given its nature as a *dignitas*, a sort of religious corporation to which women were unfit to succeed.

As the religious mystique of French kingship continued to grow, the grounds for the female exclusionary principle grew as well. Two precedents would be set in the next dozen years to fill the legislative voids uncovered in 1316 and 1328 regarding women: first, an outright declaration that females could not inherit the throne of France, and second, a related decision that women could not transfer the right to rule, which they lacked, to male offspring. Both measures were established with little formal justification other than the might of the promoters, or peers. So far (despite the misconception of many modern historians), an ancient private Frankish law code, called the Salic Law, from which later lawyers would seek to provide a juridical basis for excluding women from the crown, had not been invoked.

When the eldest son of Philip the Fair, Louis X, died in 1316 leaving only a daughter and a pregnant wife, the birth of a son still could have averted a royal emergency. But when a son was born and died in a matter of days, a crisis was thrust upon the ruling elite. The events that followed show from what fragile beginnings the firm monarchical principle of male succession arose. Louis' daughter, Jeanne, whom an earlier inheritance contract seemed to designate as heir in such a case, saw her uncle, Philip of Poitiers, quickly ease himself into the kingship as Philip V of France. The barons, called together by Philip, peremptorily declared that women did not succeed to the crown of the kingdom of France. But the decision was less than self-evident. Philip's vulnerability to the charge of usurper can be seen in the circumstances of the coronation itself. The ceremony was conducted in January 1317 behind locked gates, with armed men surrounding the city. Eudes IV of Burgundy and his mother, Agnes, the uncle and grandmother of the dispossessed orphan daughter, contradicted the right of the barons to overrule a direct heir. Agnes appealed for a full debate of the peers, or *débat contradictoire*. Their efforts were of no avail. The peers decreed that succession had to progress laterally, traveling from brother to brother (collateral succession) rather than from father to daughter (direct succession). In search of better endorsement, Philip convoked a second assembly in February, which issued a nonsensical defense of his legitimacy based on the number of intermediaries between him and Saint Louis. Behind the scenes, Philip was taking decisive action to soften the opposition of Eudes of Burgundy (and consequently the young Jeanne's claim) by marrying his own daughter to him. By March 1318 Eudes had all but relinquished his niece's rights in order to become a royal son-in-law. The king's own daughter, as one historian put it, had served to dispossess his niece. Philip V's ultimately secure kingship set the precedent for a collateral heir to replace a direct heir in the event of the deceased monarch leaving only female descendants.

Within five years, the principle of female exclusion was again invoked. In 1322, Philip V died without a male heir, survived only by daughters. He seems to have pacified a discontented younger brother, Charles of the March, with the prospect of the crown, perhaps arranging for the transfer of power to Charles upon his death, again through collateral succession, in a move that would invalidate the claims of his own daughters. Thus, in 1322, the third and last son of Philip the Fair mounted the throne as King Charles IV to no audible dissent, thrusting aside his brother's daughters, presumably with their father's consent.

SUCCESSION TRANSFERRED THROUGH WOMEN

By 1328 the exclusion of females from the royal succession was established in custom, though the principle was hardly the ancient custom the Valois would claim. There was, however, a further principle to be established. If the right of women to rule was now effectively obliterated, what could be said about the rights of their sons? Men would prove far more aggressive challengers than their mothers, who generally waived rights in exchange for compensation. In 1328 when Charles IV also died prematurely, again leaving only a female heir and a pregnant wife, a more complicated and far more persistent dispute over royal succession arose than the earlier controversy in which the antagonist, Eudes of Burgundy, had been bought off by marriage to the king's daughter. Now even the collateral line of succession had exhausted itself. When a new regent quickly established himself in 1328, as the royal family awaited the birth of the hoped-for male heir, the man in control was Philip of Valois. Neither a Capetian—the ruling dynasty since 987—nor the son of a king, but the mere nephew of Philip the Fair, Philip could never be ratified by the heredity principle. When the widow gave birth to a girl, the barons nonetheless authorized the regent Philip to accede to the throne. To do so, they established a second principle of royal succession that barred any claim to the throne based on transmission through a woman. As one Latin chronicler stated it: "Where the mother has no right, consequently neither does the son." It could be argued that if the barons had needed to reason contrarily in order to exclude Edward III of England from the French throne, they would have done so. No vassal of France who was also king of England was likely to occupy the French throne. But the unstable legal terrain on which this display of nascent patriotism rested was to be reflected in Philip and Edward's claims and counter-claims and their increasingly belligerent conduct between 1328 and 1340.

EDWARD, KING OF ENGLAND AND FRANCE

Speaking from Ghent on January 26, 1340, twelve years after he had been removed from contest for the French crown by his cousin Philip VI, Edward III provocatively assumed the title of king of France and quartered his arms with the arms of France.[4] The Ghent declaration, at least in theory, created the famous Anglo-French dual monarchy. Two weeks later on February 8, 1340, Edward went even further. In a manifesto to be affixed to church doors, the self-proclaimed king of France and England made a bid for the hearts of the French people, astutely offering them a clear alternative to the unpopular aspects of Valois rule (see Document 4). With these strategic moves in the power struggle between the two European princes, Edward opened a new phase of the escalating conflict between France and England.

How had matters deteriorated so badly in only twelve years? Was Edward's decision to claim a throne he had yet to conquer, and perhaps never would, a mere political weapon in the quest for full sovereignty over Aquitaine, as the majority of modern scholars believe? His actions from 1336 already showed him drawing closer to the brink of war, but serious tensions are discernible in the diplomatic record at an even earlier date. Edward's mother Isabella had asserted her son's right to the French throne at Northampton on May 16, 1328, and envoys had been sent to Paris in an unsuccessful challenge to Philip of Valois' bid for the throne. The young Edward, last prince of the Capetian blood, was conspicuously absent at the coronation of the first Valois king, Philip, on May 29, 1328, when the peers by convention did homage to their new king. Philip had ascended to the throne through election—a situation ever in need of validation—in a kingdom where tradition had long inclined toward hereditary monarchy. But homage and confiscation became the tools by which Philip of Valois offset the advantages of Edward's Capetian blood. Feeling in command after defeating rebellious Flanders, a French fief (a feudal estate), at Cassel in August 1328, Philip put pressure on Edward for Edward's oath of homage. At Amiens on June 6, 1329, a reluctant Edward swore simple homage, but he would not swear the more binding oath of liege homage, according to Froissart, until such time as his lawyers could see "by what means a king of England was a vassal to the king of France." Philip agreed to wait until Edward had returned home to see what "the deeds of his predecessors" showed that Edward ought to do. But by the spring of 1331 Edward was compelled to acknowledge that the force of his earlier homage was liege (or exclusive). The difficulty for Edward was that he now appeared to admit the legitimacy of Philip as French monarch, although Edward would always insist that nothing he swore at Amiens prejudiced his own rights and inheritances.

In November 1330 Edward had shed the tutelage of his mother Isabella and Roger Mortimer by coup d'état. Two years later he invalidated a treaty with Scotland on the grounds that it had been written during his minority, an argument that would also prove useful in his dynastic contest with Philip. Edward reopened war with Scotland in 1333. Although negotiations were ongoing for peace between the French and English monarchs, in May 1334 Philip rashly declared that peace in Aquitaine was dependent on Edward's suspension of war with the Scots. Edward, the overlord of the Scots, saw this as meddling in his internal affairs. The next blow to diplomatic relations was to be felt by Philip. In March 1336 Pope Benedict XII canceled Philip's five-year project for a crusade, citing as reasons the failure of both France and England to make peace and the potential of Philip's internal enemies to exploit Philip's absence. Two new problems arose. The first was the direct but unintended result of the pope's cancellation of the crusade. The French crusading fleet in Marseille was diverted to Norman ports, where it was immediately perceived by Edward as a direct challenge to England. The second was the arrival by late 1336 at the English court of the notorious Robert of Artois. In September 1336, Parliament voted to approve a war subsidy to finance Edward's increasingly obvious plans to go to war. In November, Benedict XII told Edward that Robert of Artois' presence in England was an impediment to peace negotiations. On January 23, 1337, Edward's council met in the Tower of London and agreed to seek peace, while Edward was simultaneously building up the fleet and actively seeking allies. Meanwhile, Edward imposed an embargo on the export of English wool in an attempt to force Flanders into an alliance with England. Then on May 24, 1337, Philip confiscated Aquitaine, thus inaugurating the Hundred Years War. The basis for the seizure was the expressly feudal charge of harboring Robert of Artois, the mortal enemy of his suzerain, Philip.

Edward was ready for war, but he knew that funding depended on his ability to sell his war to his own people. On August 28, 1337, the same day that Edward asked for new monies from the clergy, he laid out all his arguments for war with France in a manifesto, portraying himself—in an effort to gather support—as a champion for peace in the face of French aggression (see Document 3). Relying on the merits of his ancestry to gather allies, Edward repeatedly attacked Philip through diplomatic channels. Intermittently, at first, Edward tried out the title of king of France, simultaneously referring to his opponent as "Philip of Valois" who "calls himself" king of France. In 1338 Edward broke homage and declared in a letter of defiance that he would triumph over Philip by "force of arms." By December 3, 1339, Edward's three-year wool embargo against Flanders had accomplished its goal. For reasons of economic preservation, under the leadership of Jacob van Artevelde, Flanders broke its neutrality and aligned itself with England. This was possible because the count of Flanders, Louis of Nevers, was unable to preserve his authority and had fled to France. Edward was the clear winner in the diplomatic rivalry for Flanders. He now possessed a desperately needed staging area on the Continent from which to launch his war. But whether the Flemish, whose threatened textile industry had yielded to Edward's arm-twisting embargo, actually provoked Edward to claim the title, as is repeated in pro-French chronicles and the anonymous poem *Vows of the Heron*, is uncertain. Regardless, papal diplomacy had failed, tensions in Aquitaine had not lessened, and, if we believe Edward's pronouncement of August 28, 1337, he had come to believe that Philip was on a quest not just for Aquitaine but for "all the lands of the king of England."

Historians generally agree that a disputed Aquitaine was the immediate cause of the Hundred Years War. Philip VI wielded power over his cousin Edward III as long as the unequal relationship of suzerain and vassal prevailed. Therefore, Philip was to maintain throughout that the cause and the solution to the war lay in details relating only to Aquitaine. Increasingly, however, Edward understood that his own advantage depended on wrestling free of the Aquitaine question, the source of Philip's strength against him. Thus, Edward III's strategy in the late 1330s and 1340s was to overlay the feudal quarrel with a dynastic one, which Edward accomplished when he reopened his bid for the French crown. But the strategy does not negate the possibility that Edward also believed in the justice of his claim. Perhaps it only took Philip's expanding incursions into Aquitaine, his interference in Scotland, and his aggression at sea to convince Edward that Philip would not stop until there was one king ruling over both France and England. Then Edward could have decided that given his birthright and his dispossession as a minor, that one king should be he. In 1340 Edward III was no longer the powerless fifteen-year-old whose claims had been easily set aside in 1328 by his cousin Philip, but a buck ready to lock horns with his rival across the channel in order to protect his interests, and therein lies a final factor laying the groundwork for war.

NOTES

1. Charles T. Wood, *The French Apanages and the Capetian Monarchy, 1224–1328* (Cambridge, MA: Harvard University Press, 1966), p. 9.

2. Paul Viollet, "Comment les femmes ont été exclues en France de la succession à la couronne," *Mémoires de l'Académie des inscriptions et belles-lettres* 34, no. 2 (1893), p. 25.

3. Jules Tardif, ed., *Monuments historiques: Cartons des rois* (Paris: J. Cayce, 1866), no. 588.

4. He divided his ensign or insignia into four parts introducing the French *fleur-de-lis* into two of them.

CHAPTER 2

Popular Uprisings

The period known as the Hundred Years War was contemporary with the century of the most intense and persistent European popular revolts. Questions of cause and effect between the war and the rebellions therefore deserve special attention. Impulses toward rebellion, and even real revolts, had occurred well before the 1337 commencement of the war. These early popular uprisings, however, did not directly influence the outbreak of war. On the other hand, the constant state of war between the French and English certainly increased the likelihood of rebellions, and once they broke out, rebellions unquestionably affected the course of the war in various ways. Most uprisings had common antecedents but distinct features. Even so, upheaval often resulted when rebels fought for advantages known to have been acquired by others. Flanders mounted the longest, most successful revolts and was therefore the most influential in spreading the contagion of revolt to France and England. Contrary to the belief of earlier historians, agitators, even when peasants, were generally quite well off with upwardly mobile aspirations. They contacted each other, occasionally inspired one another, and even attempted to strengthen their positions through alliances. Especially in England, radical preachers provided an egalitarian ideology for revolt, even when pacifism had been their only clerical intention. Urban strongmen with personal agendas publicized other populist doctrines. Rebels grew in self-confidence and began to question the superiority of the nobility. Nobles, in turn, viewed the contagion of rebellion, or any signs of solidarity among the dissidents, as cause for wholesale alarm. Even kings, despite the favor and prestige of their office, were parties also surprisingly set at risk in the tumultuous fourteenth century, whether at their dinner tables, in their bedchambers, or defenseless in the open field.

Three clusters of sustained popular uprisings, in Flanders, France, and England, mark the fourteenth century as an era of rebellion by the peasantry and the rising middle social groups in western Europe. There is danger in generalizing from one rebellion to another, since different contingencies led to revolt and determined its outcome in various locales. Underlying conditions that fanned, but did not always start, rebellions included negative economic forces such as grain shortages, fixed wages, restricted access to natural resources, fluctuations in the labor market, and compromised trade routes. The conditions for revolt were sometimes aggravated by famine or plague but more often, it seems, by inadequate or outdated social structures. In the fourteenth century, peasants had their first taste of political action, sometimes demanding to rule themselves, sometimes demanding a stake in formerly closed political structures, but constantly testing the limits of their new-found power. Resistance to taxation was unquestionably the immediate cause for most fourteenth-century rebellions. In turn, the primary motive for taxation was to finance the Hundred Years War. But the rebels did not necessarily oppose the war. In France and England, on the contrary, rebels charged that monetary resources that could have led to national protection were being squandered and diverted away from the war. Their kings, they maintained, were ill-served by dishonest, profiteering ministers, local officials, and, in France, even by the royal army. Lords, nobles, gentlemen, and even the clergy were their stated enemies. During the worst years of rebellion, the case was even made that these protectors, turned oppressors, were more damaging to native soil than the foreign enemy.

FLANDERS

The territory of the medieval county of Flanders is today divided among Belgium, the Netherlands, and northern France. Flanders, situated between England and France, had a pivotal role, which is traditionally underrepresented by historians, in the Hundred Years War. Although Flanders was not a protagonist in the war, Flanders' key location and advanced industrialization quickly drew each of the rival superpowers in pursuit of its favor. Flemish rebellions had more impact on international relations during the war years than the rebellions in either

France or England had and set the standard for future rebel movements in those kingdoms. The social unrest and outright rebellion that characterized the entire fourteenth century arose out of conditions first identifiable in Flanders. Rebellions occurred there in three principal phases: maritime Flanders (1323–1328), Ghent (1336–1349), and Ghent again (1379–1382). Signs of distress and agitation were already in evidence, however, in the late thirteenth century.

England and France both saw high stakes in the wooing of Flanders. For England, Flemish ports were crucial as a first line of defense for the naval protection of England. The location of Flanders was also critical for launching an English invasion of France from the north. Flanders was the prime commercial market for English wool, and conversely, England was the chief market for Flemish textiles made with English wool. France recognized that any English alliance with Flanders would invert the balance of power of the war parties to its disadvantage. France, however, benefited from by far the longer historical relationship with Flanders and was its major grain exporter. Soon after the ninth-century breakup of the Carolingian empire, Flanders became a fief of the French crown, and the first count of Flanders was named. Flemish counts, henceforth, were vassals of the king of France. For generations, as French kings remained weak rulers and were ineffectual at centralizing power, Flanders enjoyed largely independent control over its own affairs. But as the French state expanded, its kings increasingly sought greater control over Flanders and Flemish revenues, and therefore increasingly interfered in Flemish internal affairs. In the early thirteenth century, meddling by King Philip II Augustus of France in the succession of Flemish counts saw both England and the empire intervene against this power play by the French monarch. But the crisis ended in Philip's favor when he scored a victory at the battle of Bouvines (1214).

Within seventy years, signs of distress and agitation were again in evidence. The next encroachment by the French suzerain over his Flemish vassal occurred during the reign of King Philip IV the Fair (1285–1314). Guy of Dampierre, count of Flanders since 1278, tried to break the Flemish patricians' monopoly of power by siding with their opponents, among whom were craft guild members and lesser patricians. King Philip then interfered on the side of the patricians, creating two distinct factions in Flemish politics. The nobles who rallied behind the French king were called *leliaerts*, for adopting the *fleur-de-lis* (*lelie* in Dutch) as their insignia. The supporters of the count were known as *klauwaerts* from the claw (*klauw* in Dutch) of the lion of Flanders. France's support for the *leliaerts* made the count responsive to overtures from England, threatening Philip with a more drastically altered balance of power and drawing attention to the ongoing challenge for France of keeping England at a distance. Between 1297 and 1300, the Flemish count turned his back on France and created an alliance with Edward I of England. France retaliated by imprisoning him and occupying Flanders. Flemish resentment was quickly aroused. In 1302, an attack on the French governor, known as the "Matins of Bruges," led to open rebellion and the flight of *leliaerts* and royal garrisons. When the flower of French chivalry rode into Flanders to subdue the rebels, local Flemish militias, largely infantry based, won an unheard-of popular victory at Courtrai in 1302. This clash of noble and non-noble became known as the Battle of the Golden Spurs, for the more than five hundred pairs of golden spurs, symbols of knightly prowess, recovered from the fallen French nobility and hung defiantly on the church wall at Notre-Dame of Courtrai. The commander of the French army, Robert II of Artois, died in battle. But the peace treaty resulting from the war of independence, signed at Athis in 1305 by Count Robert of Béthune, made the Flemish victors appear to have been defeated. In addition to requiring an oppressive subsidy, the king of France imposed temporary jurisdiction over the part of southern Flanders (today France) known as the Walloon castellanies (Lille, Douai, and Orchies). These centuries of Flemish resistance are the necessary prehistory for understanding the three phases of rebellion commanding attention in the era of the Hundred Years War.

In the first phase of Flemish revolt (1323–1328), a protracted rebellion, the longest of the fourteenth century, broke out against the young Count Louis of Nevers. Fault lines ran in every direction. The concessions granted in the treaty of Athis by the previous count, Robert of Béthune, and the heavy war indemnity to be paid to France were sources of great bitterness. The rural population seethed at the count and nobles, who were allied with the king of France, for exacting heavy rents and taxes and for drawing off their meager surpluses to fill the coffers of the privileged. Disgruntled antiroyalists drove out the count's bailiffs and replaced them with their own peasant captains. The rebels wanted all those who did not work with their hands—including priests—to be eliminated, and they demanded that religious houses distribute their stockpiles of grain to the poor. Despite Flanders' appearance (and even reality) of suffering, however, historian David Nicholas has argued convincingly that Flanders was experiencing "a revolution of rising expectations rather than a rebellion of the oppressed."[1] The exorbitant goal of the insurgents was to remove Count Louis from power and eliminate French authority in Flanders. Flanders would no longer underwrite the cost of French wars or France's expanding infrastructure. Violent action was pursued in the name of ending interference and eradicating aristocratic privilege. Although not true revolutionaries, inasmuch as they relied on existing institutions to define their powers, the rebels adapted those institutions novelly to their own subversive ends.[2] Notwithstanding fierce rivalries between Flemish towns and among different segments of the social hierarchy, the lower and middle groups (peasants, workers, artisans, and merchants) agreed in bringing down the nobles. Flanders erupted into open revolt in 1324. By 1325 rural rebels were formally allied with their urban counterparts in Bruges and Ypres, in a union to be duplicated later in French and English uprisings. The next year the rebels drove Count Louis out of Flanders, henceforth to rule in their own name. A peace treaty at Arques in 1326 did little to restore calm, and rebellion soon burst forth in Bruges. The situation threatened all European aristocracy, but it fell to King Philip VI, the unsteady first Valois monarch whose succession was disputed by Edward III, to quell the insurrection. With his vassals and with noble support from outside France, the French king coaxed the Flemish infantry from their defensive position atop a hill at Cassel to defeat them on August 23, 1328, during the first year of his reign. Philip's mobilization of an army in support of his vassal, Count Louis, proved how deeply France wished to maintain control of Flanders. In international terms, the French victory at Cassel gave Philip the leverage he needed to stifle objections to the new dynasty and raise his prestige. The Flemings, while still in command of their destiny atop the hill of Cassel, had capitalized on Philip's vulnerability, and taunted him as "the foundling king."[3] But soon after Cassel, an empowered Philip dared demand that his rival, Edward III, pay him homage for the English-held, French fief of Guyenne—a stronger acknowledgment still of Philip's legitimacy.

The second stage of revolt in Flanders arose from a decisive act of interference in Flemish commerce, this time not by the French king, but by Edward III of England. In August 1336, in a calculated diplomatic move, Edward imposed an embargo on English wool exports to Flanders. Predictably, Flemish merchants, whose textile industry depended on imported English wool, revolted against Count Louis of Nevers, who refused to waver in his loyalty to his French suzerain Philip. The need to end the embargo brought a member of a leading family from Ghent, Jacob van Artevelde (see biographies), to prominence in 1338. Arrogating himself special powers as captain, van Artevelde drew together a confederacy of Flemings willing to deal with the English to eliminate the embargo by bypassing the powerful aldermen. France saw its fragile ascendancy over Flanders threatened when Edward III reached an agreement with Flanders. In the move that initiated the Hundred Years War, perhaps at Flemish request,[4] Edward declared himself king of France and England from Ghent in 1340. But the tyrannical rule of van Artevelde, whose alliance with England opened him to suspicion, was not to last. In July 1345 van Artevelde was murdered. When an event in 1349 known as "Good Tuesday" returned Count Louis of Nevers to power, he was hailed by all but the members of the textile guild.

The third phase of rebellion (1379–1382) broke out in Ghent when Count Louis of Male, son and heir of Louis of Nevers, interfered in a commercial rivalry between Bruges and Ghent, which masked a power struggle between the arrogant independence of English-aligned Ghent and the pro-French count. In France the subduing of Ghent could be promoted as an issue of French national security, given its alliance with England. Philip van Artevelde, the son of rebel leader Jacob van Artevelde, led the insurgency. The French army eventually intervened, defeating the rebel forces and killing Philip in the battle of Roosebeke in 1382. The international symbolism of the victory was important: Charles VI and the French nobility recovered the golden spurs lost eighty years before. The message had been sent that to follow the rebellious example of Flanders was dangerous as well as futile. French intervention was also deemed essential for the internal peace of France, since Flemish rebellion had plausibly instigated unrest in Rouen (the *Harelle*) and Paris (the *Maillotins*). Roosebeke's calming effect on Flanders turned French thoughts to the English war. One rebel remained, though, the city of Ghent. When France harbored thoughts of an all-out invasion of England in 1385, war preparations were thwarted by interference from Ghent, with English support. Clearly no campaign could begin before Flanders was subdued. The submission of Flanders was finally achieved in December 1385 with the peace of Tournai, negotiated by the new count, Philip the Bold of Burgundy. Flemish rebellions, the gold standard of fourteenth-century revolts, subsided in that year.

THE *JACQUERIE* OF 1358

The French revolt, known as the *Jacquerie* after the peasants (nicknamed derisively *Jacques Bonhomme*) who initiated it, arose in and contributed to a period of deep political turmoil in France and of dire unpredictability for the monarchy. Chronologically, the *Jacquerie* occurred in the interval between the disastrous French military defeat at Poitiers in 1356 and France's reluctant signing of the truce of Brétigny with England four years later. While England savored its upper hand in the Hundred Years War and contemplated how it would redraw the boundaries of France, King John II's capture at Poitiers left a power vacuum in Paris. From England, prisoner-king John tried to buy his freedom by urging ruinous concessions to the English on his compatriots. When his son, the future Charles V, then lieutenant in his father's absence, proved resistant to his father's control from abroad, fears arose in Paris of a long-distance, monarch-backed coup. Charles himself, who had little political experience, was open to others' manipulation. Those surrounding him were, in the words of Edouard Perroy, a "dubious entourage." Charles, king of Navarre, in whose name the most fighting in the realm was then being waged, was seditious, unpredictable, and a maverick claimant to the French throne. Charles of Navarre was notorious for casting his lot first with one political faction and then with another as he sought his personal advantage. With the royal treasury bankrupt, the representative body, the Estates General, was demanding reforms. At its head was Etienne Marcel, Parisian provost of the merchants and a rising bourgeois demogogue who controlled not only Paris but also, increasingly, the inadequate young Charles. In France, the void at the helm left the future course of the monarchy uncertain. The outcome of the struggle for control was as yet unknown.

The *Jacquerie*, which broke out in the Beauvais region of France north of Paris, must be understood against this complex political backdrop. By the time of the uprising, which began on May 28, 1358, in the village of Saint-Leu d'Esserent on the Oise river, the key players in the political struggle had been reduced to two—the young Charles, now regent, and the Paris provost, Marcel—although the king of Navarre was very much a wild card courted by both sides. Unable to rule Paris in the face of Marcel's control of the Estates General, the regent had fled the capital to rally support among the nobles for his return to Paris. On April 10, 1358, in Provins, seven weeks before the *Jacquerie*, Charles made a speech deploring the state of France, simultaneously depicting it as cruelly open to foreign war and victim to overt rebellion at home. As chronicler Jean de Venette wrote, France was "pierced by the sword of two wars."[5] In a move seen as provoking civil war, Charles voiced support for his two murdered marshals—a sure declaration of war to Marcel—and called everyone to rally around him in the name of France.

On the first day of the *Jacquerie*, villagers, allegedly angered at the French military for "shaming" France, armed themselves with knives and staves, proceeded to a knight's house nearby, murdered him and his family, and burned his house. These events brought peasants to Saint-Leu d'Esserent from ten miles around, all prepared to wreak havoc on their foes. Nine men were killed. The insurgents eventually increased in number to as many as five thousand men, destroying chateaux and fortresses and burning records wherever they went. The *Jacques* first swept through the regions of Beauvais, Clermont, and Senlis north of Paris. In attacking the castle of Montmorency, the rebels came so close to Paris that flames could be seen from the city. The rebellion then spread eastward into the provinces of Champagne and Picardy. Numerous atrocities were reported before the end came, only two weeks after the insurrection started. By then the rebellion was concentrated in two separate towns. A savage counterassault at Mello by Charles of Navarre, who had thrown his lot with the nobles, resulted in the death of the rebels' leader, William Carle, and the immediate collapse of resistance. At Meaux, the chance arrival of a small party of the king's nobles quickly subdued the remaining rebels. The rebellion, although brief, was the most memorable French popular uprising in the later Middle Ages.

The *Jacquerie* has been considered a perplexing event, even a mystery, to historians. A well-known remark by the chronicler Froissart alleged that when the rebels were asked for what reason they rebelled, "they replied, they knew not, but they did so because they saw others do it." This quotation suggests that the *Jacquerie* was as incomprehensible to the insurgents as to their victims, but few analysts would adopt such a characterization today. Downplaying the revolt as senseless brutality was simply the aristocrats' way of reducing its threat and denying the movement an ideology. In fact Froissart also states that "they thought that by this means they should destroy all the nobles and gentlemen in the world." Undoubtedly Froissart meant to offer this testimony condescendingly, but it distinctly conveys the rebel desire to eliminate the nobility as a class. But this anti-noble sentiment should be seen as military in nature. The rebellion did not originate with serfs attempting to break their landlords' feudal power. In the prosperous farming region where the insurgency broke out, most agricultural workers were free tenants united in cooperative agreements with their lords. Rather, the conflict lay in the nobility's military vocation, to be precise, their arrogant self-appropriation of the national defense. After the humiliating defeat of the French nobility at Poitiers in 1356, the *Jacques'* resentment that these cowards were their designated protectors and defenders knew no bounds. It took only a minor ordinance by the regent, as he seized and reinforced castles surrounding Paris in a standoff with Marcel, to light the tinder of rebellion: those in possession of castles were to perform necessary renovations to serve the regent more effectively as he sought to regain Paris. If need be, they were to seek the funds from their peasants. The peasants were outraged, accusing those knights charged with their defense of fleecing them of all their possessions. Additionally, legislation in the Estates General of March 1357, allowing armed resistance in response to certain injustices, probably convinced the peasants of their right to armed resistance. Herein lay the real causes of the *Jacquerie*.

Etienne Marcel vehemently denied initiating the *Jacquerie*, but it is beyond doubt that he succeeded in partially co-opting it. The rebels were patently royalist in ideology, even carrying the royal *oriflamme* (sacred banner) and adopting "Saint Denis" as their cry. In this they were as far as they could be from Marcel's efforts to subjugate royal power to the power of the urban bourgeois elite. But from his April 18, 1358, letter to the regent (see Document 5), we can see how Marcel was able to appeal to the rebels' pride with his deep understanding of their grievances and at least partially exploit their movement. Why, after all, should their violent impulses not be harnessed to raze the castles presenting a threat to Paris? (A telling written order by Marcel to exactly that effect has survived.) In his letter of April 18, Marcel took Charles to task for directing his armed forces at Paris instead of Chartres where the enemies of the kingdom had a free hand. But the regent unquestionably saw the Paris revolution, bolstered by the *Jacquerie*, as the more immediate threat. In fact the tumultuous year of 1358 brought Charles to the bargaining table with England. At Brétigny, on May 8, 1360, almost unprecedented territorial concessions were made to Edward III.

THE PEASANTS' REVOLT OF 1381

In part because of England's relative geographical isolation, political tides swept across England later than on the Continent, including the Peasants' Revolt. The outbreak of the Great Rebellion of 1381 in England occurred four-fifths of the way through a new round of continental rebellions (1378–1382), and some impetus from mainland Europe cannot be denied. The island kingdom certainly knew about the rebellions abroad and had itself experienced unrest in the 1320s and 1340s. Yet despite similarities to the broad spectrum of violence of its continental precursors, England's situation emerged from distinctively English circumstances.

The Peasants' Revolt took place against the backdrop of English kingship, in the fourth year of the reign of the boy-king Richard II, age fourteen. Crowned as a ten-year-old in 1377, Richard ruled in the shadow of his uncle, John of Gaunt, who would eventually see to his imprisonment, deposition, and perhaps death in favor of John's own son, Henry IV, duke of Lancaster. As part of Richard's royal inheritance, he was bequeathed much popular dissatisfaction, bred of the last discrediting years under Gaunt's control of the reign of his grandfather and predecessor, Edward III. A whiff of dynastic instability was already in evidence. Richard's calamitous deposition in 1399 has allowed some historians, by contrast, to look on his handling of the rebellion with relative kindness, for talking down the rebels at a precarious moment. At the time, though, this tumultuous rebellion brought a shock capable of raising fears that the monarchy itself could be swept away. Kingship alone does not go far enough to explain the English rebellion, however.

Modern historians accept the account of the *Anonimalle Chronicle* (Anonymous Chronicle) that the English uprising broke out "because of the exceptionally severe tenths and fifteenths and other subsidies lightly conceded in parliaments and extortionately levied from the poor people."[6] Parliament had introduced three poll taxes (taxes on people rather than property) between 1377 and 1381, creating England's first universal tax system. The third poll tax tripled earlier rates, but revenue collection ran far below estimates. A silent rebellion was already under way. Tax collectors, but also sheriffs and even priors, were branded as traitors. Tax collectors became the scapegoats of the English system of taxation without representation. Despite the appearance of a fiscal crisis, with some evidence that vendettas and local score-settling may have come into play, the insurgency reflected a broader social, political, and economic malaise.

The obvious and painful overarching problem was the continuing cost of the Hundred Years War. The purpose of the poll tax was to pay for the war, but the economic issues were complex and entailed more than the refusal to pay taxes. At the Good Parliament of 1376, during the last year of Edward III's reign, citizens agreed to the king's tax "so that he can sustain his war against his enemies," but they demanded an end to the longtime misuse of war funds. The mechanism for change was to be the impeachment of evil counsellors who had betrayed both king and kingdom. Blame for England's dismal performance in the war against France was a detectable undercurrent, inasmuch as England's holdings in France since the Treaty of Brétigny (1360) had been vastly diminished. Recent setbacks included naval defeat in 1372 and a failed land campaign by John of Gaunt in 1373. A decimated English fleet and stalled shipbuilding campaign created coastal vulnerability to raids by the French and Castilian fleets. These factors fostered a pervasive sense of a kingdom unable to protect itself.

The upper classes recognized the threat of collective action by the peasants, and the consequent risk to the entire manorial system, well before the revolt of 1381. During the first year of the young Richard's reign in 1377, a petition to Parliament by landowners sounded the alarm of impending social upheaval. Villages had suddenly begun to claim that they held their lands as "ancient demesnes [lands] of the crown." The villages sought to circumvent their duties to landlords by insisting on a direct link with the king, which eliminated landlord "middlemen." The landowners rightly saw in this the threat of civil war. They stated that "unless a quick remedy is imposed, war may break out within the realm because of these acts of rebellion."[7] Action was needed "to avoid such peril as arose formerly in the kingdom of France," a clear allusion to the *Jacquerie*. They even envisioned the conflict in terms suggestive of class struggle, as "rebellion and inter-alliance among *villains* against their lords."[8]

Open rebellion started on May 30 at Brentwood in Essex. The revolt began locally but quickly grew into a widespread movement. The

Anonimalle Chronicle establishes that letters were sent from Essex invit-
ing Kent, Norfolk, and Suffolk to rise with them. Perhaps cryptic letters
by the dissident preacher John Ball had an effect on the spread of rebel
ideology also. By the time rebels appeared in Kent in early June, Wat
Tyler, who may at one time have fought in France, had been selected
from among the rebels as their leader. On June 13 at Blackheath, the
growing band of dissidents, now numbering several thousand, saw an opportunity to meet with King Richard quickly disintegrate. The band
marched on London. To deflect the danger from London, the king bravely
heard rebel demands at Mile End on June 14. There he agreed to abol-
ish serfdom. Rebels nonetheless stormed the Tower of London and de-
capitated Richard's two highest-ranking ministers, Archbishop Sudbury
and Sir Robert Hales, whom they dragged from their hiding places. In
the royal chambers they sat on the king's bed, stroked the beards of several "most noble knights," and tried to kiss the king's mother. The chronicler Thomas Walsingham notes that the king sacrificed his counsellors,
for "otherwise he knew he would have been killed himself."9 No noble
raised a hand, or even a voice. Courageously, but in an obvious struggle
for survival, Richard met Tyler and the rebels the next day at Smithfield.
Tyler's demands there show the clear imprint of an ideology, containing
ideas reminiscent of John Ball and perhaps John Wyclif. All men would
be free and "of one condition,"10 declared Tyler, except the king. Only
the Law of Winchester, deputizing home rule in each community, would
be recognized. Only the ecclesiastical holdings required for the subsis-
tence of the clergy would remain in the clergy's hands, with the rest to
be divided among the parishioners. Finally, no serf or requirement of (in-
voluntary) service would remain. Then the showdown at Smithfield
turned into a contest of strength between a roof tiler and a king, with
both their lives at risk. It was Tyler who lost the fatal contest, cut down
by sword blows (see Figure 4). Although the revolt dissolved when the
rebels were afterward rounded up, the king appears to have been, for a
time, defenseless. After Tyler's murder, it took a desperate ride to London by the mayor, William Walworth, and a single servant, calling on
the nobles to "go to help your king," to rally knights to save the king at
Smithfield. The failure of knighthood to fulfill its traditional role in
maintaining order and protecting the king is implicit in Richard's rather
startling insistence that the mayor accept the order of chivalry. Protesting that he was "only a merchant to whom it was suited to make his liv-

Figure 4. Assassination of Wat Tyler. *Courtesy Bibliothèque nationale de France, Paris.*

ing by merchandise," the mayor was registering shock at the king's willing inversion of the social order.

It is evident that before Richard II could pursue war abroad he first had to establish rule at home. Rebellion was an obvious test of his rule, and his brave words at Smithfield do nothing to hide the crisis of his kingship: "Surely you do not wish to fire on your own king," he reportedly told the rebels, "for I will be your king, your captain, and your leader."[11] But rebel ideology consistently worked in Richard's favor. The English upper classes, according to the rebels, were to be the casualties of the uprising, not the king. Once the kingdom was rid of all lords, ministers, and other functionaries, the dissidents imagined a popular monarchy wherein king and commons would be united. Tyler's watchword, "With whom holdest thou? With King Richard and the true commons,"[12] bore recognition that the "commons" in Parliament, a preserve of aristocratic interests, was misnamed and unrepresentative of the interests of society at large. Even rebels living as free tenants, such as those from Kent, fought for an inclusive "rejuvenated" commons and an end to serfdom. Ancient charters, the Law of Winchester, and petitions for the reversion of manorial lands to the royal domain all confirmed in the rebels' minds the right of ordinary people to rule themselves on the local level. The chronicler Walsingham disdainfully regarded the Rising of 1381 as a time when "swineherds set themselves above soldiers."[13] But the English rebels attacked long-term abuses in virtually all areas of society, systematically and sometimes discerningly. No longer in the world they envisioned (and partly saw enacted) would nobles siphon off the surpluses of peasants and merchants, blocking their means to economic betterment, nor would landlords continue to have judicial control over laborers' hours or access to forest and water resources; no more would the Parliament's commons be a bastion of privilege. In reality, the constitutional changes, even those agreed upon by the king, did not endure more than a few years. But within the framework of upheaval brought on by the Hundred Years War, the middle and lower social orders in England had made a partially viable effort to aid King Richard's war and provide in the meantime for their own protection.

The earliest and most serious popular rebellion of the fourteenth century occurred in Flanders because the Flemish, who had for centuries been an independent and self-governing people despite their status as vassals of the king of France, resisted increasing encroachments on their autonomy by French kings. As their financial obligations to count and king mounted, the lower social orders found new political leverage in demanding privileges—often in the form of charters—in exchange for payments. By the fourteenth century the disaffected lower groups were less intimidated by the overwhelming imbalance of power between them and the aristocracy. They saw the value of confederation and were not afraid of resorting to violence. Any danger that they would be reduced to French serfdom was offset by two factors that worked in their favor: first, the Flemish counts never had the sovereign power of kings; second, France knew that over-stringency might drive all of Flanders into the hands of the English. That Flanders' commercial needs made them dependent on both England and France only increased internal rivalries and delayed the ultimate resolution of decades of rebellion and unrest. Politically, however, Flanders long exploited France's inability to control its Flemish fief. It required an enterprising prince of the blood, Philip the Bold, to end the ineffectiveness after he inherited Flanders in 1384.

In France and England, despite fundamentally different national circumstances, their respective rebellions had "weak kingship" written all over them. In France these deficiencies would be fully overcome by Charles V, eventually known as "Charles the Wise," but in England they would result in Richard II's dethroning. In the meantime, the *Jacquerie* and the Peasants' Revolt of 1381, as in Flanders, were outcries against unfair taxation and the ill-gotten advantages of superiors. In neither kingdom did the rebels claim to reproach the king. In France, the *Jacques* rallied around the monarchy, lashing out only at lords and knights whom they reckoned culpable and disloyal. In England, the insurgents took aim at both the ministers and the military for betraying the English war effort and leaving the kingdom vulnerable to French attack. The almost perpetual state of war in Europe in the fourteenth century brought with it the eruption of social problems, but the effect of these problems on the course of the war was political. The Paris revolution, aggravated by the *Jacquerie* of 1358, brought in its wake the Treaty of Brétigny of 1360 and France's abasement. From the fiscal, political, and social turmoil that culminated in the Peasants' Revolt, England saw what it had won at Brétigny slip through its fingers in roughly the same period.

NOTES

1. David Nicholas, *Medieval Flanders* (New York: Longman, 1992), p. 216.

2. William H. TeBrake, *A Plague of Insurrection: Popular Politics and Peasant Revolt in Flanders, 1323–1328* (Philadelphia: University of Pennsylvania Press, 1993), p. 34.

3. Henry Stephen Lucas, *The Low Countries in the Hundred Years War* (Ann Arbor: University of Michigan Press, 1929), p. 86.

4. Flanders stood to gain autonomy by the replacement of their hated French suzerain with the king of England.

5. *The Chronicle of Jean de Venette*, trans. Jean Birdsall, ed. Richard A. Newhall (New York: Columbia University Press, 1953), p. 84.

6. R. B. Dobson, ed., *The Peasants' Revolt of 1381*, 2nd ed. (London: Macmillan, 1983), p. 23.

7. Steven Justice, *Writing and Rebellion: England in 1381* (Berkeley: University of California Press, 1994), p. 141.

8. Ibid.

9. Dobson, *Peasants' Revolt*, p. 172.

10. V. H. Galbraith, ed., *Anonimalle Chronicle, 1333 to 1381* (New York: Longmans, Green & Co., 1927), p. 147.

11. Dobson, *Peasants' Revolt*, p. 178.

12. Galbraith, *Anonimalle Chronicle*, p. 139.

13. Dobson, *Peasants' Revolt*, p. 172.

CHAPTER 3

CHIVALRY'S GROWTH AND DECLINE AND THE HUNDRED YEARS WAR

Chivalry, as a complex cultural construction that emerged late in the twelfth century, consisted of a polished code of ethics developed for mounted warriors. The French word *chevalier* from which the word chivalry derives originally referred only to a mounted fighter or *miles* (Latin) and was devoid of overtones of honor. No one can pinpoint the exact origins of chivalry, which influenced military culture and social life between the twelfth and fifteenth centuries, nor do scholars entirely agree on its impact on medieval warfare, yet we know that the chivalric phenomenon predates the 1337 origins of the Hundred Years War by about 150 years.

CHIVALRY IN THEORY

What made the invention of chivalry necessary? The true purpose of chivalry was to regulate the behavior of warriors. The highest virtue a knight could possess was prowess, a blend of expertise in arms and bravery that embodied the idea of military preparedness. The rigorous apprenticeship required to become a knight served as military training in an age before standing armies existed and offered princes the means to acquire a skilled fighting force. As the novice, or "bachelor," was groomed for warfare, he was taught practical military skills, but he was also

schooled in all the moral virtues. If we listen to moralists John of Salisbury and Stephen of Fougères of the twelfth century, for instance, the
lives of contemporary warriors were greatly in need of reform. Salisbury
and Fougères found warriors to be willful, greedy, excessively independent, and oppressors rather than protectors of the common people. In
short, Salisbury and Fougères believed that knights who served princes
should above all serve God. The ideal of chivalry for the moralists was
to instill Christian virtues in the warrior class for the good of society.
Fougères even conceived of knights as forming an "order" of chivalry like
a clerical order.

Although the need for chivalry was felt by princes and clerics, there is little disagreement that the origins of chivalry are to be found in literature, and
that literature was the vehicle by which the ideals of chivalry were transmitted. The interplay between literature and reality, fiction and history, is
one of the most fascinating aspects of the complex phenomenon of chivalry.
At times, it is no exaggeration to say that life imitated art. In the twelfth
century, chivalric literature blossomed into branches, of which the matter of
Britain and the matter of France, as they were called, had the greatest impact on military practice. In England the central figure of the matter of
Britain was King Arthur, whose story was first told in Geoffrey of Mon-
mouth's twelfth-century *History of the Kings of Britain*. Despite Geoffrey's
claim that he drew on a "very ancient" book, he is known as "the founding
father" of Arthurian legend. In France, the *chansons de geste*, or "songs of
great deeds," best exemplified by the epic *Song of Roland*, narrated the heroic
exploits of Charlemagne and his nephew Roland. The romances (so called
because they were written in French) of Chrétien de Troyes recounted tales
of adventure and introduced knight errantry, which was a knightly creed by
which a young man rode off in search of adventure to prove his worth in
the profession of arms.

Chivalric literature formed an integral part of a bachelor's apprenticeship. Since listening to these works of fiction might encourage men
to great deeds on the example of the ancient heroes—just as listening to
the Bible inspired Christian virtues in medieval monks—the exploits of
Arthur and Roland were used to inculcate knightly ideals in young warriors. To the aspiring knight who learned his profession well and hardened his body to the demands of knighthood, the rewards of honor, glory,
and renown were offered. Furthermore, these rewards were tied to a
knight's merits, regardless of class, as the twelfth-century real-life *Story of*

William Marshal demonstrated. The equality of knights of similar virtue was symbolized by King Arthur's "round" table. In addition, the literary myths of chivalry's origins flattered the inherent superiority of the knight, although it drew attention, as a consequence of this distinction, to his greater responsibility to society.

The books that were meant to teach chivalry "as any other science" included not only *chansons de geste* and romances, but also biographies and manuals of chivalry. They provided the order of chivalry with a high pedigree and a sense of identity around which knights could rally, but soberly emphasized the knight's double burden of vassalage to God and service to the community. In the thirteenth-century *Book of the Order of Chivalry*, the Catalan author Ramon Lull relied on a surprisingly sophisticated literary passage from Arthurian literature, spoken by the Lady of the Lake in the prose *Lancelot*, to describe chivalry's origins. Long ago, it was said, the common people had voluntarily relinquished the equality that was their birthright—inasmuch as all men are "descended from one father and one mother"—and elected those among themselves whom they judged superior in strength, loyalty, and courage to constitute a class above them in exchange for protection. In return for high rank, the knight bore the burden of having to exercise every virtue—not only on the battlefield, but also in society at large, even if it cost him his life. The significance of this myth lay in its obvious nature as a social contract, originating in the will of the people. The code of chivalry established a knight's calling as one of service rather than pure personal advancement. Arthurian legend described a rigid but subtle mechanism for pressuring knights to conform to the requirements of their duty. Each knight was bound to recount his most recent adventures, whether for honor or shame; this exposed each knight's behavior to the scrutiny of the group. A real-life counterpart was the public procession of the newly dubbed knight, who rode through town to become known, and wore identifying insignia during battle, both described in Ramon Lull's *Book of the Order of Chivalry*. In this way, the pressure to uphold one's oath of service was extended from the legendary round table to the medieval community.

CHIVALRY IN PRACTICE

The colorful tales of chivalric knights held everyone in their grip. Instead of recording exhaustive accounts of battlefield combat, the chronicler Froissart set as his only goal to record worthy feats of arms, regard-less of who performed them. To Froissart, battle was a "beautiful" sight. It was evidently the ability to view war through rose-colored glasses, under the sway of the old romances, that allowed Froissart and his fourteenth-century contemporary, poet and social critic Eustache Des-champs, to express nostalgia for the vanishing culture of chivalry.

But literature provided at best a flawed model. Only in literature was there really the luxury to prefer a tragic hero to an effective one. The *Song of Roland*, for instance, immortalized in its title not Oliver's wisdom and moderation but the futile courage of Roland which caused his death and deprived Charlemagne of his most noble warrior. From a military standpoint, to say nothing of a social or religious perspective, literature also tended to overemphasize the potentially selfish cult of individual celebrity, rashly encourage the rush to arms as a way to settle disputes, valorize violence, and, as the *Song of Roland* illustrates, promote dying as the highest sign of a man's worth. Tournaments of arms, which flourished in the twelfth century as a mechanism for military training and a breed-ing ground for glory, came under some of the same negative scrutiny. Tournaments usefully served the function of military training before the time of standing armies, and perhaps channeled martial energy in times of peace, but they were also frivolous and dangerous. Although the dub-bing ceremony by which a young man entered the brotherhood of knights was quickly infused with Christian goals and religious symbolism (the sword, for instance, represented the cross), the tournament by contrast was anathematized by the Church as diabolical and was repeatedly banned by Church councils. The Church reasoned that the vainglory and senseless killing of tournaments drew potential soldiers away from par-ticipation in the crusades. But the pageantry (often drawing directly on Arthurian models) of the tournament and the power politics, from the perspective of kings and nobles, of identifying and winning the allegiance of the best knights, to say nothing of the riches a young knight could ac-quire on the tournament circuit, did nothing to extinguish this popular medieval institution, even in view of the threat of excommunication.

Real-life battles at the turn of the fourteenth century told a different story—that of the failure of noble mounted knights in the face of chang-ing military practices. Tactical innovations, all but amounting to a mil-itary revolution, began in Flanders, spread to Scotland, and then spread to the English. The French, slow to abandon outmoded chivalric tactics, were most often defeated. At Courtrai in 1302 the French army was unexpectedly and thoroughly defeated by Flemish infantrymen. The victors' gleeful flaunting of the fallen French knights' golden spurs (tokens of achievement in battle or tournament) was in direct proportion to the unlikelihood of infantry defeating the French cavalry. At Crécy in 1346, nine years into the Hundred Years War, the French cavalry suffered devastating losses against the English in a new kind of conflict. Edouard Perroy wrote that Edward III triumphed because he refused to fight "according to the rules which he himself respected," and the evidence bears him out. There was no "level playing field," because Edward had selected a superior defensive position. Instead of a direct and unprotected cavalry charge, Edward's battle formation used sheltered longbowmen on the flanks to kill the French knights' mounts out from under them and a series of small excavations to topple the horses. This would not have been what the chivalric poet of the *Story of William Marshal* intended when he wrote: "[I]t is under the horses' hooves that the champions are to be sought."[1] Edward is also believed to have been the first to use gunpowder artillery, until then reserved for siege warfare, in the battle of Crécy. To show that the English had learned from a "suicidal" cavalry defeat at Bannockburn, Scotland, in 1314, Edward decided upon a tightknit, joint formation of dismounted knights and longbow infantrymen, against which the French made fifteen or sixteen disorganized and worthless charges. English longbowmen, benefiting from the greater speed of the longbow over the crossbow, unleased a rain of arrows on the French, which darkened the sky (see Figure 5). In disbelief at such ignoble tactics, Froissart wrote: "The might of this kingdom most standeth upon archers which are not rich men." The myth of the dominance of heavy cavalry in European warfare, sustained in part by the hero culture of romancers and poets, had been dealt a vital blow.

In the middle decades of the fourteenth century, lay orders of chivalry came into being. As formal royal institutions, with membership by invitation only, the lay orders served to tighten the loyalty to the king of his best vassals. The most familiar names of orders are Edward III's Order of the Garter (1344) and Philip the Good, duke of Burgundy's Order of the Golden Fleece (1430), but the Order of the Star created by King John II of France was possibly the most important politically, and also the most disastrous (see Figure 6). Conceived in 1344 to strengthen faltering French chivalry, the Order of the Star, with some irony, could not be in-

Figure 5. Battle of Crécy. *Courtesy Bibliothèque nationale de France, Paris.*

Figure 6. John the Good institutes Order of the Star. *Courtesy Bibliothèque nationale de France, Paris.*

augurated until 1352, delayed by the drastic chivalric defeat of the French knights at Crécy in 1346.[2] Short lived and ill conceived, the order's membership was decimated in an English ambush at Mauron in Brittany in 1352, where eighty-nine members met their death for honoring an oath not to retreat more than a certain number of feet from the enemy. The oath that allowed the French knights to overcome cowardice proved nonetheless to be of no utility to the crown.

The battle of Poitiers in 1356 provided other ironies. The French chivalry was defeated because of both its heroism and its cowardice. King John II's undaunted adherence to the tenets of chivalry resulted in his capture, an exorbitant ransom, and a disastrous ensuing decade for the kingdom. In his own way John was a second Roland, glorious but costly in defeat. On the other hand, the king had not fled the battlefield, as had the dauphin (the king's oldest son and future King Charles V) and the duke of Orleans (the king's brother)—indefensible actions in a conflict so close that their remaining on the field might have spelled the difference between victory and defeat. Furthermore, thinking they had learned an important lesson at Crécy, the French dismounted to fight. This hardly saved them from defeat, for the dismounted English clinched their victory by remounting. The English forces, under the command of Edward the Black Prince (oldest son of Edward III), backed by the military expertise of John Chandos, constable of Aquitaine, were inferior in numbers and initially uneager to fight, but they won an advantage through such conspicuously unchivalric techniques as ambushes, hiding their horses and archers, and taking advantage of the natural defense of hedges, woods, and swamp.

With as much as forty percent of the French cavalry destroyed at Poitiers alone, it is difficult to comprehend the persistence with which the French thereafter practiced a number of potentially catastrophic tenets of the code of chivalry. One of the most hallowed centered on the willingness to die (or be captured) as long as one's honor remained intact. This translated into a type of chivalric recklessness—described as an admirable trait in the *Story of William Marshal*—whereby a knight asked for no protection but his own prowess and the support of his noble peers. Another part of the creed accentuated the belief that an honorable knight never took special advantage in combat. A third compelled a noble to look upon an enemy noble (with some truth) as an equal, which led to ransoms rather than finishing off dangerous opponents.

Sparing the life of one's knightly counterpart after battle was indeed a "special quality" of chivalry. As in tournament culture, where a feast in common might conclude the day's events for the opposing sides, battle-field adversaries were known to drink a *vin d'honneur* with their aristo-cratic captives. This created an international brotherhood of chivalry—opponents were, after all, frequently cousins, in-laws, or other relatives—that was not very effective at ending wars. Jean Froissart, the foremost annalist of this "borderless" or cosmopolitan brotherhood of arms, loved to relate instances of apparent chivalric indifference to win-ning or losing, where the proper courage and courtesies were respected. At Poitiers, according to Froissart, the Black Prince assessed John II's de-feat in these positive terms: "In my opinion, you have cause to be glad that the success of this battle did not turn out as you desired; for you have this day acquired such high renown for prowess, that you have sur-passed all the best knights on your side."[3]

During the reign of John II's son, Charles V (1364–1380), the tide turned openly in favor of winning at the expense of chivalry and its im-practical prowess. By then the Hundred Years War had moved into its fourth decade and exhaustion was setting in. The French began to aban-don pitched battle and the heavy warhorse as new developments in weaponry and artillery emerged, and the dormant study of military the-ory began to catch up with actual military practice. These advances, and the personal determination of Charles V to steer clear of the disastrous course set by his captured father, brought into existence a new kind of warfare. Strategy, speed, prudence, practicality, and even "dirty tricks" were the hallmarks of the new warfare, and a petty nobleman from Brit-tany, Bertrand du Guesclin, raised on savage Breton brush warfare rather than Arthurian romance, was its commander. Charles V's decision to hand over the command and avoid personally marching into battle was equally un-Arthurian, but it assured the protection of the head of state. Charles also refused to risk his best barons needlessly. He believed in never initiating warfare unless the enemy was totally exposed, compro-mising when possible to avoid warfare, and even paying an enemy to avoid spilling blood. Refusing battle was in fact a competent defensive maneuver and Charles was quickly able to debunk the idea that signifi-cant victories rested on cavalry alone.

Mounted knights were thus forced from center stage during the reign of Charles V, and a broad strategy of siege warfare, skirmishes, and small encounters replaced them. Castle-building had reached its highest point in the thirteenth century. But since siege artillery had not changed significantly since the Roman military manual *On Military Matters*, written by the fourth-century writer Vegetius, as long as supplies held out inside the walls, the advantage generally lay with the defenders. A well-supplied town or fortress (see Document 6) could hold out for months, unprofitably immobilizing the enemy's troops. On the other hand, as du Guesclin knew, the way to gain control of a region was to capture its castle or fortress, make devastating raids of the countryside during the day, return to the safety of the castle at night, and continue until control of the vicinity was achieved. Siege warfare, therefore, became an important part of du Guesclin's offensive operations. Limited gunpowder use in Europe had begun in the late thirteenth century, and the introduction of small-caliber cannons, at first not very threatening, increased in size and effectiveness over the period of the fourteenth century. It is known that during the siege of Melun in 1359, the French army benefited from two "large" gunpowder cannons which shot lead balls and required twenty-three pounds of gunpowder to operate. It is also true that capturing an intact fortress could better serve an aggressor than a fortress in ruins, and du Guesclin deftly used diplomatic surrender, strengthened by threats and promises, as part of his repertoire (see Document 7). In the long run, this systematic, castle-by-castle strategy allowed du Guesclin to retake the majority of the territory lost by France in the treaty of Brétigny. For this he became a hero, but it must not have escaped notice that the sacrifices and casualties of warfare had in part been shifted from mounted knights to civilian noncombatants (see Document 8).

The changing nature of warfare brought alterations in the manner of recruitment and composition of late medieval soldiery. Increasingly, soldiers were not fief-holders, and the old mechanisms of military conscription, the feudal *ban* and *arrière-ban*, which required a designated number of days of voluntary service to the crown, gradually disappeared. Figures differ as to what percentage of fourteenth-century armies served on the basis of oral or written contract or worked directly for wages. But after the peace of Brétigny (1360) and the conclusion of the wars of succession in Brittany (1365), many unemployed fighters were recruited into royal armies. In France, du Guesclin was firm about the need for Charles V to pay the royal army but turned a blind eye when his men augmented their income by pillage and looting. The riffraff, who had formed a key portion of du Guesclin's men in time of need, were gradually eliminated. Nevertheless, the proportion of knights to other soldiers in the French royal army fell from sixteen percent in 1340 to eleven percent in 1382.[4] Here the change to the raid and, especially, to siege warfare tells much of the story. As it has been observed dryly, taking a fortified place required going over it (scaling walls), under it (mining), or through it (artillery).[5] There was increased need not for mounted knights, who still played a role, but for foundrymen, blacksmiths, carpenters, artillerymen, cannoneers, and simple excavators. The king now looked to a broad range of war participants; the monopoly of the nobility was clearly on the wane. The English were also practicing the devastating scorched earth technique called the *chevauchée*, which targeted the civilian population in order to force the local prince to surrender. As there was no recruitment strategy that could prevent the *chevauchée*, Charles V's response was to allow what he could not prevent, theorizing that a kingdom overrun by the English was better than a kingdom lost altogether.

THE REBIRTH OF WAR THEORY

These strange circumstances, and other moral dilemmas connected with the new warfare, were to change the way people in the Middle Ages thought about warfare. The *Tree of Battles* (1387), by the Benedictine monk Honoré Bouvet, and a later work, Christine de Pizan's *Book of Deeds of Arms and of Chivalry* (c. 1410), brought to theoretical war studies essentially the first new developments since Vegetius in the fourth century. The existence of at least three hundred manuscripts of Vegetius from the Middle Ages wrongly implies that nothing had changed in European warfare over ten centuries, and part of Bouvet and Christine's accomplishment was to make this point. In fact, some of the "new" warfare of the Hundred Years War was no more than a revival of Vegetius, which had been overshadowed by chivalry.

Bouvet's *Tree of Battles* (dedicated to Charles VI) exhibited a much broader vision of the military class than manuals of chivalry, setting out a radical program of reform derived in part from chivalry.[6] Not interested in the etiquette of the joust, the tournament, or the rules for the pursuit of individual glory through *faits d'armes* (deeds of arms), Bouvet embraced the broader subject of the soldier's role in society, a focus that has earned him the reputation as the originator of international law. By contrasting the "laws of war" (essentially the law of nations) with the "laws of arms," Bouvet moved attention to protecting the rights of all classes, not solely the military class. In arriving at the principles of a just war, Bouvet furthered the interests of the state. He argued that because sovereigns do not represent private interests but the public welfare, they alone have the right to wage war. He then added that a vassal's obligation was not to the baron from whom he held a fief, but to his highest lord, the king. Bouvet's blueprint for change represented a striking advance in the centralization of military power under the king's command.

Christine de Pizan popularized Bouvet by presenting points from the *Tree of Battles* in dialogue format in the *Book of Deeds of Arms and of Chivalry*, but also advanced her own ideas, including theoretical justifications for what was already current practice. On waging warfare, Christine agreed with Bouvet that only a sovereign could wage a just war, given the sovereign's responsibility for the well-being of his people. But she believed that the commander in the field need not be the king, noting proudly that "without moving from his royal throne" Charles V reconquered the lands that his chivalrous predecessors had lost (through the Treaty of Brétigny). On the use of cunning, significantly, Christine agreed that a commander could resort to wiles, because in the Bible the Lord helped Joshua overcome his enemies by a ruse. She argued that soldiers should receive wages, which obligated them to support the king because they took pay from him. Regarding military recruitment, she favored selection based on skill rather than lineage. Importantly, she argued that when a king desired to wage war, he should have the consent of all the people, including the common people. If he waged war without the people's consent, then he would rid himself of enemies outside only to "acquire them nearby."[7] In all things, Christine reasoned, wisdom was more important than strength and prowess.

The appearance of theoretical war studies by Honoré Bouvet and Christine de Pizan at the turn of the fifteenth century carries more importance than is obvious at first. Until the mid-fourteenth century, the chivalric nobility had succeeded in keeping the practice of warfare as its own special preserve. The Hundred Years War had made the culture of chivalry, and the knightly code of behavior on which it rested, increasingly irrelevant. Engaging in war for reasons of personal glory, placing a higher premium on honor than on winning, and swearing to preserve the life of one's opponent seemed to fly in the face of the objective of war, which was to win. But the terrible lessons of Crécy and Poitiers had not quite been learned, as the French defeat at Agincourt in 1415 was to demonstrate. Once again an overconfident French cavalry was thrown into confusion, this time by Henry V, who imitated the infantry tactics that had defeated the French before. The time was coming, however, when the principles laid down by Bouvet, Christine, and others would be increasingly reflected in practice.

NOTES

1. Georges Duby, *William Marshal, the Flower of Chivalry*, trans. Richard Howard (New York: Pantheon, 1985), p. 107.

2. Richard Barber, *The Knight and Chivalry* (Woodbridge: Boydell Press, 1995), pp. 343–44.

3. Jean Froissart, *Chronicles of England, France, Spain . . .* [etc.], ed. Thomas Johnes (London: Routledge, 1868), vol. 1, pp. 226–27.

4. William W. Kibler and Grover A. Zinn, eds., *Medieval France: An Encyclopedia* (New York: Garland, 1995), p. 510.

5. Nicholas Hooper and Matthew Bennett, *Cambridge Illustrated Atlas of Warfare: The Middle Ages, 768–1487* (Cambridge, England: Cambridge University Press, 1996), p. 162.

6. Maurice Keen, *The Laws of War in the Late Middle Ages* (London: Routledge, 1965) cited by Hooper and Bennett, *Cambridge Illustrated Atlas*, p. 168.

7. Christine de Pizan, *The Book of Deeds of Arms and of Chivalry*, trans. Sumner Willard, ed. Charity Cannon Willard (University Park: Pennsylvania State University Press, 1999), p. 19.

CHAPTER 4

THE CREATION OF ROYAL AUTHORITY IN FRANCE: THE RELIGION OF THE MONARCHY

Long before there was anything equivalent to a king of France, or any stable territory with fixed boundaries that could, with any accuracy, be called the kingdom of France, western kingdoms had to confront the problems of the creation, maintenance, and transfer of royal power. When rulers acquired new lands through inheritance, marriage, or conquest or were faced with naming their own successor, they sought ways to remove the uncertainty of their claims by legitimizing their royal authority. It is believed, in the case of Europe, that early medieval kings never merely succeeded to their thrones "as a matter of course." Mechanisms were needed to make the transfer of power something other than a blunt show of force, and religion played an important part in that process.

THE FRENCH TRADITION

France developed by far the most splendid sacred mythology around its kingship of all the kingdoms in western Europe, although the earliest known coronations occurred in Visigothic Spain and Ireland. The sacred mythology of French kingship, which came to be known as "the religion of the monarchy," first emerged during the Merovingian dynasty, in the context of a baptismal anointing rather than a sacred coronation, when Clovis, king of the Franks, converted to Christianity. From that time, kingship and the Church embarked on a joint relationship, ideally, but not always in fact, of mutual benefit. As the result of many conquests and the centralizing strategies of various kings, France ceased to be a "fluid" concept. Only then could the religion of the monarchy, which had grown apace, fed by the growth and development of formidable myths and buttressed by rich religious symbolism, be applied to the territory France (*Francia*) rather than to its people, the Franks. During the Hundred Years War, the ritual mythology, so useful to all kings during challenges to their right to rule, was at hand to be put to advantage by the king, whether of France or England, who could more effectively mobilize it to his cause. In the event it turned out that the French, master mythmakers with an ability to internalize their own fictions, carried the day. Without our understanding the concept of the religion of the monarchy and the mentality that fostered it, Joan of Arc's meteoric career becomes largely incomprehensible. The remainder of this essay, therefore, outlines the important history of sacred kingship in France to the time of the Hundred Years War. The final chapter, in taking up Joan of Arc's role in the war, will show how her unexpectedly astute use of the sacred mythology hastened England's eventual defeat.

Clovis I (d. 511) and the Franks

With Clovis, the founder of the Merovingian dynasty, begins the history of Christian kingship in France. The warrior chieftain Clovis achieved the rank of king of the Franks, reigning from 481 to 511, by the bloody elimination of other contenders in the fight for territorial supremacy in ancient Gaul. Clovis' ruthless route to power was facilitated, in his own view, by a pact he made with the Christian god whom his wife Clotilda, a Burgundian princess, already worshiped. Coming face to face with the powerful Alemanni people, Clovis put his wife's faith to the test by promising to be baptized in the new religion if the Christian god brought him victory against his enemies. Winning the battle, Clovis agreed to adopt the new religion and underwent baptism by Saint Remi, bishop of Reims. So Christian kingship among the Franks originated as a debt of gratitude for divine protection. At his baptism, King Clovis was anointed with a holy balm, or salve (see Figure 7), in a cer-

Figure 7. Baptism of Clovis by Saint Remi. *Courtesy Bibliothèque nationale de France, Paris.*

emony blending kingship and religion. According to the contemporary chronicle of Gregory of Tours, the anointing of Clovis occurred by the grace of God, prompting Gregory to draw an analogy between Clovis and the sacred kingship of David in the Old Testament. Although Clovis' campaigns were mostly about personal ambition, the first Christian king of the Franks became the protector of the orthodox faith, and the Merovingian dynasty, in that sense, acquired a special destiny.

Pepin the Short (d. 768)

The second dynasty of French kings, the Carolingian dynasty, takes its name not from its first rulers, the Pippinids, but from the most famous—Charlemagne. Pepin the Short, however, receives credit for introducing the ritual of sacred anointing, or consecration, into the installation ceremony for French kings. Adding religious ritual to the process of inaugurating new kings appears to have been an instinctive way of creating royal authority, but coronations and anointings as rituals of power, or even the use of religion itself to legitimize royal power, were not as obvious in western history as it may seem. In *Beowulf* (c. 1000), the king merely handed over his weapons as an indication of the transfer of power, and Irish chieftains were inaugurated simply by being raised on a shield, receiving a rod, or standing on a stone. Pepin, however, during a bold transfer of power, used consecration by two popes, in 751 and 754, to validate his kingship. As mayor of the palace, Pepin obtained papal approval to depose the Merovingian ruler, Clovis' descendant Childeric III, and place himself on the throne. Flaunting the requirement that all kings be descendants of Clovis, an ambitious royal administrator had usurped the throne of a reigning monarch, and the Church, through consecration, had lent support to the precarious new dynasty. As Patrick Simon has stated, Pepin's innovation consisted of "legitimizing through a religious ceremony a power obtained by force."[1] The union of king and clergy provided mutual benefit, however. An aura of prestige now surrounded the king, whom the pope called the "new David," while the pope in turn anticipated protection for the Church at Rome. The second coronation, celebrated at Saint-Denis in 754, cleverly reconnected Pepin's reign to the Merovingians through his wife, bigfoot Bertha, a descendant of Clovis, which provided fictional continuity to French kingship.

Charlemagne (d. 814)

When Charlemagne, Pepin's son, had accumulated all the vast territory that was to be added to Frankish rule during his lifetime, his authority extended across a large part of western Europe. Such political significance was nothing the Church could ignore, especially since papal authority was then threatened and in disarray. So on Christmas day 800, in commemoration of the birth of Christ, a surprise coronation took place, when Pope Leo III declared Charlemagne Christian emperor of the West, as the gathering proclaimed him "crowned of God." Charlemagne, whom his biographer Einhard described as persuaded of his own God-given mission to unite western Christendom,[2] was looked upon as king and priest (*rex et sacerdos*). Charlemagne was crowned without consecration, but as emperor he became a Christian conqueror who, with the full measure of his strength, dedicated himself to serving the faith and extending the reach of Christianity. Rome began the practice of referring to both Pepin and Charlemagne as "most Christian" kings for living up to the promise placed in them—the one as protector, the other as propagator of the faith.

Hincmar (d. 882)

Hincmar, archbishop of Reims from 845 to 882, was a learned theologian and nimble politician, whose fame in the development of sacred kingship rests on his introduction of the legend of the Holy Ampulla into the history of Clovis, four centuries after the fact. In an effort to prove the continuity of Frankish kingship and, it is commonly believed, to challenge the influence of the abbey of Saint-Denis—then successfully fusing its own history with that of the monarchy—Hincmar authorized a new myth. He is often believed to have fabricated the story himself in an attempt to expand the importance of the see of Reims. In all likelihood, he did not invent it, although he had confessed to forging other documents. The myth made the astonishing assertion that the liquid used to consecrate Frankish kings was of divine origin. A dove, the Christian symbol of the Holy Spirit, had allegedly delivered the Ampulla, or vial, of sacred liquid in its beak, when the bustling crowd at Clovis' baptism had prevented the bearer of the baptismal oil from a timely arrival at the ceremony. Through this myth the election of French kings was seen as the will of God. Furthermore, the continuity of their rule was guaranteed by an inexhaustible supply of anointing balm held in the Holy Ampulla, which could anoint French kings to the end of time.

The effect of this fiction on the course of French kingship was as vital as if it had been genuine historical fact. The legend created a dazzling identity between French kingship and the archbishopric of Reims—a convenient counterweight to the competing influence of the monastery of Saint-Denis. In 869, during the coronation and consecration of Charles the Bald, Hincmar compared the Frankish king to the kings of Israel. The Franks, according to Hincmar, were kings in the tradition of God's elect and consequently endowed with both superiority and a religious mission. But since the privilege of consecration suggested the king's resemblance to priests, a possible threat to priestly power, Hincmar clarified to Charles the Bald: "It is to your anointing . . . much more than to your temporal power, that you owe your royal dignity."[3] This was Hincmar's way of saying that through consecration prelates held control over kingship. Hincmar's fable of the Holy Ampulla became so closely linked to the essence of French kingship that after the French revolution, in a symbolic final erasure of the French monarchy, a citizen of the new republic destroyed the Holy Ampulla, breaking it against a statue of Louis XV to cries of "Vive la République!" Until then it was, in the words of French historian Colette Beaune, "an obligatory truth of French patriotism," so fundamental to the realm that the details of the legend scarcely ever varied in the retelling.[4]

Philip II Augustus (r. 1180–1223)

The reign of Philip Augustus, seventh ruler of the Capetians, France's third dynasty, was marked by astonishing territorial conquests. Focused on England as his primary enemy, in a conflict sometimes called the first Hundred Years War, King Philip eventually dismantled most of the Angevin legacy of England in France. Aquitaine was more or less all that remained of England's French dominions. By the time Philip had seized French lands from his third Plantagenet king, the king in question, John I Lackland, was being called "the king without a kingdom" and "the fifth wheel of a cart."[5] The Plantagenet dynasty survived the Capetian onslaught of Philip Augustus, although considerably weakened, while Philip nearly quadrupled the size of French lands.

By acquiring this vast territory, holding it, and effectively administering it, Philip Augustus established the foundations of French royal power in the Middle Ages. During his reign, the French monarchy, previously recognized as little more than the Paris basin, or Ile-de-France, started to take on the flavor and feel of a national monarchy. In recognition of the increasingly definable entity called France, royal correspondence during Philip's reign began to substitute the title "king of France" for "king of the Franks." By 1205 the phrase "kingdom of France" appeared. Philip was firm about matters of jurisdiction inside and outside his newly enlarged Capetian kingdom. He triumphed over his own barons, increasing royal power at the expense of the feudal aristocracy, and obtained from Pope Innocent III a declaration acknowledging that "the king of France recognizes no superior in temporal matters."[6]

Entranced by the life and imperial image of Charlemagne, to whom he must have considered himself in many ways parallel, Philip consciously patterned himself on the model of the great Christian emperor. A contemporary author, Gerald of Wales, even claimed that in a dream Philip had wondered if God would ever restore to France "the ancient breadth and greatness" of the age of Charlemagne.[7] In calling himself Augustus, Philip specifically invoked his glorious ancestor—a handy fiction, indeed, for a king needing to authorize his juridiction over newly conquered territories. In the twelfth century, Charlemagne was primarily known through literary rather than historical works. Philip had certainly listened to the popular epic poems about national heroes—the most prominent being Charlemagne—called *chansons de geste*. The *Song of Roland*, the most famous one, written around 1100, recounts the ambush of Charlemagne's rearguard at the pass of Roncevaux. Even at this early date, the poem speaks of "sweet France," as if it were a well-defined kingdom with Charlemagne its exclusive ruler, rather than the commander of the entire Carolingian empire. Philip may have taken the image of the ideal ruler depicted in the *Song of Roland* and tried to reproduce it in himself. In an evident imitation of Charlemagne's role in the *Song of Roland* as priest-king, Philip Augustus blessed his troops at the battle of Bouvines, invoking Roland and his companion Oliver, heroes of the *Song of Roland*, as examples of courage.

The Capetian dynasty, based on a usurpation which had caused the unnatural end of the Carolingian dynasty, was now ready for at least symbolic reassimilation to the Carolingian line. Therefore, during Philip Augustus' reign clerics found a way to trace the king's descent to that of Charlemagne. This was far from the only Capetian effort of its kind. At the monastery of Saint-Denis, fictions and forgeries that enhanced royal prestige—and, simultaneously, the prestige of the monastery—were commonplace during the eleventh and twelfth centuries, especially, it appears, under the direction of abbot Suger from 1122 to 1151. Suger was a realist who recognized that the fortune of the abbey had declined since the age of Charlemagne. Through strategies designed for their mutual benefit, Suger kindled in King Louis VI, who had been educated at Saint-Denis, a "Carolingian" devotion of Saint Denis. In one ritual, the royal arms were placed at the monastery's altar to receive protection from the saint before leaving for battle. In another, the military banner of Saint-Denis became assimilated with the legendary flag of Charlemagne, known as the *oriflamme* or *Montjoye*. From this fusion came the French battle cry *Montjoye Saint-Denis*. The boldest move of the era was a forged document claiming to be a charter written by Charlemagne in 813, but in all likelihood the work of the abbey of Saint-Denis during the first half of the twelfth century. Capitalizing on the popularity of Charlemagne in the *chansons de geste*, the author credited none other than Charlemagne with promises of fabulous good favor for Saint-Denis. Among the promises, Charlemagne agreed to donate all of France as a fief to the church of Saint-Denis. Placing his crown at the altar of the holy martyrs, Charlemagne offered four gold coins in acknowledgment of a vassal's submission and recognized that he "[held] the kingdom of France from God and Saint Denis alone." Finally, Charlemagne asked permission to depart, saying, "I leave behind the kingdom of France." Echoes of this curious hoax of national submission to divine protection could still be heard during the time of Joan of Arc.

Although Philip Augustus died in 1223, his obsession with Charlemagne would serve the monarchy, in a unique way, a half century later. The unofficial national French chronicle, known as the *Grandes Chroniques*, was begun by the monks of Saint-Denis in 1274 during the reign of the Capetians. In the interest of permanently placing the myth of the uninterrupted succession of French kings in the written record, the monks lent authority to a fictitious genealogy which, by an act of divine will, reconnected Hugh Capet's heirs through his wife's bloodline to their admired forebear Charlemagne. The stain of Hugh's elevation to the throne through election was thus eliminated by a fabricated return to hereditary monarchy. The broken thread of the Carolingian dynasty was reconnected, producing a chain of legitimacy unique in western Christendom. The fable was thus inscribed in the Capetian royal chronicle that the monarchy had returned, at the direction of God, to its illustrious Carolingian roots. Here was one further instance of the crafting of unshakable propaganda for the French royal house, an art at which medieval practitioners would continue to prove themselves adept in the future.

Louis IX (r. 1226–1270)

Louis IX, or Saint Louis, contributed significantly to the tradition of sacred kingship and to the development of royal administration, so much so that later generations referred to his kingship with reverence and nostalgia. Even during Louis' lifetime, he was regarded unofficially as a saint for his extravagant Christian virtues. His canonization in 1297 connected the pious king, for the only time in French history, with the dual callings of saint and king.

But Louis' reign is proof that strong monarchies often sprang from unsteady foundations. In fact, Louis' rule got off to a shaky start. His father, Louis VIII, had anticipated the risk involved in crowning a twelve-year-old and appointing his mother, Blanche of Castile, a nonnative, regent. All those in the elder Louis' immediate circle swore before the dying king to hold the coronation with all reasonable haste. When the younger Louis was coronated on November 29, 1226, three hundred armed and mounted knights fetched the Holy Ampulla, a convincing sign that they were expecting trouble. Yet during his reign, Louis IX built an ever more solid edifice around the royal authority. Two important *ordines* (liturgical scripts of the coronation ritual), written in 1230 and 1250, reveal the royal mindset. Hincmar's legend of the Holy Ampulla was permanently incorporated into the coronation ritual. As a result, it was declared, with far-reaching consequences, that because French rulers were anointed with oil sent from heaven, the king of France "outshines all the kings of the earth." Now the French could boast, as did a thirteenth-century poet named Richier, that "in all other regions [but France] / Kings have to buy their oil at the apothecary." Henceforth, French coronations were marked by a special French identity separating them from the western coronation tradition. Even the English monk Matthew Paris acknowledged the right of French kings to a certain supremacy on this basis, and was will-ing to call Louis "the king of earthly kings . . . because of his heavenly anointing."[8]

Saint Louis' reign was responsible for other innovations that strength-ened perceptions of the religion of the monarchy. In a reversal of the papal trend of the previous two centuries, which denied the ability of lay kings to perform miracles, Saint Louis revived the royal cure for scrofula (a tubercular disease), whereby the king through his touch alone mirac-ulously healed the afflicted. In an odd reinforcement of the false charter of Charlemagne, dating from the era of Philip Augustus, Saint Louis re-peated the practice of the king's vassalage to Saint Denis by performing the ritual of placing four coins on the saint's altar, and then actually trans-forming the practice into law. As others before him, Saint Louis main-tained that the consecration of French kings was intimately connected to the original anointings of Old Testament kings.

The tradition of national sainthood in France, which reached its high-est point under Saint Louis, represented a very different tradition from England, where the cults of saints either failed to reach national recog-nition or were recognized for resisting rather than supporting royal power. While politics in France maintained a firm sense of hierarchy, with God at the pinnacle, then the king, and finally the people, England, by con-trast, moved toward a constitutional political system, where eventually the king was subordinate not only to God but also to the law.[9]

Philip IV the Fair (r. 1285–1314)

Even before Philip the Fair's reign, Ramon Lull's successful *Book on the Order of Chivalry* (c. 1260) had warned the knight to aid his "earthly lord and natural country," but in France there was still reason to ques-tion where the boundaries of that "natural country" might be. The king of France had become a sacred ruler, but France still lacked true geo-graphical definition, since French kings tended to see themselves as rul-ing a series of separate possessions.[10] Strengthening the idea of a French kingdom began practically. Philip IV needed to raise an army and to fi-nance expensive wars. He promoted the idea of a unified realm so that he could then argue that its defense was required of all people "in the kingdom and of the kingdom." When Philip found himself locked in a controversy with Pope Boniface VIII over Philip's right to tax the clergy for the defense of the realm, Philip used his clever propagandists to make the case that France was a pillar of the Church, its faith being of long and unquestionable duration. In earlier reigns, the idea had already been expressed that the king's superiority implied the superiority of the king-dom, and that the kingdom was especially devout. But now the pope's challenge required a more pronounced level of defense of France's Chris-tian orthodoxy. In a context of self-defense, French propagandists rein-stated the formality—all but dropped by the popes—of calling themselves "most Christian." From their claim to be a pillar of the Church, they ar-gued boldly that an attack on France was an attack on the faith. Simi-larly, they maintained that any action taken for the defense of France benefited Christendom as a whole.

But a final piece was still to be put in place in the expanding rheto-ric of France: the assimilation, implied for centuries in comparisons with Old Testament kings, of France as a kingdom chosen by God, and its in-habitants as God's elect—ideological developments that would help to recommend Joan of Arc years later. One royal propagandist in Philip the Fair's employment wrote that "God . . . chose [France] as his own, special kingdom." Another, through a pun on the word *franks* ("the free" or "the Franks"), spoke of "Christ, the king of the free/Franks," and dared to claim that Christ carried the *fleur-de-lis* and the *oriflamme* as his ban-ners.[11] The ultimate endorsement came from Pope Clement V, who wrote in a papal bull: "Like the people of Israel . . . the kingdom of France, as a special people chosen by the Lord to carry out the orders of Heaven, is distinguished by marks of special honor and grace."[12] With this state-ment, Clement V acknowledged the new French identity, an identity, es-pecially with regard to carrying out the orders of heaven, that Joan of Arc would unhesitatingly embrace. The real question was whether this carefully constructed Christian ideology could withstand the assaults yet to be felt from the Hundred Years War.

Until the time of Charles V (r. 1364–1380), no significant develop-ments occurred in the religion of the monarchy. But the challenges faced by Charles V, who ruled at a critical juncture in the Hundred Years War, reintroduced the perennial question: How do you make a royal success story? Charles had been duly anointed in the sacred tradition of French kings in 1364, which Edward III had failed to achieve in 1359. Since the English were claiming royal jurisdiction over everything they conquered, however, Charles recognized that the theoretical structure of French kingship was no longer adequate. Through the feverish commissioning of works, Charles created a written foundation to support his kingship, pointedly focused on increasing the mystique of the throne. Although much of what Charles V accomplished was eclipsed during the reign of Charles VI, he was the strongest promoter of sacred kingship between Philip IV and Joan of Arc.

NOTES

1. Patrick Simon, *Le mythe royal* (Lille: Atelier National, Reproduction des Thèses, Université Lille III, 1987), p. 41.

2. Thomas S. Bokenkotter, *A Concise History of the Catholic Church*, rev. and expanded ed. (New York: Image Books, 1990), p. 97.

3. Marc Bloch, *The Royal Touch*, trans. J. E. Anderson (New York: Dorset Press, 1989), p. 39.

4. Colette Beaune, *The Birth of an Ideology: Myths and Symbols of Nation in Late-Medieval France*, trans. Susan Ross Huston, ed. Fredric L. Cheyette (Berkeley: University of California Press, 1991), p. 78.

5. Ernest Lavisse, ed., *Histoire de France: Depuis les origines jusqu'à la révolution* (Paris: Hachette, 1901), vol. 3, pt. 1, p. 252.

6. Jean Richard, *Saint Louis: Crusader King of France* (Cambridge, England: Cambridge University Press, 1992), p. 244.

7. Gabrielle M. Spiegel, "The *Reditus Regni ad Stirpem Karoli Magni*: A New Look," *French Historical Studies*, 7, no. 2 (1971), p. 165.

8. Cited by Jacques Le Goff, Eric Palazzo, Jean-Claude Bonne, Marie-Noël Colette, *Le sacre royal à l'époque de Saint Louis: d'après le manuscrit latin 1246 de la BNF* (Paris: Gallimard, 2001), p. 156.

9. Sergio Bertelli, *The King's Body: The Sacred Rituals of Power in Medieval and Early Modern Europe*, trans. R. Burr Litchfield (University Park: Pennsylvania State University Press, 2001), p. 38.

10. A. W. Lewis, *Royal Succession in Capetian France: Studies on Familial Order and the State* (Cambridge, MA: Harvard University Press, 1981), cited by Richard A. Jackson, *Vive le Roi! A History of the French Coronation from Charles V to Charles X* (Chapel Hill: University of North Carolina Press, 1984), p. 70.

11. Joseph R. Strayer, "France: The Holy Land, the Chosen People, and the Most Christian King," in *Medieval Statecraft and the Perspectives of History: Essays by Joseph R. Strayer* (Princeton: Princeton University Press, 1971), p. 307.

12. Strayer, "France," p. 313.

CHAPTER 5

THE WAR AND JOAN OF ARC

There is scant evidence to reveal what Joan of Arc understood about the broad conflict known as the Hundred Years War. But since she came to believe herself divinely appointed, not so as to dedicate herself to a life of prayer, or to offer prophetic advice to royalty, for which there were ample precedents for women, but to conduct a political and military mission in the kingdom of France, that evidence is of genuine importance. Therefore, after providing the fundamental background, this chapter does not ask the conventional questions about who Joan of Arc was and what she did, but rather what she knew and understood about the war and her own position in it.

In the year 1412, when Joan of Arc was born in Domrémy, on the eastern frontier of the French monarchy, France and England were in the seventy-fifth year of the Hundred Years War. Forty-one years still remained in the war. Few historians would admit that nationalism as yet existed, but the conflict that had begun as both a dispute over Aquitaine and a dynastic quarrel for the crown of France had, perhaps from the sheer duration of the struggle, been altered, for some, into an essentially nationalistic war. French patriotism had certainly been aroused, although the sentiment would lack for a name in French until the end of the century. Instead, the focus of pride in one's country was the king.

Two kings named Charles had most recently succeeded each other as rulers of France. The first, Charles V (1364–1380), after an unfavorable start, had become a powerful ruler. The second, Charles VI (1380–1422), began his reign with a disastrous minority (interim rule for a minor), but when conditions might have improved, he was struck with mental illness, and competition for the reins of power led to civil war. There was as yet no thought of the rule of a third Charles. Two older princes, Louis, duke of Guyenne, and John, duke of Touraine, stood to inherit the crown before the nine-year-old Charles, count of Ponthieu and future Charles VII. The last stabilizing influence disappeared from the realm in 1404 with the death of Philip the Bold, duke of Burgundy, the mad king's brother. Hatred between the opposing factions in the civil war escalated after the murder of Louis of Orleans in 1407. Louis' cousin and rival, John the Fearless, the new duke of Burgundy, confessed to the crime, but his political career nevertheless survived through an arrogant self-defense brought before the Parisians, which few, if any, must have believed.

At the time of Joan of Arc's birth, the civil war between the Armagnacs and Burgundians, which then influenced all politics in France, produced the strangest episode yet in the Hundred Years War. The rival factions were locked in conflict so bitterly that they forgot England was the mortal enemy of France, and each side took a turn negotiating with the English on its own behalf. Each faction believed that alliance with England might be the "deciding factor" in their struggle for power against one another. The duke of Burgundy was the first to approach Henry IV, offering his daughter's hand in marriage. The Armagnacs, on the other hand, agreed to grant to England important territories then under their control, despite the growing sense at the time that kings could not alienate (that is, detach or separate) any part of the realm. In this case, though, the king was indisposed because of his illness. When the rival factions finally came to their senses and signed the Treaty of Auxerre on August 22, 1412, renouncing all foreign alliances, it was too late. Henry V came to power in England in 1413 and quickly recognized the opportunity presented by civil war in France. Optimistic about the potential for power, Henry resurrected Edward III's claim to the French throne as pretext for an invasion. After no English campaign had troubled French soil since 1380, English troops now arrived on the Norman coast and the Hundred Years War resumed.

In October 1415, Henry V achieved a stunning victory over the French army at Agincourt. Henry's intimate advisers urged the king to see the English victory as God's blessing on his efforts.[1] Joan was then three years old and not yet ready to contest this view, but the war had reached her corner of the world. Edward, duke of Bar, whose duchy lay across the river Meuse from Domrémy, was among the estimated 10,000 French deaths.

Around this time, two misfortunes were added to the calamities already devastating France. The three royal princes, Louis, John, and their little brother Charles, had been shuttled around the kingdom for years for their safety and to prevent the duke of Burgundy from abducting them in his own quest for power. Louis and John, each named dauphin in turn, died in 1415 and 1417. This left Charles the unexpected heir. Significantly, for the infamous disinheritance that would soon take place, the young Charles was immediately named dauphin, or heir to the throne, "with all the privileges attached to the title." He was clearly a prince in good standing.

Before Joan set out on her mission in 1429, there were two more tragedies in store for France. In apparent recognition that a house divided cannot stand, the dauphin Charles met John the Fearless on a bridge at Montereau to negotiate a peace. Despite the professions of good will and intricate precautions for safety, on the day of the meeting (September 10, 1419), the dauphin's men hacked the duke of Burgundy to death. Later, pointing to the hole in the Burgundian prince's skull, someone declared, "This is the hole through which the English entered France." In effect, on May 21, 1420 (in the ultimate act of alienation of the royal kingdom), Charles VI, his queen Isabeau of Bavaria, Henry V, and the new duke of Burgundy, Philip the Good, all signed the Treaty of Troyes (see Document 10). The treaty stipulated that after the death of Charles VI, the entire kingdom of France would pass to Henry V and his heirs. The peace between England and France that would follow was to be secured by the marriage of Henry V to Charles VI's daughter Catherine. The dauphin Charles was excluded from the proceedings where his fate was decided, stripped of the title of dauphin, and disinherited—the sole explanation given being the "horrible and monstrous crimes and transgressions" he had perpetrated in the kingdom of France (the murder at Montereau). Since the disinherited dauphin still held most of France south of the Loire, Henry prepared to conquer his "inheritance" in France by force.

To those who believed in the dignity and the rights of the French crown, the last forty years, culminating in the Treaty of Troyes, had brought France to the point of heartbreaking desolation.

The voices were for the king of France. The question posed by Joan's early years is when and how her own participation in the Hundred Years War arose. Joan grew up in a region of exceedingly complex jurisdictions at the crossroads of the duchies of Bar, Lorraine, and Champagne, all three owing fealty to the Anglo-Burgundians. Her own village of Domrémy had been a dependency of the French crown since 1328, but her local parish was divided between French loyalists residing in Domrémy and Burgundians from Bar and Lorraine. The nearby town of Vaucouleurs was the local seat of government for territory owing allegiance to the king of France. This small pocket of Anglo-Burgundian resistance has been compared to the Mont-Saint-Michel, a fortified monastery off the coast of Normandy, loyal to France although surrounded by Anglo-Burgundian territory. The monastery maintained its loyalty to France by its fortifications and ocean protection, but the inhabitants of Joan's town maintained their loyalty to France by sheer strength of will.

As to what exact circumstances led Joan of Arc to believe that she was destined to participate in the Hundred Years War, not as an observer but as an actor, our curiosity can only be partially satisfied. We rely for an answer on the two trial records—the condemnation trial (1431) and the nullification trial (also rehabilitation trial) of 1456, neither of which was written for this purpose. The condemnation trial, surviving in two versions (the contemporary French *Minute* and a Latin version of 1435), reflects the bias of Joan's foes, who put her to death for crimes of heresy on the basis of this testimony. The condemnation trial is also marred by Joan's understandable reluctance to provide her judges, through fully truthful answers, with the means to condemn her. The nullification trial suffers from the opposite bias. Designed to nullify the act of condemnation of 1431, the testimony consists of only flattering judgments by village friends, acquaintances, and relatives, all wishing to prove that their local heroine was no heretic. Twenty-five years after Joan left Domrémy, they presented crystal clear memories of her youthful piety and disdain of superstitious practices, and they outdid themselves describing how she was "just like the other girls." By and large, this is not a good way to learn what prompted her to go to war. Despite these limitations, much can be inferred.

From the age of thirteen Joan received directives she believed to be supernatural, telling her to be good. The first hint that this mystical experience was war related came when Joan "learned that the voices were for the king of France."[2] This knowledge caused her to dislike the Burgundians and to consider that "they would have war, if they did not do as they ought." When Joan saw the boys from Domrémy return home bloodied after fighting their Burgundian counterparts in the neighboring village of Maxey, she was watching, however small the scale, the same struggle that was in progress all over France.

In the meantime, the presence of soldiers in the region was a fact of life. Joan's father dreamed that she might go away with some men-at-arms, a prospect that infuriated him. Cattle often had to be herded into a walled fortress for protection from hungry soldiers. In fact, livestock had been stolen from Domrémy and neighboring Greux in 1425. But the most memorable war incident of Joan's early life must have been the attack by a pro-Burgundian force from Champagne in July 1428, when Domrémy was burned. Joan stayed temporarily in nearby Neufchâteau "partly for fear of the Burgundians."

Joan testified that the English "were already in France when the voice first spoke to her." Her judges then asked her "if in her youth she had a great desire to defeat the Burgundians," to which she answered that "she had a great desire that the king should have his kingdom." It was part of Joan's genius to perceive as simple truths realities that were, in actuality, considerably more complex. Without necessarily knowing about the Treaty of Troyes or the dauphin's disinheritance, Joan saw as fundamental and self-evident that a king should have a kingdom. She must have known full well that kings were crowned and anointed at Reims, roughly four days' journey away, although no such ceremony had taken place since 1380. Her own parish church was, in fact, dedicated to Saint Remi, who according to the legend had brought the miraculous chrism to Clovis. Since she insisted on calling Charles "dauphin" until his coronation, she realized that the sacred ceremonies at Reims conferred legitimacy, or, simply put, make a royal heir a real king. Whether or not this is what she was referring to when she stated that she "knew things" she couldn't tell a Burgundian cannot be determined. But Joan, by 1428, was preoccupied by the idea that she must go "into France" to reveal what she knew to the dauphin.

There were, at the time, two prophecies in circulation that may have predisposed Joan or her potential supporters in her favor. The first promised that a maid would come from the Lorraine borderland "who would work miracles." The second, according to Joan's relative Durand Laxart, she herself used to convince him to take her to the dauphin. "Has it not been said," she reportedly told him, "that France will be lost by a woman and shall thereafter be restored by a virgin?"[3] Later, at Vaucouleurs, Catherine Le Royer (in whose home Joan boarded), on hearing Joan relate the prophecy, remembered having heard it and was "stupefied." It appears that "losing" France alluded to the transfer of the kingdom to

England, under the Treaty of Troyes, and "restoring" France referred to a military recovery. Here is a strong hint that Joan may already have understood Isabeau of Bavaria's instrumental role in the dauphin's disinheritance, the queen being clearly indicated in the prophecy, as Joan could have learned by asking. The prophecy also permits a reading contrasting the sexual promiscuity of one woman (Eve) with the virginity of another (Mary). With Joan's focus on moral behavior and the emphasis she placed on her own virginity,[4] knowledge of the prophecy may have helped her sharpen the focus of her future role.

Whatever the specific influence of this prophecy on Joan, during those months in 1428 when she sought support for her mission, one striking incident stands out. Charles II of Lorraine got wind of Joan and provided safe conduct for her to visit him in Nancy. They spoke at cross-purposes: she intent on her mission, he focused on a cure for his ill health. But already now, Joan had traveled on horseback, accompanied at least part way by a future devotee, Jean de Metz, to a nobleman who recognized her for special talents, and had come home with the gift of her own horse. These scattered facts are all we can really learn from her youth in Domrémy that foreshadow her religious mission and explain her understanding of her role in the war.

More substantial information about what Joan knew (or had learned) comes from testimony relating to Vaucouleurs, the town where she convinced Robert of Baudricourt to send her to France. It was there, according to the nullification testimony of Bertrand of Poulengy, that Joan allegedly made this powerful statement to Baudricourt: "The kingdom of France is not the dauphin's but my Lord's. But my Lord wills that the dauphin shall be made king and have the kingdom in custody."[5] How much greater already is Joan's understanding of her mission. She understands that it is God's will that the king will have his kingdom, but she describes the kingdom, in a sophisticated metaphor, as a divine fief, and the king as a vassal of God. These are not ideas that would have been beyond Joan's grasp. Everyone knew that God determined the winners of battles and even wars. And since God ruled heaven and earth, it followed that France belonged to God. A peasant could understand the idea of feudal land tenure—a vassal held land for his own use that belonged to someone better placed in the social hierarchy. So it is not inconceivable that Joan could imagine her king designated by God as his vassal. That said, it is most unlikely that Joan would have known of the false, twelfth-century Carolingian charter that, through the offering of four gold coins, turned French monarchs into vassals of God (see Chapter 4).

Take me to Orleans and I will show you the signs. Joan reached the dauphin in Chinon after finally receiving from Baudricourt escorts, equipment, and the parting comment "Come what may." When she asked to speak to the dauphin Charles, she was undoubtedly unaware that there were historical reasons for permitting her a royal interview as well as for refusing one. French kings listened to female clairvoyants, but they knew the risks involved. Behind Joan's back, the king's counsellors weighed the pros and cons of her claims. The archbishop of Embrun, Jacques Gelu, in possibly the earliest surviving opinion of the Maid, warned that it was important that Charles not "make himself ridiculous in the eyes of foreign nations, the French having quite a reputation for the ease with which their nature leads them to be duped."[6] The archbishop specifically warned the dauphin not to speak to her alone (advice not heeded) and that she not come too close to him. Gelu noted that as a shepherdess, Joan herself might easily be duped, and that "as a girl" she was ill-suited to bear arms and lead captains. Nonetheless, Gelu admitted, based on the model of the Old Testament heroines Deborah and Judith, that it was easy for God, even by the exploits of girls and women, to bring about victories.

From the time of Joan's arrival at Charles' court, it becomes impossible to distinguish her original mission from a potentially expanding one, once she found herself in the midst of a vastly enlarged circle of French loyalists. Information flowed in both directions. By then Joan understood not just that a king must have his kingdom, but that the young Henry VI, with his half-English blood, could not represent, as she put it, the "blood royal." In fact, when the duke of Alençon joined the king at Chinon she told him: "You are very welcome; the more men of the blood royal of France that are gathered together, the better." Once in the company of the Bastard of Orleans (later Count Dunois), Joan would have learned that Orleans, under attack for six months, belonged to the bastard's half-brother, Charles, duke of Orleans, who could not defend it after being captured by the English at Agincourt. Did Joan know that it was a violation of chivalric code to attack the lands of a prisoner? The simple injustice of the duke's plight was enough to raise Joan's indignation, and some versions of Joan's mission now included crossing the channel to free the duke from captivity. Moreover, by talking to the captains as she bided her time waiting for the battle, Joan must have learned the strategic importance of the city and the need to break the stalemate. Orleans was the gateway to the north—and therefore Paris—for the dauphin. By the same token, it was the gateway to the south for the duke of Bedford, who had been in charge of the English advance since the death of his brother Henry V in 1422. Rumor even had it that the dauphin had vowed in a prayer that if he lost Orleans, he would retire to Spain, Scotland, or Dauphiné.

After Charles' immediate advisers had interrogated Joan, they escorted her to Poitiers to be questioned further by a larger body of theologians. Joan may have thought they were taking her to Orleans, but once she understood what was ahead, she exclaimed: "In God's name, I know I will face a challenge!"[7] It is doubtful that Joan ever understood that the clerics were testing her, according to prescribed religious principles, to determine if her inspiration was angelic or diabolical. But when they demanded a sign to confirm her mission, she was willing to barter. If they would stop bothering her with their tiresome questions, she would *prove* her mission by raising the siege: "In God's name, I am not come to Poitiers to make signs; but take me to Orleans, I will show you the signs for which I have been sent."[8]

Surrender to the Maid who is sent here by God. On March 22, 1429, Joan dictated a letter to the English (see Document 11). It is cast as a military summons which, if issued at all in the fourteenth and fifteenth centuries, was a diplomatic formality that served as a first contact with the enemy. Often it simply amounted to a declaration of war. Joan's letter differs significantly from medieval models and is subtler than it appears. Evidently, in her salutation she means to expose the emptiness of English claims to France. She refuses to call Henry VI king of England *and France*, and she undermines the pretensions of his commanders by prefacing their titles with "who call yourself." This appears to return the insult of the Treaty of Troyes, where Charles was labeled the "so-called dauphin of Vienne."

The letter also exhibits Joan's unusual, even unprecedented, sense of French national boundaries. Joan clearly has her sights on something bigger than victory at Orleans. In fact, her letter anticipates nothing less than the end of the war itself—as can be seen by her order that the English leave *all* France. (In her letter to Troyes, she promises the submission of "all the cities that *should* belong to [France].") According to the logic expressed in the letter, the English have a country, as do the French. If the English wish to avoid war, then they should "go away to [their] own country, in God's name." Bowing to legal procedure, Joan also demands that they return the keys of the occupied towns and pay damages for holding them illegally.

In addressing the English, Joan seems to acknowledge the Old Testament origins of the military summons and even appears to echo the book of Deuteronomy on the laws of war. In Deuteronomy 20:16, God told the Jews to pursue their God-given inheritance ("the cities which are given to you"), but to ask for peace first. If the enemy refused, then God promised to fight for his people and deliver the city into their hands. Joan's letter repeats the "if . . . then" pattern found in Deuteronomy. Joan also boldly compares the French, about to receive divine aid for the recovery of their rightful inheritance (the kingdom of France), to the Israelites recovering their lands in the Old Testament. This letter, therefore, is a powerful and unusual extension of the concept of the religion of the monarchy so forcefully emphasized by previous generations of French monarchs, including through links to the Old Testament.

At its most basic level, the letter reveals the same Joan who knew at Domrémy that the Burgundians "would have war, if they did not do as they ought."[9] But the real power of the letter lies in how Joan manages to raise the level of discourse from petty earthly politics to God and divine will—with herself as the sole interpreter. God, the king of heaven, is a mightier king than Henry VI, and Joan has been "sent by God" to say that Charles is the true heir of France.[10] Therefore Charles, not Henry, will hold France from God. Here, in the feudal vocabulary of the ancient tradition of Saint-Denis, Joan has (again) used the metaphor of Charles as God's vassal and France as his divine fief. Furthermore, Joan points out the futility of trying to fight divine will with soldiers and artillery. As the poet Christine asked, similarly, in her poem on Joan of Arc: "You don't have sufficient strength! Do you want to fight against God?"[11] Joan ends her letter with an invitation to the duke of Bedford to join Charles in a crusade, a reminder of the special role that the French attributed to themselves, also from the time of Charlemagne, as protectors of the faith. There is no way to determine how much Joan's letter may have been modified by members of the king's inner circle, but it is one of the most extraordinary documents to be written on either side of the war. It justifies the remark of a French historian that Joan of Arc lived the religion of Reims "to the letter."

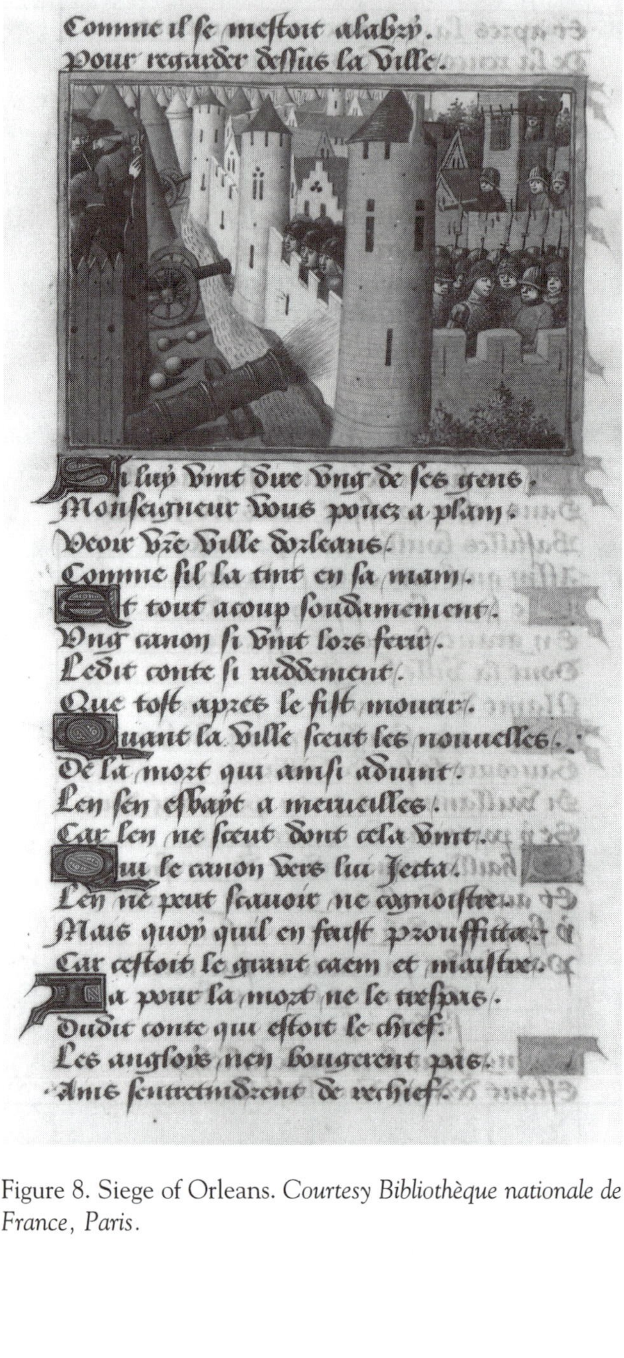

Comme il se mestoit alabry.
Pour regarder dessus la Ville.

Il luy vint dire ung de ses gens.
Monseigneur vous poues a plain.
Veoir vre ville dorleans.
Comme sil la tint en sa main.
Et tout acoup soudainement.
Ung canon si vint lors ferir.
Ledit conte si roiddement.
Que tost apres le fist mourir.
Quant la ville sceut les nouuelles.
De la mort qui ainsi aduint.
Len sen esbait a merueilles.
Car len ne sceut dont cela vint.
Qui le canon vers lui Iecta.
Len ne peut sauoir ne congnoistre.
Mais quoy quil en feist prouffita.
Car cestoit le grant caem et maistre.
Qui pour la mort ne se trespas.
Dudit conte qui estoit le chief.
Les anglois nen bougerent pas.
Ains sentretindrent de rechief.

Figure 8. Siege of Orleans. *Courtesy Bibliothèque nationale de France, Paris.*

Figure 9. Siege of Orleans. *Courtesy Bibliothèque nationale de France, Paris.*

The siege of Orleans took place from May 1 to May 8, 1429. Joan found herself in conflict with the captains over strategy. She favored the most direct route to the enemy, the route straight to Talbot, relying on what she called the "better help" of God. In the end, the conflict ceased when the English stockade was breached by cannon and the French poured into the city (see Figures 8 and 9).

Solely at the recommendation of Joan the Maid. After the French had successfully reclaimed Orleans in less than a week, many people were satisfied that Joan had performed a miracle, but some professional soldiers grumbled, and the English were, in any case, not among the believers.

Following Orleans and a successful sweep through the Loire valley, Joan's next challenge was to convince Charles and his council that he should now set his sights on Reims and a proper royal coronation, not Normandy—which could then have led to Paris—as his nobles urged. It all boiled down to the question of the capital or the coronation. Inadequate men and money, as well as the danger of the enterprise, had been given as arguments against a Reims campaign, but Joan eventually won the day. At the end of June, Charles set out at the head of the royal army on the coronation campaign. In the meantime, a rumor circulated in

Paris that the Armagnacs were about to attack. The Parisians apparently anticipated that Paris would be Charles' next strategic target. From that day on, according to a Parisian bourgeois who kept a journal, the Parisians strengthened and fortified the walls "day and night."

The French army was first thwarted at Troyes in their advance to Reims. This was the city where Charles' parents had notoriously signed the Treaty of Troyes, excluding Charles from the crown (and consequently, from a Reims coronation). Joan knew about the murder at Montereau that had resulted in Charles' disinheritance; it was the thorn on the rose. Her sorrow, as well as her dilemma in mounting a heavenly campaign for a man tainted with murder, are preserved in the French *Minute*:

> Asked whether she thinks and firmly believes that her king did right in killing or causing to be killed my lord of Burgundy [John the Fearless], she answered that this was a great tragedy for the kingdom of France; and whatever there had been between them, God had sent her to the help of the king of France.[12]

It was Joan's mission to maintain—and even to publicize—that God wanted Charles to be king *despite* Montereau. What better way to accomplish this, especially in Troyes, than to drive home the point about France's sacred mission? On July 4, 1429, therefore, Joan wrote a letter to the inhabitants of Troyes trumpeting that "King Jesus" was coming to aid "the holy kingdom" of France. Joan claimed to have her information from the highest source, not Charles, but "the King of Heaven, her sovereign and liege lord, in whose service royal she is every day."[13]

The royal army, however, did not gain immediate access to Troyes and contemplated a retreat. The council vacillated until Robert Le Maçon set things in perspective. When the king undertook this mission, he said, he did not do it based on the strength of the army, or on the money he had to pay for it, or even because the campaign seemed possible, but "solely at the recommendation of Joan the Maid . . . because it was the desire and the will of God." Plans for retreat were abandoned. The next day Troyes surrendered and the French continued on to Reims.

By my staff, I want to see Paris closer than I have until now. From the day of Charles' coronation on July 17, 1429, the moment of Joan's second great triumph, her star began to fall. But she did not, as yet, know it. She probably knew nothing either about the shaky alliances that the dukes of Burgundy had entered into with the kings of England since before she was born. All such agreements, of course, were contracted out of pure self-interest. After the murder of John the Fearless at Montereau, John's son Philip the Good had signed an alliance with England—even after a memorandum his councilors drew up honestly noted that, as the principal vassal of the French crown, "it was his duty to protect, not alienate it."[14] Although Philip's military support to the English was always handsomely paid, his loyalty was always in question.

As the murder at Montereau receded from Philip's memory, he found his loyalty to the English increasingly burdensome. But the day of Charles' coronation, as Joan was drafting a reproachful letter to Philip for failing to appear at the ceremony and failing to reconcile his differences with Charles as a prelude to peace with England, Philip was spending the week in Paris making public appearances with Bedford. Among Bedford's not-so-subtle efforts to re-cement the relationship with Philip was a dramatic reenactment of the murder at Montereau. Clearly, neither the king nor Joan knew of Philip's double-dealing.

Through Joan's efforts, Charles was able to validate his kingship at Reims and be reabsorbed into the line of his ancestors. Bedford, not to be outdone by the French, organized Henry VI's English coronation in fewer than four months. Held at Westminster on November 6, 1429, the attempt to mount a ceremony on a French scale was unmistakable. The ceremony included borrowings from a coronation book, or *ordo*, composed for Charles V, which Bedford obtained from the royal library of the Louvre, then in Anglo-Burgundian hands. Henry was anointed with sacred oil brought by the Virgin, England's answer to the miraculous oil of Clovis. A pastry decoration at the banquet depicted Henry VI flanked by Saint Edward and Saint Louis, in recognition of Henry's dual ancestry and his saintly French forebears.[15] Joan must not have known anything of this, however apparent her influence.

In the meantime, the day of Charles VII's coronation, while Philip the Good was in Paris, his envoys arrived in Reims to begin secret negotiations with Charles for a Franco-Burgundian peace. First came a two-week truce, which greatly displeased Joan when she heard about it. Next came a more extensive truce, signed in secret on August 28, 1429, and Charles' increasing reluctance to sustain Joan or the military campaign. In a letter she wrote to the inhabitants of Riom, on November 9, 1429, Joan asked for emergency gunpowder and war material. In another letter, to the people

Ou la pucelle et les francoys.
Y arriverent sans turgier.
La y eut courtes escharmuches.
Et saillies qui assez durerent.
Si advint qua unes approuches.
Les francoys treffort reculerent.

Coment la pucelle fut prinse devant
compiegne et vendue aux angloys.

Lors au conflictes par surprise.
Comme chascun tiroit arriere.
Ladicte pucelle fut prinse.
Par ung picart pres la barriere.
Ledit picart si la bailla.
A luxembourg les assistant.
Qui la vendit et rebailla.
Aux angloys pour argent content.
Si en firent apres leurs monstres.
Comme ayans treffort besongne.
Et ne leussent donnee pour londres.
Car cuidoient avoir tout gaigne.
Chascun delle si fut marry.
Depuis poton a son enseigne.

Figure 10. Capture of Joan of Arc at Compiègne. *Courtesy Bibliothèque nationale de France, Paris.*

of Reims, on March 28, 1430, Joan was forced to acknowledge that "many wicked people" were trying to betray the city and "install the Burgundi-ans." Doing her best to encourage her friends in Reims, Joan reported that Breton soldiers were about to join the royal forces. But by now she was tilt-ing at windmills. Insufficiently equipped and minimally supported, she was captured at Compiègne on May 23, 1430, pulled from her horse by an archer who tugged at her cloth-of-gold *huque* (see Figure 10). After being tried and condemned as a relapsed heretic by an Anglo-Burgundian court at Rouen, Joan of Arc was burned at the stake on May 30, 1431.

On December 2, 1431, the young Henry VI made his royal entrance into Paris. The pageantry included representations of the Nine Male Worthies, a popular grouping of ancient warrior heroes. More unusual were the Nine Female Worthies, all Amazons. At the coronation two weeks later, Philip the Good was not in attendance. Yet it would be four more years before the reconciliation between Charles VII and his cousin Philip—a mandatory step before the English could be driven out of France—would take place. In 1435 Philip hosted the congress at Arras where, on September 21, the twenty-eight-year-old quarrel between the two princes, which Joan of Arc had tried to end both by pleas and by war, was formally concluded. The duke of Bedford had died eleven days earlier; Isabeau of Bavaria died a few days later. Although there is no record that anyone spoke of Joan of Arc at the congress, the winter of 1435 was especially cold. A memorandum by town authorities recorded the array of snowmen that arose that winter in the streets of Arras, in-cluding the notation of a snow sculpture of Joan of Arc at the head of her men.[16]

NOTES

1. C. T. Allmand, *Henry V*, repr. (Berkeley: University of California Press, 1992), pp. 338–39.

2. W. S. Scott, trans., *The Trial of Joan of Arc*, repr. (London: Folio Society, 1968), p. 74. This is a translation of the French *Minute*.

3. Régine Pernoud, *Joan of Arc: By Herself and Her Witnesses*, trans. Edward Hyams (New York: Stein & Day, 1966), p. 33.

4. Joan preferred to be called *la Pucelle* (the Maid) rather than her given name.

5. Willard Trask, *Joan of Arc: In Her Own Words* (New York: Turtle Point Press, 1996), p. 15.

6. Deborah Fraioli, *Joan of Arc: The Early Debate* (Woodbridge: Boydell Press, 2000), pp. 18–19.

7. Anatole France, *The Life of Joan of Arc*, trans. Winifred Stephens, repr. (Amsterdam: Fredonia Books, 2004), vol. 1, p. 186.

8. Pernoud, *Joan of Arc*, pp. 55–56.

9. Scott, *Trial*, p. 74.

10. The term "true heir" is often thought to refer to rumors of Charles' bastardy. Here the term undoubtedly refers to his right to rule rather than the circumstances of his birth.

11. Christine de Pizan, *Ditié de Jehanne d'Arc*, eds. Angus J. Kennedy and Kenneth Varty (Oxford: Society for the Study of Mediaeval Languages and Literature, 1977), p. 48.

12. Scott, *Trial*, p. 126.

13. France, *Joan of Arc*, vol. 1, p. 419.

14. Richard Vaughan, *Philip the Good: The Apogee of Burgundy*, repr. (Woodbridge: Boydell Press, 2002), p. 3.

15. Bertram Wolffe, *Henry VI*, new ed. (New Haven: Yale University Press, 2001), p. 51.

16. Vaughan, *Philip the Good*, p. 67.

CHAPTER 6

CONCLUSION

It could be said that since there is no more feudalism, nor are there powerful kings, because rulers do not settle their differences by marrying their daughters to their enemies, and peasant girls have ceased to approach heads of state with revelations from God, the lessons of the Hundred Years War, whatever they might be, are no longer relevant. But as long as political power, sovereignty, national identity, and war are pertinent, and as long as traits such as honor, pride, glory, greed, envy, hatred, and revenge are part of human nature, the Hundred Years War remains entirely relevant.

What were the causes of the war? Why did it last so long? These are the enduring questions. Certainly territorial expansion lay at the heart of the Aquitaine quarrel, which was the conflict that sparked the war. In the fourteenth century, France sought control of this province, lying geographically at hand, which had once belonged to France and had passed into the hands of the rival English with the second marriage of Eleanor of Aquitaine. Yet territorial conflicts bore the complicated imprint of feudalism. Recent historical opinion has questioned the impact of feudalism, and even whether it actually existed, but the control of vassals by suzerains, the requirements of homage, and the loyalty and subservience that homage entailed definitely existed. As royal power increased in the late Middle Ages, the clash of feudal jurisdictions with central governments also increased. Especially where kings were involved, feudal practice had become outmoded and unworkable. War also originated in the general failure of kingdoms—as well as smaller political units—to establish firm principles of succession. Two affiliated problems were the lack of a uniform system of inheritance rights, in general, and the lack of either succession or inheritance statutes specifically relating to women. Although France had long shown a preference for male rulers, modern historians are quick to point out that there was no clear body of law to indicate that the royal domain, or kingdom, was any different from other property, which women could and did inherit. Women appear not to have contested their exclusion from the throne, although they depended regularly on champions, often with contradictory motives, to protect their inheritances. But the issue did not end there. The sense of insult, resentment, and wounded honor that motivated Edward III and Charles of Navarre, key players in the war for decades, was at least in part due to the belief that their mothers' rights, and consequently their own, had been transgressed. The strictly emotional dimension that this lack of gratification and unfulfilled entitlement gave to their political and military actions seems hard to deny. Even if the sense of mistreatment and injustice was at times feigned—for such complaints often proved effective mechanisms of diplomacy—that does not diminish the role that the phenomenon of injured sensibilities played in history. The French, as it has been seen, were often quite willing to give great swaths of territory to make Edward III refrain from using the three words "king of France." Of course what really worried the French was Edward's refusal to forswear the aggression that the words implied, but Edward's use of the French title took on the value of a powerful myth in its own right.

The French, however, did not lack for myths of their own, which they developed and refined throughout the war to serve French monarchical interests. The sacred myths of Saint Remi, the *fleur-de-lis*, and the *oriflamme*, evolved into the "religion of the monarchy," and were used to excellent effect, especially under Charles V and Charles VII (whose debt to Joan of Arc in this was significant). Whereas every kingdom believed that God granted military victory, French myth was also used to authorize and promote French jurisdiction over other kingdoms, and even, in certain instances, over the pope himself. On occasion, the French even convinced their enemies to acknowledge that France was most favored by God. Nothing was more telling of the internationally understood relationship that sacred coronation bore to French kingship than Edward III's Reims campaign in 1359. After he failed to achieve a Reims coronation, which would have reinforced his claim to French kingship, he agreed to the Treaty of Brétigny, thereby terminating an important phase of English conquest.

What were the factors that perpetuated war once it started? Mainly that, for a variety of different reasons, varying with time, the opponents remained quite evenly matched. Sometimes this only meant that, exhausted and without resources, they were equally unable to fight. Contradictorily, at any given time, war continued precisely because of the *un*equal strength of the antagonists. One kingdom would reignite war whenever it sensed an advantage, whether through the aid of allies, improved military technology, new tax revenue, or other circumstances. Had one kingdom been more powerful than the other for any length of time, it would have realized a lasting victory. Each phase of the war, therefore, can be seen as a consequence of the shifting balance of power. England began the military phase of the war after Flanders agreed to recognize Edward III as king of France. On the other hand, France employed the fleet from its canceled crusade to threaten England. And so it went throughout the entire Hundred Years War. Because of constantly changing conditions, territories once seized often reverted to one's opponent. This was true of France's losses at Brétigny in 1360 and England's relinquishment of the same territory between 1369 and 1375. The pattern was repeated in 1415 and 1417 when Henry V invaded France but was reversed again, this time for good, in the era after 1429, when Joan of Arc's influence in raising French spirits made the eventual repossession of northern France possible.

Among the potentially alterable variables of war were personalities, diplomacy, alliances, civil war, rebellion, taxation, the military, national mythologies, and codes of behavior. Other factors were among the unalterable or circumstantial conditions, such as death, royal minorities, bad weather, insanity, and plague. The factors responsible for the return to war after periods of military inactivity often demonstrated no ideological change, just the sheer ability to resume warfare. Planning for war, whether by strengthening the treasury, the armed forces, the arsenal, or the national defenses, probably continued during all intervals of peace, sometimes even simultaneously with the peace talks themselves.

A modern reader can be justifiably amazed at the level of treason, back-stabbing, seemingly senseless aggression, reopened dormant claims, and aggression against next of kin that characterized the war through a number of generations. Few actors in the war, for more than one hundred years, could ever let bygones be bygones. It is astonishing, for instance, that Henry V could suddenly lay claim to Normandy after it had

been in French hands for two centuries. Readers may be equally per-
plexed by the behavior of Charles VII, who failed to pursue an imposing
military advantage and naively negotiated with his faithless cousin Burgundy, for all practical purposes behind Joan of Arc's back. To many, however, one of the hardest developments to understand is French conduct
during the civil war, when uncontrollable animosity drove the Armagnacs and Burgundians simultaneously to the enemy for aid in their fight
against each other—their own blood relatives.

Other factors, too, impacted the duration of the war. France came
somewhat belatedly to concepts of centralized government. Its princes
were powerful and rarely wanted to submit to the yoke of royal control
which was so badly needed in time of war. Furthermore, both France and
England had monarchs who were alternately, or even simultaneously,
committed to peace. But the progress toward peace between Richard II
and Charles VI, for instance, was soon reversed by Henry V and Charles
VII. The number of truces that were signed in the course of the war is
remarkable, but because these interludes were used to rest and retool for
war, they perpetuated the general conflict instead of leading to peace. As
many a military leader—including Joan of Arc—has argued, sustained
warfare to the point of resolution might have led more reliably to the
end of war. But when one looks at the minor pretexts that served to ini-
tiate armed conflict, or the lengths to which the parties involved were
willing to go to press their often illegitimate cases, it appears that there
were always fresh reasons at hand to restart war.

Joan seems to have recognized, better than most, a special historical
circumstance that was prolonging the war. This was, precisely, that the
era in which the English presence in France would be tolerated had
drawn to a close. Joan had said, as early as the *Letter to the English*, that
war would end when the English left "all France." The desire to rid France
of the English presence, for anyone who had suffered under the English
occupation, was more than likely self-evident, but it was Joan who told
the English they had no right in France and backed it up with military
action that *to her* was a pure expression of divine will.

Biographies

Bertrand du Guesclin (c. 1320–1380)

Born around 1320, Bertrand du Guesclin was the offspring of minor nobility in Brittany. In 1370, at the acme of his career, King Charles V designated du Guesclin constable of France. The appointment made him second-in-command in the kingdom, an unlikely honor for a man of his origins. Today du Guesclin is arguably the best-known French warrior hero of the Hundred Years War. His patriotic example is praised in French schoolchildren's textbooks. Du Guesclin's reputation rests on his recovery of extensive French lands from the English. Born to a mother who allegedly denied giving birth to such an ugly infant, Du Guesclin's famed homeliness is confirmed in manuscript illuminations and by his own motto: "Courage supplies what beauty withholds." Bred for military life on jousts and skirmishes in the Breton wars of succession (1341–1364), du Guesclin was noticed by the then regent (the future Charles V) for his bravery at the siege of Melun in 1359. In 1364, the year of Charles' accession to the throne, du Guesclin delivered the monarch's first victory at the battle of Cocherel. Charles V, who lacked a warrior nature and sought to avoid the rashness of his father John II's capture at Poitiers (1356), was not a king for the battlefield. Thus the prince and du Guesclin were appropriately complementary. Du Guesclin employed a "new" brand of chivalry (construed by some as "dirty tricks") designed for maximum efficacy. Disguise (once as woodcutters), ambush, feigned retreat, hastily seized opportunity, and enviable mobility were the mechanisms of his success. Unlike the knights who rode to their slaughter at Crécy (1346) and Poitiers (1356), du Guesclin was a practical strategist who harassed the enemy piecemeal and avoided pitched battle. When forced into pitched battle, he usually lost, and his four captures obliged Charles V to pay exorbitant ransoms.

Du Guesclin's fame may rest on his ability to function equally well in the aristocratic world of Charles V and the world of the new breed of everyday soldier, mostly mercenaries. His respect for the needs of those who served under him—which could mean turning a blind eye to looting—allowed him to exert control over their unruly ranks. This was a fitting skill for the second phase of his career.

In 1366, Charles V sent du Guesclin on an expedition to Spain under the guise of a crusade against Muslims and Jews. The campaign's real objectives were to replace Pedro the Cruel, king of Castile, with his half brother Henry of Trastamara and to divert the unemployed mercenaries who were ruthlessly plundering the French countryside to Spain. The poet Cuvelier, du Guesclin's epic biographer, claims that du Guesclin assured his men a crusader's death (with the promise of heaven) and better booty than in France! French alliance with Henry later proved invaluable when the Castilian fleet scored naval victories against England. In 1378 du Guesclin's chivalric oath to serve his king required a campaign undertaken against his native Brittany. To this day some Bretons deem him a traitor, periodically blowing up the statue erected in his honor in his hometown square. His second wife, Anne of Laval, championed his posthumous glory among poets, whose laudatory verse survives. Du Guesclin is buried at Saint-Denis next to his king.

Charles V (1338–1380, r. 1364–1380)

In 1349, at the age of eleven, Charles became the first heir to the throne to bear the title dauphin, when negotiations on behalf of Philip VI resulted in the acquisition of Dauphiné (southeastern France), and the king conferred the title and territory on his grandson. There were two capital events in the early manhood of the future King Charles V, both in 1356. The first was the seizure during a banquet and imprisonment of Charles of Navarre by the young Charles' father (John II) and the slaughter of several other dinner guests, at the same ill-fated banquet, on suspicion of treason. The second was his father's capture at the battle of Poitiers, when Charles was eighteen. Thus the dauphin was left to rule France in the turbulent and humiliating years following the French defeat of 1356. King John tried to maintain his authority from captivity, pursuing in particular a conciliatory diplomacy directed at his release, which his counsellors publicized as they moved about France allegedly collecting the king's ransom. But the dauphin, serving as lieutenant for his captive father, found that the Estates General not only refused to permit the king's concessions to England, but also demanded the release of Charles of Navarre and laid numerous restrictive ordinances upon John's rule. In the spring of 1357, following their lead, Prince Charles annulled his father's orders.

On February 22, 1358, the dauphin watched helplessly as a mob, under the direction of rising Parisian leader Etienne Marcel, murdered his close advisers, the marshals of Normandy and Champagne, in his chambers. The dauphin fled the capital to prepare his retaliation, restaking his claim on the capital the next month from Provins. A fast conclusion to the *Jacquerie* (May–June) and the assassination in July of Etienne Marcel raised the dauphin's stature and enabled his return to Paris. The signing of the truce of Brétigny in 1360, however, granted one-third of France to England and set a reduced but still ruinous ransom for John II. On John's death in 1364, Charles was crowned and anointed at Reims, where he also celebrated the first victory of his reign, Bertrand du Guesclin's defeat of Charles of Navarre at Cocherel. This military leadership by proxy became the pattern for Charles' entire reign, as du Guesclin wielded his sword on behalf of his king. By the mid-1370s, du Guesclin had won back virtually all of France's lost territory, using tactics abhorrent to chivalry, such as ambushes, deception, and guerilla warfare, yet nonetheless effective. For this efficacy contemporaries labeled both the armchair strategist Charles V and his wily commander du Guesclin valiant knights. Du Guesclin also helped Charles solve the problem of unemployed mercenaries, who devastated France after the peace of Calais, by leading them on a campaign into Spain. In 1374, Charles V instituted ordinances guaranteeing an army, and regulating currency and taxation. A truce was agreed upon at Bruges in the summer of 1375. With the truce between France and England that followed, English hopes of continental conquest all but died until the time of Henry V.

Charles V is known for more than the remarkable recovery of his reign. He also raised the prestige of the monarchy through the use of elaborate rituals, the creation of political doctrine, and renewed emphasis on the divine origins of the French monarchy. In particular, his paid writers argued France's superiority over other nations as a result of the kingdom's special favor from God. Charles also commissioned numerous translations of scientific, literary, and religious works, furthering the efforts of his father John to establish the royal library. The impetus to expand the library, however, like much of the headway made during his reign on so many different fronts, largely died with him on September 16, 1380. His final act was a bad deathbed decision to lift taxes, which left his son and successor, Charles VI, facing serious riots when taxes were inevitably reinstated.

Charles VI (1368–1422, r. 1380–1422)

Charles VI, the king who, at the age of fifty-two, signed the kingdom of France over to the Lancasters of England, was called both Charles the Well Beloved and Charles the Mad. His three older sisters, the first three children of Charles V and Jeanne of Bourbon, died before 1365. The royal couple finally produced a male offspring in 1368 who was destined to survive, but not without falling victim to recurrent bouts of mental illness from the age of twenty-four. When his father and namesake died in 1380, Charles was placed under the guardianship of his four uncles, the dukes of Anjou, Burgundy, Berry, and Bourbon, in an arrangement that only partially reflected the deceased king's wishes. Philip the Bold, duke of Burgundy, emerged as the supreme authority in the realm by 1382, after suppressing the *Maillotin* tax protest in Paris. Charles' marriage to Isabeau of Bavaria in 1385, first discussed between Philip the Bold and her uncle during a French campaign in Flanders, produced twelve children. Two of their daughters were married to English monarchs: Isabella to Richard II coincident with a truce between France and England in 1396, and Catherine to Henry V to secure the agreement reached between France and England in the Treaty of Troyes of 1420. However, Charles VI's reign was marked by aggression toward England at its moments of strength. After plans to mount a landing on the south coast of England were postponed, while Philip the Bold stamped out the last Flemish rebels in 1385, French policy quickly inclined toward an English invasion the following summer. A great armada gathered at Sluys in preparation for the attack. In November 1386, however, the invasion was called off for reasons no one could blame on Charles VI—first Philip the Bold's illness, and then an unforgiving winter sea ("too dark, too cold, too wet and too windy"). The English, acting like "frightened hares," according to one English chronicler, had been spared.

In 1388, as Charles VI approached his twenty-first year, backed by supporters, this "perpetual minor" decided to end the uncles' rule. He then brought back the career administrators, known as Marmousets and handpicked by his father, to advise him. But on August 5, 1392, an event interrupted his advance toward independent rule. While riding in the forest of Le Mans, a brief encounter with a stranger and the piercing sound of a lance striking a knight's helmet initiated what would become an intermittent but eventually disabling mental illness. To implore God for good health, the king made a pilgrimage accompanied by vast numbers of children to the shrine of the Mont-Saint-Michel off the Norman coast in July 1393. Several years later, the queen pledged the first child born after the king's attack, their four-year-old daughter Marie, to the convent of Poissy outside Paris, where she lived out her life. These appeals through faith were to no avail. Within no time the uncles were back, each fighting to outmaneuver the other. When Philip the Bold died in 1404, in view of Charles VI's disability, his brother, Louis of Orleans, and his cousin, John the Fearless (heir of Philip), inched toward civil war in a contest for power. In 1407, after each antagonist committed himself to thwarting the other, John the Fearless had Louis of Orleans assassinated.

In England, Plantagenet rule ended in 1399 when Henry IV of Lancaster usurped the throne from Richard II. Charles VI's daughter and Richard's bride, the young Isabella, was initially retained in England. She returned home minus her jewels and dowry, a belated installment, so Henry said, on John II's ransom.[1] The usurpation disrupted England much as the civil war did France. Henry IV, who rose to power backing a war platform, was unable in his lifetime to carry out his threats against France. But Charles VI faced the invasion that the first Lancaster had dreamed of in the second Lancaster king, also a Henry, in 1415. Henry V's aptitude for military effectiveness brought Charles VI to the peace table in only five years. In the meantime, the growing anarchy in France was exacerbated by the murder of John the Fearless in 1419, by accomplices of the king's son, the dauphin Charles. Philip the Good, John's son, quickly threw his weight with the English. Under the terms of the Treaty of Troyes of 1420, the ailing Charles VI turned the entire kingdom over to Henry (at first as regent) in a pitiful exchange for the right to bear the title "king of France"—a right not acknowledged by the English for many years—during his remaining years. On October 22, 1422, Charles VI died, leaving his nine-month-old grandson, Henry VI, as the unique ruler of England and France. Henry V, the instigator of this strange circumstance, had died two months before.

Charles VII (1403–1461, r. 1422–1461)

Charles VII of France, whose greatest fault has been considered to be his lack of determination, was incongruously the king who finally won the Hundred Years War. The third of three sons to survive among the twelve children of Isabeau of Bavaria and Charles VI, Charles VII nevertheless acceded to the throne. An early household record notes a toy brass cauldron was made for him to dispel his bad moods. He grew up in turbulent times, and was often spirited to safety with his brothers as bouts of civil war struck Paris. In 1417, after the death of his second brother, Charles VII became heir to the throne. By the age of sixteen, he was himself embroiled in the civil war, and on September 10, 1419, he was the party responsible for the murder of John the Fearless, duke of Burgundy, as the two cousins met at Montereau to negotiate peace. The king and queen disowned him for the crime. On May 21, 1420, they signed the Treaty of Troyes, which designated Henry V regent and heir of France and their adopted son.

Nine days after the death of his father Charles VI on October 21, 1422, the dauphin Charles took the title "king of France." The French people now divided their loyalty between Henry VI of England north of the Loire and Charles VII south of the Loire. Charles was disparagingly called the "king of Bourges," after the town in which he took refuge, yet he was still recognized as king by half the kingdom. After a French victory at Baugé in 1421, Charles' army met defeat at Cravant (1423) and Verneuil (1424). The earl of Salisbury, Thomas Montague, who had triumphed at Verneuil, was killed at Orleans in 1428 by cannon fire, thus removing a skilled English captain from the war arena.

It was Joan of Arc's arrival that proved to be, as it was quite literally believed, the real godsend. Her mission, which she claimed to carry out at God's command, was to restore the kingdom of France to Charles. Before placing faith in her, Charles subjected her to a formal examination by theologians, which included a test of her virginity. Until his coronation on July 17, 1429, Charles consented to conduct his military campaign according to the dictates of Joan's voices, but he gradually became disenchanted with her, perhaps under the influence of favorite Georges de la Tremoille. Joan represented the war party, but Charles now decided to pursue peace with Burgundy, by means of truces, the first one signed on August 28, 1429. Six weeks later, Bedford named Philip of Burgundy lieutenant general of the king of England for the kingdom of France, second in command after himself. This move, and others that followed, were hardly peacemaking gestures, but it took Charles almost a year to recognize the strategy of deceit and underhanded politics in Philip's truces. In May 1430, King Charles issued a manifesto laying bare the bad faith of the duke, who "diverted and deceived us for some time with truces." Charles' recognition that he had been duped came too late to save Joan of Arc, who disapproved of the truces and had threatened to break them. She was captured in the same month, on May 24, 1430. Her imprisonment in enemy territory offered Charles little chance of delivering her, although he has often been charged with abandoning her.

After years of failed attempts, Charles reconciled his differences with Philip the Good through the peace of Arras on September 21, 1435. The French hastened the agreement by bribing members of the duke's council. In 1436, Paris fell to Arthur of Richmond, who had replaced the royal favorite La Tremoille in the king's affections. After Charles subdued a revolt by the barons in 1440, known as the *Praguerie*, he began to think seriously about reconquering Normandy and Aquitaine. In 1449, after several years of truces, Charles invaded Normandy. Rouen fell in 1450. Once Rouen was in French hands, Charles launched an investigation into Joan of Arc's trial and burning. The final objective of the war was to expel the English from Aquitaine. Master gunners Jean and Gaspard Bureau used early gunpowder artillery to turn the tide in favor of Charles, as the longbow had done for the English in the early years of the war.

In 1456, a second trial for Joan of Arc—this time by the French—nullified the verdict of Joan's condemnation trial of 1431. Plagued by subversive activity among his nobles in the later years of his reign, Charles found that even his son, the future Louis XI, had plotted against him. Despite the sense of apathy Charles sometimes projected, he strengthened his resolve and eventually carried out reforms in taxation and the military. He died at Mehun-sur-Yèvre on July 22, 1461.

Charles of Navarre (1332–1387)

Charles of Navarre was a prince of royal French blood driven by a sense of injustice, who aggravated the general circumstances of the Hundred Years War by maintaining his own slender claim to the throne of France and playing one side of the war against the other. The story of Charles II of Navarre begins before his birth in 1332. His mother, Jeanne of Navarre, only surviving child of French king Louis X, was denied the crown by her uncle King Philip V on the false grounds that French legal tradition excluded women from the royal succession. She also lost her inheritance of the rich counties of Champagne and Brie to the king in exchange for the more meager compensation of Normandy and Angoumois. But she retained the kingdom of Navarre in the Iberian Peninsula, an inheritance from her mother. In 1349, the year of her death, Jeanne agreed to trade Angoumois to King John II for other fiefs, but the land transfer never took place.

Charles, nicknamed the Bad for his cruel repression of a minor rebellion in Navarre, had an equally unscrupulous career in France. He claimed to have a clearer right to the French crown than either Philip VI or Edward III because Capetian blood flowed in his veins from both parents. But he was born four years too late. The royal succession had been decided in favor of Philip VI of Valois in 1328. Cynical and ambitious, but probably more sincere in his bid for the crown than has been acknowledged, Charles II bitterly dedicated himself to vengeance against the French crown. Yet he was wholeheartedly French and only played a double game with the English when it suited his immediate purposes. His wiles and personal charisma drew diverse enemies of the French royal administration into his party. Charles' inherent sense of injustice quickly evolved into a life of conniving and intrigue, wars of acquisition and vengeance, and even murder. Most observers duly acknowledge his repeated mistreatment by the French crown, however little they condone his behavior.

In June 1350 Charles was crowned king of Navarre. Two years later, aged twenty, he was married to the daughter of King John II, who may have viewed the union as a hedge against trouble. But trouble broke out in January 1354 when the king's favorite, the constable Charles of Spain, was ruthlessly murdered in Normandy, and Charles of Navarre calmly accepted responsibility. The granting of Angoumois by John to his favorite, while technically still owned by Charles II, figured significantly in the murder, but Charles justified it more broadly as good for the realm. Under pressure to reconcile despite the murder, John II put the public interest—and the fear that Charles would make his alliances elsewhere—before his vendetta against his son-in-law and agreed to Charles' terms at Mantes in February 1354. When rumors circulated that King John was preparing to seize Charles, the prince traveled to Avignon to complain to the pope. There Charles met Henry, duke of Lancaster, and quickly promised him military aid in Normandy against France. On September 10, 1355, Charles again made peace with the French king John, repeated his oath of loyalty, and was rewarded with new territories. On April 15, 1356, John II finally took his revenge. Fearing collusion between his son Charles (the future Charles V) and his son-in-law, Charles of Navarre, the king stormed into a dinner at Rouen hosted by his son. Charles II was taken prisoner and the count of Harcourt and others were unceremoniously executed. Philip of Navarre took up the cause of his brother and issued a letter of defiance to King John in May, declaring, "I see and understand that reason and equity hold no weight with you." But when John was captured by the English at the battle of Poitiers in September 1356, immediately there were calls for Charles of Navarre's release from prison. An arranged prison escape occurred in 1357. The king of Navarre gained immediate popularity, drawing sympathetic crowds in Amiens and Paris. At a public speech held at Pré-aux-Clercs (November 30, 1357), Charles argued his right to the French crown and dispensed his antiroyalist politics.

During the social upheaval in Paris in the 1350s, the bourgeois leader Etienne Marcel dealt intermittently with Charles of Navarre, as both were opponents of the monarchy. In a move favoring the nobility, however, Charles turned an apparent alliance with the peasant rebels of the *Jacquerie* into an outrageous slaughter near Montdidier in June 1358, effectively ending the peasant movement. In Paris, a weakened Marcel sought Charles' help, but this did not prevent Charles from simultaneously playing games behind the scenes with both the kings of England and France. Apparently committed in August 1358 to a joint campaign with Edward III against France, Charles performed an about-face later that month at Pontoise, where he signed a treaty with the regent Charles, promising to be a "good Frenchman" and fight against England.

By 1361 Charles II had returned to Navarre. The career of the French knight Bertrand du Guesclin was on the rise. In Charles II's absence in 1364, du Guesclin seized the king of Navarre's cities of Mantes and Melun and then took effective control of Normandy from him with a victory on May 16 at Cocherel. The king of Navarre's last years brought (unverifiable) accusations against him of poisonings and attempted poisonings. He died on January 1, 1387, possibly by accidental burning in a sheet soaked in *eau-de-vie* (brandy). Although he died having fallen short of fulfilling any of his grandiose goals, through his own deviousness and the intercession of powerful supporters he had managed to avoid the consequences of most of his nefarious acts. By his wit and cunning he had indeed managed to manipulate even the kings of France and England to his own ends and did so throughout his life.

Christine de Pizan (1364?–1430?)

Christine de Pizan was the daughter of an Italian astrologer who served Charles V. She therefore grew up at the French court where she profited—although indirectly, since she was a woman—from the educational and cultural opportunities of her exceptional circumstances, and became an unusually well-educated woman for her time. Widowed at the age of twenty-five, Christine was forced to support herself, her mother, and three children by her writing, in order to rescue her "little household." The first French woman of letters to live by her pen, Christine was dependent upon patrons in order to earn her livelihood. Her father Thomas had been lured to the French court by Charles V, where he was highly prized as a royal counsellor and friend of the king. But after Charles V's death (1380), Thomas lost stature and the family found itself in reduced circumstances. When her father died (c. 1387), followed by her husband Etienne du Castel (1390), Christine was forced to seek out new benefactors, principally Duke Louis of Orleans and Duke Philip the Bold of Burgundy, brothers of Charles V. At least eight of Christine's early works, mostly in verse, were dedicated to Louis of Orleans. After she failed to place her son Jean du Castel in the duke's household, Christine dedicated no further works to him, although politically she would remain a supporter of his party rather than the Burgundians.

Many of Christine's best-known works, such as her letters in the debate on the *Romance of the Rose* and *The Book of the City of Ladies*, directly relate to the condition of women. But given the political milieu in which she lived and wrote, as well as the commissions of patrons, new works on kingship, knighthood, the politics of war and peace, and even political theory emerged increasingly from her pen. In a letter of 1405, searching for a solution to France's misfortunes, Christine pleaded with Isabeau of Bavaria to intervene in the rivalry between the dukes of Orleans and Burgundy, which was then deteriorating into civil war, to no avail. In 1410 Christine fruitlessly implored the duke of Berry, in another letter, to lead France and restore order. A few years later, she looked with hope to the reign of the dauphin Louis of Guyenne in *Le livre de la paix* (The Book of Peace), but the boy died at the age of twenty in 1415, the year after she finished her book. When Christine finally wrote the *Ditié de Jehanne d'Arc* (The Song of Joan of Arc) in 1429, a verse composition celebrating the arrival Joan of Arc, its tone was justifiably triumphant. The political appeal for a savior for France, which Christine had launched for almost three decades on behalf of her adoptive country, had finally been answered—not by royalty, but by "a simple shepherdess."

It is believed that Christine, who communicated such confidence in 1429 that Joan would produce the sweeping victory needed to reclaim all France, probably died before she could learn of the Maid's capture on May 23, 1430. As Christine was a female writer, her career was unconventional, but her works were well respected by her contemporaries. Both the poets Eustache Deschamps and Martin Le Franc praised her in their poetry. Although her writings have been brought to a broad audience only in the last fifty years, today her talent and political discernment are almost universally recognized. Christine was, after all, among many other accomplishments, the first writer to devote a significant literary work to her more famous female contemporary, Joan of Arc.

Edward III (1312–1377, r. 1327–1377)

In 1327, as a boy of fourteen, Edward III was thrust into the role of English monarch. His mother, Isabella, had been sent to France in March 1325 to negotiate a settlement between her husband, Edward II, and brother, Charles IV, king of France, after war broke out in Aquitaine in 1324. To save Edward II the humiliation of swearing homage to the king of France, the young Edward did homage for Aquitaine in September 1325. Instead of returning to England as foreseen, Isabella and an escaped

English rebel, Roger Mortimer, gathered a small force and invaded England in 1326. Edward II was deposed and died in prison, presumably murdered on Mortimer's orders. Once rid of Edward II, Isabella and Mortimer ran the affairs of the kingdom as they pleased, even resorting to the execution of the young Edward's uncle, the earl of Kent, to control dissent. Edward might have caved in to the pressures of his early circumstances and become a weak man. Instead he seized power from Mortimer, who was tried and executed in 1330, and sent his mother into retirement on rich estates.

In February 1328, one year into Edward's reign, Charles IV died in France, leaving no male heir. Edward's French cousin Philip of Valois was hastily elected king. In May 1328 Isabella made the case to Parliament that Edward's right as French heir should be recognized. When the claim was put forward by ambassadors, the French rejected it, arguing that women could not transmit to their sons rights which they themselves never possessed. Edward refused to accept this decision, at least outwardly, and his insistence on his right to the French crown became a hallmark of his politics. Scholars still disagree as to Edward's sincerity in asserting his right to the French throne.

Facing war in Scotland in 1333, Edward did not immediately provoke war with Philip VI. Instead he maintained a foreign policy of prudent duplicity with regard to France. At the Tower of London in January of 1337, he urged his council to seek peace, but at the same time he built a fleet and counted his allies. On August 28, 1337, Edward made the case before his council that any war against France would be a defensive war, in view of Philip's naked aggression. Soon after he concluded a hard-won alliance with Flanders, Edward publicly proclaimed his title to the throne of France in February 1340. It was the first English claim to a dual monarchy. Edward's first campaign to secure his new kingdom ended in failure; he signed the truce of Esplechin in September 1340. After 1342, Edward found a pretext for war against Philip VI in the duchy of Brittany, after Philip decided the disputed ducal title in favor of his nephew Charles of Blois. In June 1344, the English parliament voted war subsidies that allowed Edward to set sail for France to "take what God may bestow upon him."[2]

After a papal peace conference at Avignon failed to reconcile the two cousins, Edward invaded Normandy in July 1346, defying French expectations of an attack on Aquitaine. Counting on the destructive English tactic known as the *chevauchée*—a raiding maneuver developed in the Scottish wars that targeted civilian populations—instead of direct military confrontation, Edward III was nonetheless forced into pitched battle against the French at Crécy. There he scored a glorious victory against superior French forces in August 1346. That October he defeated the Scots at Neville's Cross, and he took Calais the following year. Edward then returned to England, where he began to build the foundations of a stable monarchy. Through domestic concessions, generally viewed today as a clever policy to keep his French aspirations alive, he ceded powers he did not need in exchange for taxes to sustain his foreign wars. (By contrast, across the channel, neither John the Good nor the Estates could raise the revenue in France needed to confront the English threat.) Edward's son, the Black Prince, initiated new hostilities from Bordeaux in 1355. The following year, two English armies threatened to converge on Normandy. At Poitiers, the Black Prince was overtaken by the French army and forced into pitched battle. Edward's son beat the French, however, in September 1356 and escorted John the Good from the battlefield as his captive. Edward III, not present at the battle, was in his glory. In 1359, he launched a military campaign in France aimed at Reims. As powerful testimony to the strength of the mythology of sacred French kingship, Edward had decided that his legitimacy as French monarch depended on achieving a proper French coronation. After the campaign failed, Edward signed the treaty of Brétigny in 1360. Although the terms set a generous ransom for John II and granted Edward sovereignty over a larger, reconstituted Aquitaine, Edward lost his northern provinces of Anjou, Touraine, and Maine and was forced to renounce his alliance with Flanders.

The French, increasingly in the ascendancy, resumed war against England under Charles V in 1369. By 1371, the Black Prince had been immobilized by illness, and John of Gaunt proved to be no match for the French. In June 1375, a general truce was signed at Bruges. The great conquests of Edward's reign had virtually all dissolved, and by the 1370s the power of the throne had passed to others. But Edward had adhered to a broad vision of his role as monarch and ruled for fifty years. He died on June 21, 1377.

Edward the Black Prince, *Prince of Wales* (1330–1376)

Edward of Woodstock, so named after the place of his birth, also carried the titles of earl of Chester (1333), duke of Cornwall (1337), prince of Wales (1343), and prince of Aquitaine (1362). Both his father Edward III and son Richard II were kings of England. Either the elder Edward lived too long, or the younger Edward died too soon, for the hero who wore black armor never wore the crown of England.

As a sixteen-year-old, the Black Prince earned a reputation for valor at the battle of Crécy in 1346, where his father assigned him command of the first battalion. Froissart tells a tale, contradicted by another chronicler, that when Edward fell in battle, his father refused help, saying, "Let the boy win his spurs!" However it was that Edward learned courage, Shakespeare would say of him: "In war was never lion rag'd more fierce." Approximately two years later, Edward became an original member of the king's brotherhood of knights, the Order of the Garter. Appointed lieutenant of Gascony, Edward led a ruthless campaign through southern France in 1355. At the battle of Poitiers in 1356, he captured King John II, but insisted on personally serving his prisoner, whom he viewed as a true knight despite his defeat. An English campaign conducted as a *chevauchée* in 1359–1360 (in which the Black Prince and his three brothers took part), whose object was a Reims coronation for Edward III, failed to meet its goal. Aquitaine was reconstituted as a principality in 1362 with Edward as its prince. His third major battlefield triumph came at Nájera in 1367, where he temporarily reinstated Pedro the Cruel on the throne of Castile. The Black Prince did not receive the money promised him for Nájera, and he resorted to levying harsh taxes on his subjects in Aquitaine to recoup his losses. This led the powerful count of Armagnac and his nephew to seek recourse against the Black Prince in the Parlement of Paris. Infuriated by Charles V's willing intervention in the affairs of Aquitaine, the English declared war in 1369. In one of the contradictions of chivalry, Prince Edward conducted a savage attack on Limoges in 1370, where "all were put to the sword," puzzling Froissart, who noted the severity of the Prince's response. It was an illustration of Shakespeare's understated comment about the Black Prince that "when he frown'd, it was against the French."

In deteriorating health, Edward returned to England in 1371, where he died five years later. His copper effigy can be seen in Canterbury Cathedral.

Etienne Marcel (c. 1290–1358)

The life and public career of Parisian bourgeois Etienne Marcel, probably born in the 1290s, are inseparable from the politics of mid-fourteenth-century France and the weakness of the French monarchy under the early Valois kings. Marcel, like most popular leaders of the period, died violently as a result of his recourse to violence during his lifetime. The sheer brutality of Marcel's tenure as the provost of the merchants of Paris (equivalent to mayor) has obscured the evidence that Marcel espoused a genuinely revolutionary ideology, plotting to transfer power from the monarchy to the city of Paris. This was all the more daring inasmuch as Paris drew its influence from being the seat of the monarchy. Marcel's career can be divided into two periods: first, public life until the murder of the marshals of Normandy and Champagne in the dauphin's chambers; and second, his association with Charles of Navarre.

Born into a prosperous, upper-middle-class draper family, Marcel advanced in stature and wealth by his marriage to Marguerite des Essarts (c. 1345), who came from a family with royal connections. Having attained the post of provost of the merchants around 1354, he took an active role in the "reformist" coalition in the Estates General. After the humiliating defeat at Poitiers in 1356 and the capture of King John, there was widespread demand for change. In the calls for reform heard in the Estates Generals of 1355, 1356, and 1357, Marcel may not have been prime architect or even a very major player. Powerful nobles in the assemblies were equally indignant at the corruption and wide-ranging fiscal malfeasance of royal advisers, and equally dogmatic about the need for power sharing with a popular assembly. By December 1356, however, Marcel's importance was signaled by his receipt of a letter from King John acknowledging (and critical of) his war politics. On December 5, 1356, the dauphin departed Paris for Metz. Two days later an ordinance declaring a significant monetary devaluation was announced, which Marcel vehemently opposed. The dauphin returned on January 14, 1357, to a tumultuous Paris packed with revolutionary fervor and led by Etienne Marcel. A strike against the new coinage ordinance ended in the dauphin's capitulation on January 20, 1357.

Suddenly, on February 22, 1358, as royal forces gathered outside Paris, Marcel showed a new side of his character, shattering the illusion of the provost as disinterested reformer or moderate. That day he led a throng of three thousand men straight to the king's chambers in the grand palace next to the Sainte Chapelle. There he unleashed his mob to do their "business." The dauphin's friends and closest advisers, John of Conflans, marshal of Champagne, and Robert of Clermont, marshal of Normandy, were cut to pieces. In derision, the dauphin was made to don the red and blue hood of Marcel's rebel party.

In April 1358 from outside his capital, Charles decided upon a block-ade of Paris as the most effective strategy for wresting Paris from Marcel's grasp. Apprised of the strategy, Marcel wrote an impassioned response to Charles in which he demonstrated great diplomatic resourcefulness in the face of adversity (see Document 5). During a two-week peasant rebel-lion, known as the *Jacquerie* of 1358, Marcel sent minor reinforcements to the rebels, but he was not in sympathy with their cause. The king of Navarre, whom Marcel would soon court for his ability to rally anti-monarchical partisans, would in fact crush the rebellion on June 10 at Montdidier. By prior agreement between Marcel and Charles of Navarre, the latter entered Paris on June 14, 1358, and was proclaimed "captain." Marcel had ceded his place to a prince of the blood. In July 1358, Paris experienced preposterous circumstances. While the nobility exhibited its indignation at the Paris-Navarre confederacy, the dauphin prepared to besiege his own capital. In the meantime, Parisians were objecting to having English and Navarrese mercenaries secure their defense instead of being treated as enemies and resisted. In Paris on July 31, 1358, a mas-sive antirevolutionary demonstration took place. That same day a mob cornered Marcel and cut him down.

Henry V (1386?–1422, r. 1413–1422)

It must not have seemed likely that Henry V would become king of England. He was only the grandson of John of Gaunt, who was the third son of Edward III. Edward's second son, the famous Black Prince, had died in 1376, and the throne had devolved to his son, Richard II. But Richard was deposed by Henry IV of Lancaster, father of Henry V, and as a result of Henry IV's inauguration of the Lancastrian dynasty and his own kingship, the young Henry became Prince of Wales and heir. From

1400, the young prince learned the art of war fighting a rebellion in Wales, overseeing the military operations by 1404. His father's reign, based as it was on the shaky legitimacy of usurpation, encountered challenges, controversy, and rebellion. As late as June 7, 1406, nearly seven years into Henry IV's kingship, a debate and declaration of the legitimacy of his rule were necessary. Even his son had differences with him, a specific point of friction being how England should respond to the civil war in France. Veiled rumors that the young Henry might try to seize power before his time prompted the elder Henry to remove his son from the royal council in 1411. Representatives from both the Armagnac and Burgundian factions appealed to Henry IV for his support in 1412, but whereas Henry IV leaned toward the Armagnacs, his son favored the Burgundians. In 1413 Henry IV succumbed to ill health and died, leaving the direction of the kingdom to his son, who was now King Henry V.

The civil war in France placed the English king, who had clear designs on France, in an enviable position. Because France was already divided, Henry had only to enter the breach and conquer. But he couched his militarism in terms of what he called "a just peace" and became its determined broker. To him justice for England required that France return not only lands lost during the Hundred Years War but also the ancient territories that had slipped away when Philip Augustus seized vast domains from king John in the twelfth century. Henry's aims might have seemed delusional, but he was by nature determined, well organized, and attentive to detail. This enabled him to back up his grand schemes with effective action on the battlefield.

The first outward sign of Henry's decision to make war on France came in June 1415, when he abruptly dismissed a French embassy engaged in negotiations at Winchester. During July, Henry readied his fleet for embarkation, arriving in Normandy in mid-August. From the fleet's strategic naval position at the mouth of the river Seine, Henry first besieged the port of Harfleur. Taking Harfleur on September 22 without French interference, Henry minimized the danger to English ships in the channel and gained control of maritime traffic to Rouen and Paris. The French army, however, mobilized in the meantime, blocked the return of Henry's troops to Calais and forced him to give battle at Agincourt. In the hostilities that followed on October 25, Henry scored an unlikely but resounding triumph over a French army so large that to English scouts it seemed "an innumerable host of locusts."[3] Agincourt was the last of the

stunning English victories of the Hundred Years War. The number of pris-
oners was so overwhelming that, despite chivalric custom, Henry ordered
their slaughter. Among those valued enough to be spared was the duke
Charles of Orleans. Henry reportedly approached his high-ranking captive the evening of the battle, and with a strengthened sense of mission
after the day's events, told Charles that God had granted him victory to
punish the "wicked vices" then "holding sway in France."[4]

After laboring for more than three years to forge an alliance with the
changeable Burgundian duke John the Fearless, Henry succeeded in arranging a meeting at Calais in October 1416. The Anglo-Burgundian understanding that issued from this encounter, if anything concrete issued
from it at all, came only a year after two of the duke's brothers had per-
ished at the hands of the English on the fields at Agincourt. An accord,
preserved only in English archives, promised that John the Fearless would
"recognize" Henry and his descendants "as heirs of France," four years in
advance of the Treaty of Troyes. This document is presumably no more
than a draft that the English *hoped* John would sign. If John was not now
a clear ally of England, even his neutrality, confirmed in the events,
boosted the English position.

Henry V's second major campaign, now clearly for the crown of
France, began in lower Normandy in August 1417. By January 19, 1419,
Rouen had surrendered. In the meantime, John the Fearless had driven
the Armagnacs out of Paris in 1418. But in the same year that Rouen
was taken, John the Fearless was brutally murdered at Montereau by the
dauphin Charles' companions. If John's loyalty to England had often appeared in question, his son and successor, Philip the Good, lost no time
in vengefully linking himself to Henry V. The following year Henry saw
all his plans fall into place. With the signing of the Treaty of Troyes on
May 21, 1420, Charles VI, Isabeau of Bavaria, and Philip the Good all
recognized Henry V as heir to the throne of France upon the death of
Charles VI, and regent until that time. To further unite the two realms,
Henry V received the hand of Catherine of France in marriage. From this
union, in Shakespeare's words (*Henry V*), they would "compound a boy,
half French, half English,"[5] whose heirs would join the kingdoms forever
and usher in a perpetual peace.

Henry's third and last campaign in France, launched in June 1421, was
directed at the dauphin's control of the French heartland. After con-
tracting an illness in camp, Henry died on August 31, 1422, at the age

of only thirty-five. His marriage to Catherine had produced one child, a son, who became King Henry VI at nine months old upon the death of his father.

Isabeau of Bavaria (c. 1370–1435)

This queen of France has received a terrible reputation in the annals of history, which some scholars now are convinced she did not deserve. Isabeau was the daughter of Stephen II, duke of Bavaria, and Taddea Visconti. She arrived in France on July 14, 1385, believing she had been sent on a pilgrimage. In fact, she had been sent by her father for marriage consideration, in the hope that Charles VI would consent to take her as his wife. Her name had been put forward by Philip the Bold, duke of Burgundy. A wedding took place three days later, confirming Charles' endorsement of the young Isabeau. Among the twelve children produced by the marriage, the future Charles VII was the eleventh, born in 1403. By that time Charles VI had already experienced bouts of madness, which had begun in 1392. But each time they ended, Charles VI resumed life with the queen, and no fewer than seven children were conceived after his first episode of insanity.

The queen was politically aligned with Philip of Burgundy, who held control of the monarchy until his death in 1404. Within the next year she drew closer to Burgundy's political rival, Louis of Orleans. She and the duke of Orleans became increasingly unpopular for their decadent lifestyle, but facts confirming rumors of an affair are lacking, despite periodic claims that Charles VII and even Joan of Arc were bastard offspring of their relationship. In fact, the biggest political issue facing the queen was how to replace the king during his mental absences. In the tug of war for power that ensued in France, the dukes of Burgundy and Orleans competed with one another while Charles VI made decisions in his lucid moments, and Isabeau watched out for her own interests. Only months after the disturbing November 1407 murder of Louis of Orleans by John the Fearless, duke since his father's death in 1404, two new ordinances placed the royal heir Louis of Guyenne explicitly under the control of Isabeau. The duke was excluded from any part of the rule of France. In 1419 when the dauphin Charles' men retaliated by murdering John the Fearless on the bridge at Montereau, Isabeau acted decisively and within two days had sent couriers to Burgundian towns urging their loyalty to the crown. By 1420 she had entered into the agreement, known as the Treaty of Troyes, which disinherited her son, the future Charles VII. According to the treaty, the royal couple's daughter Catherine was to marry Henry V of England, and on the death of Charles VI the kingdom of France would be handed over to Henry, their newly "adopted" son. Because of this agreement Isabeau came to be known, in a widely circulated prophecy, as the woman who had destroyed France, and Joan of Arc the woman who saved France. But Isabeau's denial of Charles' legitimacy in the Treaty of Troyes referred not, as people commonly believe, to his illegitimate birth. That line of thinking belonged to later anti-French rumors. The treaty referred instead to the "illegitimacy" of his right to rule based on his having caused the murder of John the Fearless. After the death of her husband in 1422, little more is heard of Isabeau. She seems to have lived the rest of her life in relative seclusion at the palace of Saint-Pôl in Paris. A touching exception is the report by a Parisian chronicler that when the nine-year-old Henry VI was brought to Paris in 1431 to be anointed king of France, his procession passed by the former queen's palace, who, upon being saluted by her young English grandson, "turned away weeping."[6] The duke of Bedford and Isabeau of Bavaria, both principal players in the civil and foreign wars that divided France during their lifetimes, died within two weeks of each other in September 1435. By chance, during that same month of September an agreement was reached at Arras to end the civil war.

Jacob van Artevelde (c. 1290–1345)

On January 3, 1338, van Artevelde was among five men elected by their parishes as "captains" of Ghent. Van Artevelde, made chief captain, rapidly inverted the power structure, in which the aldermen had the ascendancy. Emergency circumstances, presumably due to the need for price controls caused by a food shortage, quickly allowed van Artevelde to bypass the governance of the city's aldermen and assert his own local authority. Moreover, van Artevelde sought to replace Louis of Nevers' meddling control as count of Flanders with his own, in part by diverting monies collected for Louis to civil coffers at his disposition. Van Artevelde's mechanisms for wielding control have been characterized by the chronicler Jean Froissart as violent, tyrannical, and dangerous. According to Froissart, nobles were banished and opponents were killed. Political problems facing van Artevelde's regime included how to deal with English pressure to join in an alliance, since Flanders was still very obligated to the French crown. It was decided to grant English armies free passage through Flanders but still to maintain neutrality in the great rivalry between England and France. Nonetheless, van Artevelde engaged in secret diplomacy with Edward III, and it has been suggested that van Artevelde, not Robert of Artois, provoked Edward to assume the title of king of France. Van Artevelde's alliance with England reopened access to English wool. The failed siege of Tournai in 1340 by the combined Flemish and English armies, at which van Artevelde was present, demonstrated the inadequacy of England's Flemish alliance to provide the means for a successful invasion of France. At Esplechin in 1340, Edward III signed a truce; at Malestroit in 1342, he signed another. Although Edward had restored the supply of wool to Flanders, the van Artevelde alliance with the English crown had yielded fewer benefits than expected. Even before 1342, urban dissatisfaction with van Artevelde had begun. But in that year, during the absence of the leader from the city of Ghent, a market-place assembly of the citizenry, led by the deputies of the corporations, demonstrated their rising disenchantment with van Artevelde's rule. The main accusation Froissart cited against him was lack of fiscal accountability. Van Artevelde had spent nine years' revenue as he pleased and seemed also to have sent money to England, a decision with which some citizens disagreed. Rising grain prices, competition among the crafts of the textile industry (drapers, weavers, and fullers), and van Artevelde's autocratic rule from Ghent bred further discontent. By 1345 the populace deemed van Artevelde worthy of death, and upon his return to Ghent a mob gathered in the street, stormed his house, and murdered him on July 17. The Flemish did what they could to mollify the anger of Edward III, who had lost an ally. The era of Jacob van Artevelde gradually ended. Louis of Nevers, however, who had fled, did not immediately dare return to Flanders.

The life of Jacob van Artevelde illustrates not only the dictatorial rise of a local strongman in a time of crisis—whom citizens came to resent as much as they had once revered him—but also the critical importance of Flanders in the French and English rivalry for allies in the Anglo-French conflict. Flanders could indeed tip the balance of power in favor of one kingdom or the other. Although van Artevelde's attempt in the 1330s and 1340s to shake off the feudal control of the king of France might seem a failure, rebellion in Flanders had broken the monopoly of noble power and would serve as an example for emulation in later French and English rebellions.

Jean Froissart (1337–c. 1404)

Jean Froissart is best known for his *Chronicles* recounting the history of his times from approximately 1327 to 1400. Froissart's narrative relies heavily on the chronicle of Jean le Bel until 1361, after which time Froissart gathered his own material including the accounts of eyewitnesses. Written in four books, the only complete edition, edited by Joseph Kervyn de Lettenhove between 1867 and 1877, runs to twenty-six volumes. The four books record events up to 1377, 1387, c. 1390, and c. 1400, respectively. Froissart is often regarded as a French chronicler and poet, but technically speaking, he was born outside France in the northern county of Hainault. His birthplace, Valenciennes, is today part of France. Although of simple bourgeois origins, Froissart wrote to please aristocratic patrons, playing to their fascination with great deeds and chivalric attitudes, as the spirit and ideals of chivalry took root in his own mind in the process. After an ecclesiastical education, Froissart became secretary to Queen Philippa of Hainault, a compatriot, who had married King Edward III of England in 1328. For years French kings considered Froissart's writing too sympathetic to English interests, but his panoramic view of the events of the Hundred Years War later resulted in the production of French manuscripts of his *Chronicles*, sometimes with a pro-French bias detectable in the manuscript illuminations. Froissart's cosmopolitan outlook grew out of a life of tireless travels that took him to Scotland, Gascony (in the company of the Black Prince), Italy, and the Low Countries. Froissart's conviction that deeds of prowess deserved to be recorded irrespective of the actor's nationality ("without bias . . . on whichever side they occur") was further proof of his cosmopolitanism. Scholars have accused Froissart with some justice of allowing his love of chivalry to deform his historical accuracy. It can be shown that he made up dialogue, embellished his narrative to appeal to his aristocratic readers, and wrote biased accounts of rebellions such as the *Jacquerie* (1358) and Wat Tyler's rebellion (1381) whose rebels he held in contempt. Froissart also displays an unnerving fascination with warfare as spectacle, frequently characterizing violent combat as "beautiful" or "a pleasure to see." But the *Chronicles* present a broad tableau of European events, almost an aerial view, complete with color and sounds, from decorated banners to the clash of steel. The complicated chronology of the different books of the *Chronicles* and their various recensions ends with the Rome manuscript, a recasting of the earliest section of the first book but written as late as 1400 and reflecting the historian's most mature (and sober) thoughts on the age he chronicled. Despite their shortcomings, Froissart's exhaustive annals stand as the most important chronicle source for the Hundred Years War. Current scholars are more willing than previous generations to attribute to him a more complex understanding of his times. Reassessments of his work have emphasized that he was far from frozen in an idealized past and that he was more capable than previously thought of seeing and recording reality. Froissart also deserves recognition as a poet. Two manuscripts of his rich poetic output survive, as well as a long verse romance in the Arthurian tradition called *Meliador*.

Joan of Arc (1412?–1431)

At the time of Joan of Arc's birth, reports of despair emanated from the dauphin's court. Charles was derisively labeled the king of Bourges, from the town south of the Loire where he had convened his makeshift government after taking flight from Paris in 1418. By all accounts, Charles lacked the finances as well as the morale to mount a serious campaign against his enemies, who then held approximately half of France. It was commonly believed at the time that victory rested solely in the hands of God, and because the French believed they had often received divine aid in the past, they therefore could not discount that God might again intervene on their behalf. How the young Joan came to believe that she was the messenger destined to bear God's promise of salvation to the French remains largely a mystery. However, it was the strongest recommendation she could have made for herself.

Despite the popular perception that Joan had appeared out of nowhere, she in fact had a small personal history and a family, including two brothers who eventually rode with her in battle, one of whom was captured at her side at Compiègne. Almost everything we know about Joan personally, before she met the dauphin Charles at Chinon in March 1429, is

derived from the testimony of thirty-four men and women from her birthplace, witnesses at the nullification trial of 1456. Their sworn statements
reveal a girl who was teased for being too pious, "liked working," and
"undertook all sorts of jobs." She was remembered as a child who did
everything "gladly."[7]

According to her godfather, Joan had been baptized in the church of
Saint Remi, named for the saint who baptized Clovis, first Christian king
of the Franks. From annual sermons praising Saint Remi, Joan probably
learned the little she knew of the pious myths of Charlemagne and Saint
Louis, and the rudiments of France's tradition of sacred kingship. Yet it
was apparently to a man she referred to as her uncle (the husband of her
first cousin), rather than her parish priest, that she first spoke of her mission. Uncle Laxart stated under oath that Joan, alluding to a prophecy,
had confided in him that she wanted to go to France to have the dauphin
crowned. "Was it not said," he recalled her asking, "that France would
be ruined through a woman, and afterward restored by a virgin?"[8] He was
apparently an unsophisticated man, good-hearted enough to help the
young Joan make contact with the captain of Vaucouleurs, who eventually arranged her journey to the dauphin.

Joan made the trip from Vaucouleurs to Chinon in eleven days, with
her escorts Jean of Metz and Bertrand of Poulengy, sometimes traveling
by night to avoid the English and Burgundians, and pausing only twice
to hear Mass. She later testified that she traveled in men's clothes, and
described her party as consisting of a knight, a squire, and four servants.

After waiting impatiently for two days in Chinon, Joan was granted a
private interview with the king. There she revealed the secrets she knew,
destined only for him. In all likelihood, her message was one of reassur-
ance, that it was God's will that he have his kingdom. Charles, swayed
by her words, quickly arranged an informal interrogation of Joan by those
who knew better than he how to judge self-proclaimed prophets. Her case
called for a more extensive investigation, which took place in Poitiers
where Charles' most qualified clerics were assembled. The verdict, to
quote the official summary of their findings, declared that "in her is found
no evil, only goodness, humility, virginity, piety, honesty, and simplic-
ity."[9] Her virginity, in fact, had to be verified by, among others, the
dauphin's mother-in-law, Yolanda of Aragon, to eliminate the possibility
of sorcery.

Once Joan was approved to join the army, she immediately wanted to head for the besieged town of Orleans. She felt it a grave injustice that the duke of Orleans' city was besieged while he was an English prisoner, claiming that "[God] would not suffer that the enemies have the body of the duke of Orleans and his city."[10] From the time Joan dictated her famous *Letter to the English* on March 22, 1429, it took nearly fifty days for the battle to begin, but only eight days to liberate Orleans. On May 8, as the French tensely anticipated another battle, the English turned and fled. A spontaneous parade formed proceeding to the cathedral to give thanks for the victory. Charles of Orleans authorized payment from England for a handsome scarlet garment and deep green tunic for the "good and agreeable service that the said Maid performed for us against the English."[11]

The victory quickly persuaded the dauphin to keep the campaign going. By June 18, after a striking victory at Patay, all the occupied Loire towns had been recaptured. Joan believed that God had an appointed time for all actions. Her persistence convinced Charles to advance to Reims, where he could be anointed as a true French king. On the march to Reims, gates opened to Charles with little difficulty. On July 17, 1429, between 9 A.M. and 2 P.M., Charles was duly anointed and crowned at Reims. Now Joan could properly call her dauphin "king." Joan stood beside the altar during the ceremony, in acknowledgment of the role she had played.

A letter to Yolanda of Aragon, written the day of the coronation, announced the king's departure for Paris the next day, but a surprising event caused a serious change of plans. The same day a Burgundian embassy arrived in Reims seeking a truce. The envoys offered Charles a tempting proposal—the promise of a bloodless transfer of power in Paris at the end of a two-week truce. But Joan was right to have interpreted the duke's failure to attend the coronation as a sign of Burgundian bad faith. When the king agreed to the Burgundian truce, he unwittingly relinquished an eight-day lead over the Anglo-Burgundians on the march to Paris. As Charles lingered northeast of Paris, English reinforcements, diverted from the crusade for which they had been mobilized by Henry Beaufort, bishop of Winchester, made their way to Paris, arriving July 25.

To Joan, as well as to most military authorities, Charles' naïve trust in the Burgundian truce, at a time of such obvious French momentum, was incomprehensible. Writing to the citizens of Reims on August 5, 1429,

Joan declared that if she kept the king's truce it would only be "to pre-serve the king's honor," but she confessed to being "not at all content." Going further, Joan also said that she herself would hold the French army together and in readiness, lest the truce fail. Such big talk was no doubt only a reflection of Joan's disappointment that Charles now ignored her counsel. However, the king was not devoid of gratitude. The previous week, he had formalized a tax exemption for Greux and Domrémy for "the services she has rendered us and renders each day in the recovery of our kingdom." As Joan lost favor with Charles, her reputation among simple people continued to grow. Even a hostile witness admitted that the common people called her "the angelic one" and invented songs and fables about her. Meanwhile, Bedford and Charles played a cat-and-mouse game marked by roundabout maneuvers, as the king made hardly any attempt to reach Paris.

According to Perceval de Cagny, a chronicler and participant in the French campaign, Joan felt that Charles had become "content" and lacked the will to "undertake anything else." Growing tired of inactivity, on August 23, she, the duke of Alençon, and a company of men made for Paris. From Saint-Denis, where Joan arrived on August 26, her men made two or three skirmishes a day at the gates of Paris, eventually at-tacking the city on September 8, 1429 (see Figure 11). The Parisian re-bellion from inside the walls of Paris against the Burgundian occupation that Christine de Pizan had hoped for (see Document 12) never materi-alized. "Instead of the keys [to Paris]," wrote a Paris bourgeois, "they sent an arrow through [Joan's] thigh." Charles, not wanting to jeopardize ne-gotiations with Philip the Good, seems to have actively thwarted the army's success. When forced to abandon the siege of Paris, Joan left a suit of armor at Saint-Denis, according to her later testimony, "because it was the battle cry of France" (*Montjoye Saint-Denis*). By September 21, Charles had retreated (with Joan) south of the Loire. Cagny commented bitterly that "in this way were the will of the Maid and the king's army broken."

The king kept an eye on Joan after the failed campaign of Paris to make sure that she observed his second truce with the duke of Bur-gundy, signed on August 21 for four months, and then extended until April 16, 1430. She joined Charles at Sully-sur-Loire in March, at the family castle of her chief detractor La Tremoille. During March it was learned that the duke of Burgundy was about to attack Compiègne. In

Figure 11. Joan of Arc and the siege of Paris. *Courtesy Bibliothèque nationale de France, Paris.*

late April, determined to block Burgundy's move, Joan returned to the field without even taking leave of Charles. She drove the English out of several towns on her way to Compiègne. There, whether betrayed by Burgundian sympathizers in the town or by her own disregard for her personal safety, Joan was captured on May 23, 1430, taken by an archer. The archer turned her over to his lord, the Bastard of Wandonne. He, in turn, presented her to Philip the Good, who eventually sold her to the English for a handsome price. The enemy rejoiced at her capture and wrote letters declaring her guilty of horrible crimes and fiendish influence. Far away in London, a chronicler noted simply under the rubric 1430: "In this year, on May 23, a certain woman called the *Maid of God*, was captured by the English at the town of Compiègne."[12]

Moved from castle to castle, Joan finally arrived at Rouen on December 23, 1430. There, the Maid was tried in a partisan trial and condemned as a relapsed heretic, on a technical point involving her refusal to abandon male clothes. She was burned at the stake in Rouen on May 30, 1431, at the Old Marketplace.

John II the Good (1319–1364, r. 1350–1364)

King John II of France, called "the Good" for embodying the quintessential chivalric virtues, has paradoxically been portrayed as a classic example of royal ineptitude. This unfavorable image may owe in part to his bad luck at having ruled during one of the darkest periods of French history. His reign began four years after the ignoble French defeat at Crécy. During his own reign, and under his own direction, the French army suffered a still more humiliating defeat at Poitiers, where John himself was taken prisoner. The economic effects of the Plague, which struck France two years before John took the throne, and the pervasive sense that the nobility was depleting the royal treasury without providing military security in return, added to the sense of national calamity. Growing up under one set of ideals, John saw the world embrace new principles, more practical than chivalric, and was unable to adapt in time to the new order.

It must not be forgotten that the good King John was often partial to brutal violence. One of the first acts of his reign was the execution of his constable, Raoul de Brienne (1350). Later on, almost paranoid in his fear of treason, John burst in on a banquet given by his son at Rouen, seized Charles of Navarre, and executed the count of Harcourt without formal charges or trial (1356). But by then the king had lost his constable and confidant, Charles of Spain, to assassination instigated by Charles of Navarre (1354), his son-in-law of two years. Whereas John II had a reputation for impetuousness and bad temper, there were an equal number of signs that he wished to act and treat others honorably—including the poor. His administration attempted many new initiatives rarely credited to him, often with safeguards for the most vulnerable. To stimulate commerce and industry in France, he abolished the privileges restricting free trade of waterways, broke the monopoly of suppliers to the court, and deregulated the trades, promoting competition. After exercising the royal privilege of manipulating coinage to his advantage early in his reign, John later worked to establish a stable currency, instituting the (gold-standard) franc, and incorporated protections for debtors from their creditors. In order to surround himself with trustworthy counsellors, John appointed administrators of modest backgrounds and admitted them to his royal council. Then to secure the loyalty of the nobles, who had lost their accustomed domination of his council, he established a chivalric order, called the Order of the Star. Thoughtfully designed to create tighter bonds of loyalty between crown and knighthood, as the bonds of feudal vassals progressively weakened, in practice the order proved to be fantastically impractical.

John II also seems to have envisioned the royal benefits of money spent on the arts, by starting the royal library collection, paying for manuscript illuminations, and engaging painters and musicians. In a practice later characteristic of the humanists, he even commissioned a translation of a work by the Roman historian Livy. The famous Italian poet Petrarch held John II in high intellectual regard, higher than his father Philip VI, whom Petrarch claimed "held his son's teachers as his personal enemies." Petrarch even journeyed to Paris to return a gold ring lost by John at the battle of Poitiers.

John's son, the dauphin Charles, knew his father's shortcomings at close range, and Charles' experience sets in relief the damage of John's reign. The tumultuous years the young boy spent with the weight of the kingdom on his shoulders, while his father dwelled in "golden handcuff" captivity in England, are an important part of John's legacy. Intoxicated with impractical notions of courage, King John had remained on the field at Poitiers after his son Charles took flight. The cost of John's bravery to the kingdom was incalculable. In the absense of stable leadership, agitators of all stripes sought to fill the vacuum—Etienne Marcel and Charles of Navarre among the most notable. During the Paris revolution the young dauphin saw his marshals murdered before his eyes, and was himself ousted from the capital. Moreover, in England John made ridiculous concessions to Edward III in the two treaties of London, confidently signing away as much as two-thirds of the kingdom in exchange for his freedom, and flew into a rage when the Estates General courageously refused him.

John II's measured efforts to reform the royal administration, take an active hand in affairs of the realm, balance the interests of his subjects to prevent rebellion, and build the economy—especially once crippled by his ransom note—suggest the outlines for at least part of his contribution to history. Although captured at Poitiers in 1356, John was blamed neither by his people nor even by the English, who went to great lengths to honor his courage. But by refusing to lose a battle, he nearly lost the kingdom. He died in captivity, having returned to England when his son, a royal hostage while the ransom was being raised, escaped. John had bled his people for ransom money but still died in captivity.

John the Fearless (1371–1419; Duke of Burgundy 1404–1419)

John the Fearless was the son of Philip the Bold, duke of Burgundy, and Marguerite of Flanders. Seemingly well endowed by fortune, John inherited the duchy of Burgundy in 1404 from his father, and the following March, on the death of his mother, the county of Flanders. But John had already paid the price for his Burgundian heritage when, as an inexperienced military commander aged twenty-five, he was sent on a crusade in place of his father to aid Sigismund, king of Hungary, against the Ottoman Turks. The Ottoman Empire had at that time reached as far west as the Hungarian fortress of Nicopolis on the Danube. Impetuous minds had opted for a cavalry charge instead of a more cautious plan, and John, lucky to survive, spent two years imprisoned before being ransomed. This adventure earned him the nickname John the Fearless.

After 1392, the year of Charles VI's first attack of insanity, a severe rivalry had developed between John's father, Philip the Bold, and Louis of Orleans, uncle and nephew respectively of Charles VI. When John acceded to the duchy of Burgundy, the rivalry of the two first cousins, John and Louis, escalated still further. A point of no return was reached on the evening of November 23, 1407. Louis of Orleans, who had dined with Queen Isabeau of Bavaria, his sister-in-law, was returning home when suddenly he was set upon by masked men. With swords, clubs, and axes, they hacked the duke of Orleans to death, causing his brains to spill out on the pavement. Although John the Fearless was among the most vocal mourners, he soon confessed to his uncles, the mad king's brothers, that he had succumbed to the temptation of the devil and was the responsible party. He was allowed to escape but returned to Paris, and on March 8, 1408, he defended his crime to the court, with the utmost arrogance, through his spokesperson Jean Petit. The text of the defense, which Petit needed four hours to read aloud, argued that John the Fearless had murdered for the public good. "This extraordinary document," wrote John's biographer, Richard Vaughan, "stands out as one of the most insolent pieces of political chicanery and theological casuistry in all history."[13]

After surviving the crisis of the murder of Louis of Orleans, John the Fearless began to play a double game, siding with either England or the French royal family as it suited his interests or secretly with the two sides simultaneously. First he joined in a truce with Henry IV of England in

1411, although it applied only to Flanders. Overtures by Henry V for a complete accord with the duke failed in 1414. Talks between England and Burgundy were reopened in 1416, but they went nowhere, prompting a chronicler for Henry V to declare that the duke "detained our king all this time with evasions and ambiguities" and was "a double-dealer, one person in public, and another in private."[14]

On the night of May 28–29, 1418, the Burgundians seized control of Paris. A prime opponent of John of Burgundy, Bernard VII of Armagnac, whose name was synonymous with the Orleanist party, was removed from action by his death in the Burgundian seizure. Already in November 1417, John had facilitated Isabeau of Bavaria's removal from Armagnac custody. On February 16, 1418, already governing from Troyes, the pair had declared the French Parlement reconstituted in Troyes and that of Paris abolished. By 1418, with John the Fearless master of Paris, Henry V, who had accomplished a decisive victory over the French at Agincourt in 1415, was eager to deal with him. Now, however, the duke faced challenges to his power from Henry V, who was as intent as Edward III had ever been on claiming the crown of France, as well as from the dauphin Charles, the French heir. The dauphin turned out to be the greater threat. On a bridge at Montereau, where the dauphin and duke met to sign a peace agreement, John the Fearless was brutally assassinated. The details were never clear, but there is no incontestable proof that Charles had orchestrated the murder. As John's enemy Louis of Orleans had met his death, so too did he.

Philip VI (1293–1350, r. 1328–1350)

Philip of Valois was appointed regent after the death of his cousin, King Charles IV of France, with the expectation that if Charles' pregnant widow gave birth to a daughter, Philip would succeed to the throne. When a daughter was born to Jeanne of Evreux, Philip was crowned king at Reims (May 1328). This distinction had eluded his father, Charles of Valois, who was the son, brother, uncle, or father of six French kings. Philip, however, owed his crown to an election by the princes whose favor he thereafter needed to maintain. The principal contender to the throne was Edward III of England, denied consideration because his claim depended on the transmission of his right through a woman.

Philip's reign began with a military victory over rebellious Flanders at

Cassel in August 1328, which reinstated his vassal and loyal ally Louis of Nevers as count of Flanders. In 1329 Philip obtained Edward's reluctant homage for Aquitaine. A bitter feud with Robert of Artois caused Robert to transfer his allegiance from Philip to Edward III. In retaliation, Philip confiscated Aquitaine in 1337. Although the duchy had been confiscated twice before, this seizure started the Hundred Years War. The Avignon popes had already attempted to avert full-scale war, but Philip's reckless insistence that Scotland be involved in any peace settlement ended promising peace talks. In such an uncertain political climate, Pope Benedict XII canceled a crusade by Philip, who rashly escalated a tense situation by threatening the coast of England with the same fleet that had been assembled for the crusade.

A serious French naval defeat at Sluys in 1340 was followed by a humiliating defeat of the French cavalry at Crécy in 1346. More losses were at hand for Philip and his allies. Scotland lost badly to the English at Neville's Cross in 1346, and the following year, the English captured Charles of Blois, the French-backed claimant to the duchy of Brittany, at Roche Derrien. Adding to French discouragement, the town of Calais surrendered to the English in 1347 after a long siege. The truce of Calais was signed in September 1347, concluding English campaigns in France—for the remainder of Philip's lifetime, as it would turn out—although raids continued in southwestern France. Looking for additional funds for war, Philip faced an angry meeting of the Estates General in November 1347 where he was told that, by the counsel he had followed in his wars, he had "lost all and gained nothing." As historian Robin Neillands has observed, "defeated kings are notoriously short of credit."[15] Still, the Estates finally agreed to his request. Then an epidemic, afterward labeled the Black Death, suddenly broke out in Marseille in December 1347. It continued the devastation of the kingdom where the English had left off.

Although Philip made substantial additions to the royal domain, including the acquisition of the city of Montpellier and the province of Dauphiné (a future endowment for royal heirs) in 1349, he is no doubt better remembered for what he lost, principally the battle of Crécy and the fight for Calais. A determined ruler, Philip VI was often too willful or too undiscerning to meet the challenges of his reign, yet he extended France's western border to the Alps. He died at Nogent-le-roi on August 22, 1350.

Philip the Good (1396–1467; Duke of Burgundy 1419–1467)

Philip the Good was born in 1396, the year John the Fearless, his father, was defeated and taken prisoner at Nicopolis, ending a crusade against the Ottoman Turks. Philip was the only legitimate son of John the Fearless and Margaret of Bavaria. Philip was only sixteen when his father was murdered at Montereau on September 10, 1419. The grisly murder, carried out by emissaries of the dauphin Charles, left Philip and his mother stunned and grief-striken. A letter written on behalf of the young Philip, a week after the murder, revealed his fragile state, noting that because Philip "has suffered . . . extreme grief and distress . . . it is quite impossible for him to deal with the matters mentioned."[16] Philip's mother made it immediately clear that she expected her son to avenge his father's death. As we know from a contemporary memorandum, Philip contemplated the pros and cons of an alliance with England almost immediately. The memorandum recognized that, as first peer of France, Philip should protect the realm by calling a meeting of the Estates, not arbitrate against it. Linking himself to Henry V's conquest of France was demonstrably dishonest. But rationalizing that if he rejected England's offer, then the dauphin might accept it, Philip sealed two separate pacts with England in December 1419 at Arras. Burgundian counsellors soon drew up arguments to justify the duke's English leanings. The culmination of Burgundian cooperation with England was the signing of the Treaty of Troyes in May 1420, which provided the title to the lands Philip already held in France.

In the summer of 1420, Philip joined Henry V in a military campaign that won towns able to bridge the gap between English-held France and the duchy of Burgundy. Philip's support was immensely helpful to Henry V, but the duke remained a reluctant ally. As Pierre Champion put it, Philip was "French in origin, Flemish at heart, and English by self-interest."[17] Yet to the extent that the two princes were able to work with each other, while still managing to work for themselves, the alliance held. When Henry V died in August 1422, Philip declined the regency of France (for nine-month-old Henry VI), deferring to John, duke of Bedford, the deceased king's brother. A marriage the following year between Philip's sister Anne and Bedford helped to maintain Anglo-Burgundian harmony.

From 1422, however, Philip became increasingly susceptible to entreaties from the French. In 1429, during the Anglo-Burgundian siege of Orleans, the besieged inhabitants offered their town, in the name of their lord (and Philip's cousin), the imprisoned Charles of Orleans, to Philip in exchange for "abstention from war."[18] Once informed, however, Bedford immediately neutralized the deal, claiming that he did not beat the bushes so others could take the birds.[19] In response, Philip summoned his troops and abandoned the siege. On the other hand, there was no love lost between Philip and Joan of Arc, whose Reims campaign deep into Burgundian territory insulted and threatened the duke. On July 17, 1429, the day of Charles VII's coronation, Joan expressed disappointment in a letter to Philip that he had failed to appear for the ceremonies. A two-week truce between Philip and Charles was in the works as she wrote, followed by another in effect from August to December 1429. Lacking support, the French military offensive languished. Georges de la Tremoille, lieutenant general for Burgundy under Charles VII, who was charged with handling all Franco-Burgundian negotiations, had no more use for Joan than the duke Philip. He was able to keep her out of action at his chateau at Sully during much of the winter of 1429–1430, apparently so that she would not threaten Franco-Burgundian negotiations. By May 30, 1430, Philip's arch-enemy, Joan, had been captured. For purposes of propaganda, Philip quickly composed a letter denouncing the error of her ways.

In the meantime, Philip had married Isabel of Portugal on January 7, 1430, and at the same time founded the Order of the Golden Fleece. His land holdings during the decade after the Treaty of Troyes had grown significantly, with the addition to his domains of Brabant, Hainault, and Holland, and the Order became a mechanism for binding his distant territories together. At the same time, the coalition with Bedford was weakening. After the death of Philip's sister Anne in 1432, the alliance started to crumble. In the Burgundian city of Arras, in 1435, Philip was finally reconciled with his cousin Charles VII for the murder at Montereau sixteen years before. Philip's wife Isabel served as an effective mediator at Arras, but she was unable at Gravelines in 1439 to make peace between Philip and the English, who were furious at Philip's defection and violation of the Treaty of Troyes. Isabel did secure a commercial trade agreement, however, which restored commerce between England and Flanders. The following year Burgundian intervention obtained the release of

Charles of Orleans after twenty-five years of captivity in England. Consistent with the recommendations of a fascinating memo of September 10, 1436, by Hugh of Lannoy, ducal adviser, detailing Philip's post-Arras game plan (see Document 13), Philip, the son of murderer John the Fearless, sought Charles of Orleans, the son of John's victim, as an ally, with the hope that a Burgundian-Orleanist alliance would improve his position relative to Charles VII of France. The last major project Philip undertook was an unsuccessful effort to launch a crusade against the Ottoman Turks, who had taken Constantinople in 1453. Philip's crusading vows were undoubtedly sincere, but they also offered the prospect of avenging his father's defeat at Nicopolis.

The richness of Burgundian archives under Philip the Good provides detailed knowledge of his ducal achievements and striking personality. The exceptional advancement of the arts under Philip's tenure included the sponsorship of an official chronicler, Georges Chastellain, and many writers, painters, miniaturists, translators, and musicians. In his leisure, Philip was a tinkerer who loved to solder broken utensils and repair glassware. The necessary gadgetry for his hobby accompanied him as he moved from castle to castle, as did his jewels, his spices, and his son's toys. This scheming potentate, who raised the duchy of Burgundy to its highest stature, was also a practical joker. His expense accounts provide insight into this side of his personality. In 1433 he had a number of mechanical contrivances at the castle of Hesdin refurbished. Hesdin held a special gallery containing a distorting mirror, a fake book of ballads that squirted soot, devices that sprayed unsuspecting guests with water, rings to pull that showered guests with flour or soot, an elaborate system of pipes under the floor "to wet the ladies from underneath," and even a weather room that made rain, thunder, lightning, and snow.[20]

Philip the Good died on June 15, 1467, after dining on an omelet and a few sips of almond-milk. He left a throng of bastard children and a single surviving legitimate son, who succeeded him as Charles the Rash.

Robert III of Artois (1287–1343)

In the early years of the reign of King Philip VI of France, Robert of Artois first served as trusted counsellor to the king, lost favor, changed sides, and then became as trusted an adviser to King Edward III of England in making war on France as he had previously been confidant to

Philip VI. To this role Robert owes his place in history. Born in 1287, Robert had the hapless distinction of being the only prince of his generation to lose a contest of disputed inheritance to a woman, his aunt Mahaut of Artois. Claimed by the chronicler Jean le Bel to have been the most instrumental person in Philip VI's accession to the French throne, Robert must have believed that a king who owed his crown to the successful exclusion of claims through the female line would look with equal favor on Robert's own attempts to acquire Artois from his aunt. A first appeal in 1315 was unsuccessful, in part because two powerful princes, married to the daughters of Mahaut, coveted the inheritance. A second appeal to Philip in 1330 was embellished with inheritance documents that soon proved to be forged. When the subterfuge became known and Philip's confidence in Robert turned to virulent hatred, Robert fled France, and between 1334 and 1336 found asylum with Philip's rival, King Edward III of England.

Once in England, Robert appears to have personally incited Edward III to reclaim France as his rightful inheritance. A degree of uncertainty surrounds Robert's direct involvement. An important source of information is a satirical poem titled *The Vows of the Heron*. In the poem, Edward's knights make humorous vows of bravery on a heron, the symbol of cowardice. Outlining the possibly fatal consequences of royal cowardice, Robert of Artois provokes Edward into vowing that he will invade France, but how much historical truth lies beneath the buffoonery of the poem is unclear.

On December 26, 1336, Philip VI demanded that Edward expel Robert from England. The grounds were feudal: the mortal enemy of the suzerain is by right equally the enemy of the vassal. Therefore, Edward, as Philip's vassal, had no right to harbor Robert of Artois, who was, in feudal terms, their mutual enemy. Robert was accused of having tried to kill Philip, first by magical incantations and then by hired assassins. There were also accusations that he had tried to poison his own aunt. Papal record verifies the attempts on Philip's life and confirms that Robert was considered a lethal accelerant in the Anglo-French conflict. When Philip announced the confiscation of Gascony on January 7, 1337—the event that precipitated the Hundred Years War—he cited Edward's insubordination as a vassal in continuing to harbor the king's mortal enemy Robert of Artois. In 1343 Robert died at sea of battle wounds sustained while fighting for England near Vannes in Brittany.

NOTES

1. Edouard Perroy, *The Hundred Years War*, trans. W. B. Wells, repr. (New York: Capricorn, 1965), p. 214.

2. Jonathan Sumption, *The Hundred Years War I: Trial by Battle*, repr. (Philadelphia: University of Pennsylvania, 1999), p. 452.

3. Desmond Seward, *The Hundred Years War: The English in France, 1337–1453*, repr. (New York: Penguin Books, 1999), p. 162.

4. Ernest Lavisse, *Histoire de France depuis les origines jusqu'à la révolution*, vol. 4, pt. 1, *Les premiers Valois et la Guerre de Cent Ans (1328–1422)*, A. Coville (Paris: Hachette, 1902), p. 370.

5. William Shakespeare, *Four Histories . . . Henry V*, ed. A. R. Humphreys, repr. (New York: Penguin Books, 1994), p. 859.

6. Régine Pernoud and Marie Véronique Clin, *Joan of Arc: Her Story*, rev. and trans. Jeremy duQuesnay Adams, ed. Bonnie Wheeler (New York: Saint Martin's Press, 1998), p. 144.

7. Régine Pernoud, *The Retrial of Joan of Arc*, trans. J. M. Cohen (New York: Harcourt, Brace, 1955), p. 4.

8. Pernoud, *Retrial*, p. 77.

9. Deborah A. Fraioli, *Joan of Arc: The Early Debate* (Woodbridge: Boydell Press, 2000), p. 206.

10. Jules Quicherat, "Chronique de la Pucelle" in: *Procès de condamnation et de réhabilitation de Jeanne d'Arc, dite La Pucelle*, vol. 4 (Paris: Renouard, 1847), p. 219.

11. Quicherat, *Procès*, vol. 5, p. 113.

12. Quicherat, *Procès*, vol. 4, p. 475.

13. Richard Vaughan, *John the Fearless: The Growth of Burgundian Power*, repr. (Woodbridge: Boydell Press, 2002), p. 70.

14. Ibid., p. 214.

15. Robin Neillands, *The Hundred Years War*, rev. ed. (London: Routledge, 2001), p. 110.

16. Richard Vaughan, *Philip the Good: The Apogee of Burgundy*, repr. (Woodbridge: Boydell Press, 2002), pp. 2–3.

17. W. P. Barrett, ed. and trans., *The Trial of Jeanne d'Arc: Translated into English from the Original Latin and French Documents*. With Pierre Champion "Dramatis personae," trans. Coley Taylor and Ruth H. Kerr (New York: Gotham House, 1932), p. 409.

18. Henri Martin, *Histoire de France depuis les temps les plus reculés jusqu'en 1789*, vol. 6 (Paris: Furne, 1865), pp. 129–30.

19. Régine Pernoud, *La libération d'Orléans* (Trente journées qui ont fait la France, 8 mai 1429) (Paris: Gallimard, 1969), p. 105.

20. Vaughan, *Philip the Good*, p. 139.

PRIMARY DOCUMENTS

DOCUMENT 1
Homage Texts

The following texts demonstrate the influence of homage as a social and political force. Homage was used not only as a mechanism to regulate complicated feudal relationships, as in the case of John of Toul (on p. 115), but as a political instrument in the battle for ascendancy between the monarchs of France and England.

TREATY OF PARIS OF 1259

The Treaty of Paris of 1259 is frequently cited as a major, though distant, cause of the Hundred Years War. The redistribution of territories agreed to in this contract, signed by two kings who were brothers-in-law, Henry III of England and Louis IX of France, concluded a long power struggle between the royal houses of England and France. As French kings had increasingly sought to bring the lands of Francia under their control, they had constantly clashed with the powerful rulers of England, who held vast territories in western France known as the Angevin Empire. There were those on each side who thought that the treaty gave away too much. The French, unable to wrest the duchy of Aquitaine from English authority, officially relinquished it to the Plantagenets who, in turn, surrendered the French provinces of Normandy, Anjou, Maine, and Poitou, effectively breaking up the Angevin Empire. From Louis IX's viewpoint, the agreement was advantageous because the king of England became his vassal, and thereby came under his control, which had not been the case before.

Paris. Tuesday, May 28, 1258

. . . And in exchange for what the king of France gives the king of England and his heirs, in fiefs and domains, the king of England and his heirs will do liege homage to the king of France, and to his heirs, [future] kings of France; and also for Bordeaux, Bayonne, and Gascony, and all the land that he holds beyond the England Channel, as fiefs and domains; and for the islands, if there are any, that the king of England holds, which are in the kingdom of France, and which he will hold from [the king of France] as peer of France and duke of Aquitaine. And of all the aforesaid things . . . the king of England will render agreeable service, until it is determined which services should be rendered; and then he will be obliged to perform them. . . .

And the king of France will absolve the king of England, if he or his ancestors ever did him wrong by holding his fief without doing homage to him or performing his service. . . . And they will pardon and excuse each other all evil intention relating to quarrels or war, and for all damages and all expenses incurred on either side, in war or otherwise. . . .

The king of England . . . will swear to uphold these things . . . and for this the king of England will make formal promise . . . just as the king of France will make to him. . . . And this formal promise will be renewed at ten-year intervals at the request of the king of France, or his heirs, kings of France. And also the king of France will be obliged, as will his heirs . . . and will swear . . . to keep the peace in good faith, as befits each party.

And we . . . agents of the king of England . . . have sworn on the soul of our lord the king of England, that he will firmly maintain and loyally guard [the aforementioned items] . . . nor will he go against them . . . and that he has done nothing, nor will he do anything, by which the strength of these things, in whole or in part, should be diluted. . . .

Completed in Paris, in the presence of the king of France . . . in the year of Our Lord 1258.

Source: Joseph de Laborde, ed., _Layettes du Trésor des Chartes,_ vol. 3 (1246–60), _Archives nationales Inventaires et Documents_ (Paris: Plon, 1863–1909), no. 4416, pp. 411–13. Trans. Deborah A. Fraioli.

THE HOMAGE OF JOHN OF TOUL

*The need to modernize the archaic system of feudal relationships is evi-
dent in the homage oath of John of Toul, who held land from four lords. The
practice of liege homage was designed to create a hierarchy of fidelity for the
vassal who had multiple overlords. However, when the relationships were as
complicated as the case of John of Toul, compromises were necessary.*

I, John of Toul, make known that I am the liege man of the lady Bea-
trice, countess of Troyes, and of her son, Theobald, count of Champagne,
against every creature, living or dead, saving my allegiance to lord
En[gu]rand of Coucy, lord John of Arcis, and the count of Grandpré. If it
should happen that the count of Grandpré should be at war with the countess and count of Champagne on his own quarrel, I will aid the count of
Grandpré in my own person, and will send to the count and the countess
of Champagne the knights whose service I owe to them for the fief which
I hold of them. But if the count of Grandpré shall make war on the countess and the count of Champagne on behalf of his friends and not in his
own quarrel, I will aid in my own person the countess and count of Champagne, and will send one knight to the count of Grandpré for the service
which I owe him for the fief which I hold of him, but I will not go myself
into the terrritory of the count of Grandpré to make war on him.

Source: Oliver J. Thatcher and Edgar H. McNeal, eds., *A Source Book for Mediaeval History: Selected Documents Illustrating the History of Europe in the Middle
Age* (New York: Scribner's, 1905), no. 213, pp. 364–65.

EDWARD'S REPLY TO THE REQUEST FOR HOMAGE

*After Philip VI's shaky legitimacy as French monarch was strengthened
by victory over the Flemish at Cassel in 1328, Philip decided to bring Edward III to heel by requiring of him an oath of homage for his French fiefs.
All the peers of France had paid homage at Philip's coronation except Edward. The following is an excerpt from Edward's reply to the French king's
request.*

April 14, 1329

My most serene prince and lord, to whom I wish every success and
every happiness, I desire to inform your magnificence that I have long

since had the desire to pay you a visit in France, in order to fulfill my duties as was fitting; but, as a result of the hindrances and difficulties, which beset me in my kingdom, as you must be aware, I have not been able, up to now, to accomplish the project which I had formed. As soon as I am free, and God willing, I shall come in person to pay you the homage which I owe you.

Source: Edouard Perroy, *The Hundred Years War*, trans. W. B. Wells, repr. (New York: Capricorn, 1965), p. 82.

EDWARD'S OATH OF HOMAGE TO PHILIP VI

The following is the key passage regarding the oath of homage sworn before Philip VI at Amiens in 1329.

I become your man for the duchy of Aquitaine and its appurtenances that I hold of you as duke and peer of France, according to the peace treaty made in the past . . . and then the hands of the King of England were put between those of the King of France and the kiss was given by the King of France to the King of England. This was done at Amiens in the choir of the cathedral on 6 June 1329.

Source: Anne Curry, *The Hundred Years War: 1337–1453* (New York: Routledge, 2003), p. 20.

FROISSART DESCRIBES HOW EDWARD III CAME TO ACKNOWLEDGE PHILIP'S REQUEST FOR LIEGE HOMAGE

Once Edward III had performed simple homage to Philip VI, the French began to demand liege homage, a more binding oath. Liege homage required that Edward forswear his own foreign policy interests in deference to those of Philip in a case of conflict of interest. This was a mechanism by which Philip VI could control the freedom of action of Edward, rival to the French throne. French ambassadors were retained in England throughout the winter of 1329–1330 before the homage was indeed determined to be liege.

It appears to me, that king Edward at that time did homage by mouth and words, but without placing his hands in the hands of the king of

France. . . . And the king of England, by the advice of his council, would not proceed further in this business, until he should be returned to England, and have examined the privileges of old times, to clear up this homage, and see by what means a king of England was a vassal to the king of France. The king of France replied, "Cousins, we do not wish to deceive you; what you have hitherto done has been very agreeable to us, and we will wait until you have returned to your own country and seen, from the deeds of your predecessors, what you ought to do." Many in England murmured, that their king should do homage to Philip, who had not so near a right to the crown of France as himself.

Source: Jean Froissart, *Chronicles of England, France, Spain, and the Adjoining Countries, from the Latter Part of the Reign of Edward II, to the Coronation of Henry IV,* trans. Thomas Johnes (London: Routledge, 1868), vol. 1, pp. 32–33.

Philip Finds a Cause for War in the Case of Robert of Artois

In a letter dated December 26, 1336, Philip VI of France, after banishing Robert of Artois from France, wrote to Edward III from Paris, through the intermediary of the English seneschal of Gascony, objecting strenuously to the safe haven Edward had granted Robert in England. Philip demanded that Edward hand the traitor over to him.

Earlier . . . we wrote our said cousin [Edward III] in our other letters that we had heard that . . . he retained with him and in his company Robert of Artois, knight, our mortel enemy, [a person] banished from our kingdom, which astonishes us greatly. And we pray, by these our letters, that he let us know the truth about this. . . . We are particularly astonished. . . . since [Edward] knows that he is bound to us, both through nearness of kinship, and because he is our liege man and peer of France, and owes us faith and loyalty in this case; and we also beg him now, through other letters, as strongly as we can, that regarding these things he reveal plainly his will, and accordingly, that . . . he send us the said Robert, who is our mortal enemy, and who must, for that reason, rightly be his.

Source: Eugène Déprez, *Les préliminaires de la guerre de cent ans (1328–1342)* (Paris: Fontemoing, 1902), p. 414. Trans. Deborah A. Fraioli.

DOCUMENT 2
Female Succession

The following documents describe in historical sequence the development of political theory on the exclusion of women from the throne of France. Since the right to inherit land bore a relationship to the right to inherit the throne, pertinent information on the property rights of Eleanor of Aquitaine is also included. At the time of these disputes over royal succession, there was in fact no legal justification for barring women from the crown.

ELEANOR OF AQUITAINE

Before William X of Aquitaine died in 1137, he bequeathed the duchy of Aquitaine to his daughter Eleanor, his only heir. Anticipating, if not actually arranging for, the marriage of Eleanor to King Louis VII of France, William nonetheless strictly specified in his will that Eleanor's inheritance should not be incorporated into the royal domain of France. On the order of the father, the daughter's inheritance would remain independent and be reserved for her heirs alone.[1] In this way Eleanor of Aquitaine's inheritance was protected by her father. In the event, when the marriage between Eleanor and Louis VII was dissolved for lack of a male heir, Eleanor left the marriage with her domains intact. After Eleanor's second husband, Henry II of Plantagenet, became king of England in 1154, Aquitaine was transferred to English jurisdiction, becoming a source of conflict between England and France from then on.

PHILIP V SUCCEEDS HIS BROTHER KING LOUIS X
THE VERSION OF THE CONTINUATOR OF GUILLAUME DE NANGIS

King Louis X of France died in 1316, leaving the succession to the throne uncertain. Despite an adultery scandal involving his first wife, Marguerite of Burgundy, Louis acknowledged the legitimacy of their daughter, Jeanne, who was legally free to inherit the crown of France. His second wife, Clemence, who was pregnant at the time of his death, gave birth to a son who died within a week. Immediately, Philip of Poitiers, brother of the deceased King Louis, made a bid for the crown. In order to succeed his brother as king of France, Philip had to invalidate his niece's claim to the throne. In the following passage, the Latin continuator of the chronicle of Guillaume de Nangis (writing between 1316 and 1339) describes how Philip V became king.

Everyone approved the coronation of King Philip equally, and they swore an oath to obey the king and after him his son Louis, his heir and legitimate successor by primogeniture in a like manner. The masters of the university of the city unanimously approved, although not with an oath. Then it was declared that a woman could not succeed to the throne of France.

Source: Chronique latine de Guillaume de Nangis . . . continuations, ed. H. Géraud (Paris: Renouard, 1843), vol. 1, p. 434. Trans. Kenneth J. Pennington.

THE VERSION OF THE GRANDES CHRONIQUES DE FRANCE

The Grandes Chroniques de France *(Great Chronicles of France) were the official history of France, written by the monks of Saint-Denis. According to the author of this section of the* Chronicles, *the decision to elect Philip V was not unanimous. The duke of Burgundy, Eudes IV, and his mother Agnes spoke out for the right of Jeanne, daughter of the deceased King Louis (and Eudes' niece), to inherit the throne.*

[Clemence] who was pregnant . . . gave birth to a son named John who quite soon died, which was why Philip, count of Poitiers took possession of the kingdom. But the duke of Burgundy and his mother were against him, and they said that the daughter of his brother, King Louis, should inherit. But the others said that women cannot inherit the kingdom of France. For that reason Philip was crowned king.

Source: Les Grandes Chroniques de France (Société de l'Histoire de France), ed. Jules Viard (Paris: Champion, 1934), vol. 8, pp. 334–35. Trans. Deborah A. Fraioli.

A DIFFERENT VERSION IN A SINGLE MANUSCRIPT OF THE GRANDES CHRONIQUES

[Clemence] gave birth to a son . . . but he lived only two or three days. And from that time, the count of Poitiers ruled the kingdom as its king. But the duke of Burgundy challenged him on behalf of his niece who should have had the kingdom by right, as the nearest daughter to the king. But he was told that women could not succeed to the kingdom of France, a thing that could not be clearly proven. And for that reason, the duke and the duchess [mother of the duke] sent letters to several barons with the request that they not agree to the coronation of Philip, count of Poitiers. And nonetheless the count of Poitiers, with a large company of men-at-arms, went to Reims, and had the gates of the city closed, and in this manner he had himself consecrated and crowned by the archbishop. But the count of Valois, his uncle, did not wish to be present, and also Charles, count de la Marche, his brother [the future Charles IV], would not deign to be there but left Reims that morning in indignation. And when this was done, the newly crowned king went to Paris, and was received by the Parisians with great honor and reverence.

Source: Ibid., vol. 8, p. 334. Trans. Deborah A. Fraioli.

Froissart on the Contested Succession Following the Death of Charles IV

After the death of the last Capetian ruler Charles IV, who was the third son of Philip the Fair to leave no male heir, Charles' sister Isabella, who was married to king Edward II of England, and her son Edward III were excluded from the French throne. Froissart finds the cause of the Hundred Years War in the disputed succession that arose. This places Froissart at odds with most modern historians, who view the confiscation of Aquitaine as the cause.

All these [Louis X, Philip V, and Charles IV] were kings of France . . . by legitimate succession, one after the other, without having by marriage any male heirs. Yet on the death of the last king Charles, the twelve peers and barons of France did not give the kingdom to Isabella, the sister, who was queen of England, because they said and maintained, and still do insist, that the kingdom of France is so noble, that it ought not to go to a woman, consequently, neither to Isabella, nor to her son, the king of England. For they hold that the son of a woman cannot claim any right of succession, where that woman has none herself. . . . Thus it seemed to many people [that] the succession went out of the right line, which has been the occasion of the most destructive wars and devastations of countries.

Source: Froissart, *Chronicles*, vol. 1, p. 5.

DOCUMENT 3
Edward III's Case for War
August 28, 1337

The examination of Edward III's diplomatic correspondence reveals how pressure built toward war during the 1330s and tensions between England and France escalated. In the following document Edward III outlines the measures that he has already taken for preventing war between England and France. Edward portrays himself as having given in to every conceivable compromise but, through no fault of his own, being unable to negotiate a peace with his stubborn and imperialistic cousin Philip VI of France. Edward has proposed marriages under increasingly generous circumstances, offered outright payments of money, and reduced his preconditions for joining Philip's crusade. Edward's stance is that of a tireless defender of peace.

One of many documents in which Edward presented his case for war, this one is somewhat unusual in that it is directed at a domestic audience. As Edward moved closer to war with France, the case had to be made to the English people in order to obtain the necessary finances. On this August day, Edward directs the archbishop of Canterbury, and others, to clarify to the clergy and the people these matters touching upon the defense of the realm. In this document, which is framed as a request for further suggestions on how to secure peace, Edward in fact makes the case that Philip VI's seizure of Aquitaine (May 24, 1337) was an act of aggression, exposing the French king's real goal of conquering all England. By alluding to the threat to the homeland, Edward seeks to depict war with France as a defensive war. Edward does not stake his claim on France here, and refers throughout to Philip as king of France. Although partisan, the document summarizes events of the past decade, testifying to the approaching military conflict.

These are the offers made to the King of France by the King of England to prevent war.

In the first place, the King of England sent to the King of France diverse solemn embassies, requesting him to restore the lands that he withheld from him, willfully and against reason, in the duchy of Guienne; to none of which requests did the King of France consent; but at last he promised that, if the King of England would come to him in person, he would show him justice, grace, and favour.

Trusting to this promise, the King of England passed privately into France [in 1331] and went to him, humbly requesting the return of those lands, offering and performing to the King what he was bound to do and more; but the King of France gave him words only and not deeds, and, moreover, while the negotiations were going on, encroached wrongfully more and more on the rights of the King of England in that duchy.

Also the King of England, seeing the harshness of the King of France, in order to have his good will and that which he wrongfully kept from him, made him the great offers below mentioned; that is to say, when one was refused he made him another:

First, the marriage of his eldest son, now Duke of Cornwall, with the daughter of the King of France, without dowry;

Then, the marriage of his sister, now Countess of Guelders, with his son, with a very great sum of money;

Then, the marriage of his brother, the Earl of Cornwall, whom God absolve, with any lady of the blood royal of France;

Then, to make redemption for disturbance, he offered him as much money as he could reasonably demand;

Then, since the King of France gave the King of England to understand that he wished to undertake a crusade to the Holy Land, and greatly desired to have the company of the King of England, and that he would do him grace and favour therefor, the King of England, in order that the prevention of the crusade might not be attributed to him, offered to the King of France to go in force with him on the crusade; provided, however, that before going, he make full restitution to him of his lands;

Then, he offered to go with him on crusade, on condition that he made restitution of half or a certain part of his lands;

Then, afterwards, he offered, with still greater liberality, to go with him on condition that, on his return from the Holy Land, he made full restitution.

Then, to stay the malice of the King of France, who tried to put upon the King of England the blame of preventing the crusade, he declared himself ready to undertake the crusade, on condition that, on his return, he did him justice.

But the King of France, who endeavored in all ways that he could to injure the King of England and all his subjects, that he might keep what he unjustly withheld and conquer more from him, would not accept any of these offers, but seeking occasion to injure him, gave aid and support to the Scots, the enemies of the King of England, trying to prevent him, by the Scottish war, from seeking his rights elsewhere.

Also, then, from respect to the King of France and at his request, the King of England granted to the Scots a cessation of the war and a truce, with hope of bringing about the peace;

But, during the truce [in 1335], the Scots killed the Earl of Atholl and others, and took prisoner many nobles faithful to the King of England, and besieged and took castles and other places from the King and his subjects;

And, recently, at his request, he offered to the Scots a truce for four or five years, on condition that they restored what they had taken during the former truce, in order that the crusade might take place in the meantime;

To which restoration the King of France would not consent, but supported the Scots in their malice with all his power, and made open war without just cause on the King of England, and sent to sea his galleys and navy which he had prepared under pretense of the crusade, with a great number of armed men, to destroy the navy and subjects of the King of England;

Which men have taken in war and despoiled many ships of England and killed and taken the men who were in them, and have landed in England and the islands of the King of England, committing arson, as much as they could.

Also then the King of England by the counsel and advice of the magnates and wise men of the realm, wishing to prevent the war if possible, sent solemn embassies to the King of France, to offer him all he could without losing greatly of his inheritance, to obtain peace;

But the King of France, hardened in his malice, would not suffer these ambassadors to be brought before him, nor consent to peace or negotiations for peace; but sent a great and strong army to take into his hands by force the duchy before mentioned; declaring, untruly, that the duchy was forfeited;

Which army did great evils in the duchy, besieging and taking castles and towns as far as they could.

Also the King of France, to cover his malice, did try to misinform the Pope and the other great men of Christendom with regard to the King of England; aiming at conquering, as far as he can, not only that duchy, but all the lands of the King of England.

These proposals and others the King of England and his Council could think of, have been made to the King of France to secure peace, and if any man can find any other suitable way, he will be bound and ready to accept it.

Source: Translation reprinted with permission from Clifford J. Rogers, ed., *The Wars of Edward III: Sources and Interpretations* (Woodbridge: Boydell Press, 1999), pp. 51–53.

DOCUMENT 4
Edward III's Proclamation to the French People
February 8, 1340

As England and France continued to move toward war, Edward sent letters with the appearance of diplomatic test balloons, designed to assess the strength of his support and the loyalty of his allies by the reaction the letters provoked. For instance, Edward announced in a letter of October 19, 1337, that he intended to conquer "our inheritance" by force of arms, leaving unclear exactly what he meant by these words. The same was true of his gradual assumption of the verbal and visual symbols of the French kingship—for instance, the title "king of France" or the English arms quartered with the French fleur-de-lis—which he used selectively as he pressed his claim for the throne of France. Increasingly, Edward argued the superiority of his blood right over Philip's kingship by election.

On February 8, 1340, Edward produced the startling manifesto below, written in French for the French people, in which he publicly laid claim to the title "king of France." In this manifesto, Edward presents the case for his hereditary claim to the French throne, arguing that he is the nephew of the deceased king rather than a mere first cousin, as was Philip VI. He carefully avoids the question of whether the right to rule can be transmitted through a woman. Since Edward now claims to be the legitimate heir, he refuses to call Philip VI king, referring to him only as Philip of Valois. As the self-proclaimed king of the new "double" monarchy, Edward presents an attractive program for governing his French subjects, designed to win them over. He deftly presents his claim to the throne of France as the fulfillment of God's will (the duty to rule falls to the legitimate heir). For the people, he promises a return to the justice of Saint Louis and freedom from burdensome taxation. He assures the French—quite disingenuously considering the state of his own treasury—that he is wealthy in his own right and has no need of their money. He pledges respect for the liberties of the Church, and with the resources freed by ending the war between France and England, he plans to mount a new crusade against the infidel. Twelve years into the reign of Philip VI, Edward hopes to capitalize on the dissatisfactions of a decade, presenting himself as an alternative to Valois rule.

LETTER OF FEBRUARY 8, 1340

About the kingdom of France transferred by heredity to the king: Declaration of the King

The King to all peers, prelates, dukes, counts, barons, nobles, and commons of the kingdom of France, of whatever estate or condition they may be, hear this truth. It is well known that Charles [IV], of agreeable memory, formerly king of France, died in legal possession of the kingdom of France; and that we are the son of the sister of the said lord Charles, after whose death the said kingdom of France, as is well known, was handed down and devolved upon us through the right of succession; and that Sir Philip of Valois, son of the said lord Charles' uncle, and thus of a more distant degree of kinship than we are, seized the said kingdom by force, against God and justice, during our early years, and thus holds it by extortion. Therefore, after deep and careful deliberation, and placing faith in God and the good people, we have taken title to the government of the said kingdom, as we ought. And it is our firm purpose to deal graciously and kindly with those wishing to do their duty toward us. And it is not at all our intention to take away your rights unjustly, rather we intend to do justice to everyone, and to reinstate the good laws and customs of the time of our ancestor and progenitor, Saint Louis, king of France.

Nor is it our desire to increase our own wealth at your expense, either through devaluations of the coinage, exactions, or arbitrary taxes, for, thanks be to God, we have enough money to maintain our state and honor. Thus, we want to relieve our subjects as much as possible, and we want to defend and maintain in particular the liberties and privileges of all, and especially of holy Church, as much as it is in our power. However, it is our desire, in the business of the kingdom, to consult with and follow the advice of the peers, prelates, nobles, sages, and our faithful subjects in the said kingdom, never . . . acting hastily or unilaterally. And we must reiterate that we greatly desire that God, through our work and that of the good people, grant peace and love among Christians, and especially among you, so that Christian armies can hasten to the Holy Land, to deliver it from the hands of evil men, a project to which we aspire, with God's help.

And please be aware that we have often proposed to the said lord Philip several reasonable paths to peace, but he agreed to none of them, nor made any proposal of his own. Instead he made war on us in our other lands . . . and therefore we are driven of necessity to defend ourselves and seek our rights. But truly we do not seek to kill or to impoverish the people, rather we desire that they and their possessions be saved.

For this reason we wish and petition, through our grace and kindness, that all the people in the said kingdom, of whatever estate or condition they may be, address themselves to us, as our dear and faithful people, as the good people of the county of Flanders have done, in acknowledgment of God and our right, and recognize us as their rightful king, and do their duty to us between now and the upcoming celebration of Easter, that they be received in peace and under our special protection and defense, and that they keep their possessions and their goods, movable or immovable, completely, without losing anything or being harmed for things done against us in the past.

And because the things stated above cannot be proclaimed easily to each of you individually, we have had them publicized, posting them on the doors of churches and in other public places, so that they may come to the notice of all, to the comfort of our faithful followers and to the terror of those who rebel against us, and so that, henceforth, no one can use ignorance of the said things as an excuse.

Given at Ghent, on the 8th day of February [1340]

Source: Thomas Rymer, ed., *Foedera, conventiones, litterae et cuiuscungue generis acta publica* (London: [n. p.], 1816–1869), vol. 2, prt. 2, p. 1111. Trans. Deborah A. Fraioli. The author has also consulted the translation by C. T. Allmand, ed., *Society at War: The Experience of England and France during the Hundred Years War* (Woodbridge: Boydell, 1998), pp. 147–49.

DOCUMENT 5
Etienne Marcel Warns the Regent That the Parisians Are Murmuring

This remarkable letter from Etienne Marcel to the duke of Normandy, the future Charles V, is little known, but profoundly important for laying out the causes of national malaise six weeks before the outbreak of the Jacquerie. Events leading up to the letter began on April 10, 1358, in the provincial Champagne town of Provins. On that day, at a regional meeting of the Estates—which was held outside Paris because Marcel's commune controlled the capital—Charles let it be known that he was launching a campaign to retake Paris from the bourgeois syndicate of Marcel. Days later, Charles seized fortresses and placed garrisons at Meaux and Montereau. He also had artillery, stockpiled for the defense of Paris, removed from the Louvre to bolster the military strength of the garrisons. Marcel was not deceived as to the purpose of these military maneuvers, which were directed against him and which prompted this letter. He knew that Charles was systematically cutting off all rivers and roads by which food and supplies could reach Paris. The seizure of castles encompassing Paris would create a stranglehold designed to starve the city into submission.

Marcel must have been infuriated, as well as alarmed, by the duke's sudden move to unseat the Paris commune. But his letter is a model of calm and reason and consequently a strategic masterpiece. Were this the only document to survive about Marcel, we would have no hint of his darkly brutal reign over Paris. Although Marcel's personal interest in the letter is solely to lift the blockade of Paris, he sympathetically lays out the grievances of citizens in the provinces when it bolsters his own case against the monarchy. According to Marcel, the target of the royal soldiers should be the foreign enemy near Chartres, not regions living in peace that raise no suspicion, maintain their fortresses properly, and cost the royal treasury no money. Marcel portrays Parisians as loyal to the crown, but he offers a startling rationale for the Parisian revolution based on the theory of a broken covenant: when the monarch fails to provide protection and defense, his subjects are released from their obligation to honor and obey him. Marcel's sensitive exposition of rural complaints against the monarchy clarifies how his propaganda made the leader of the Jacques, William Carle, perceive him as an ally. Lest anyone, however, doubt Marcel's true feelings, his indignant response to royal soldiers who call Parisians villeins says it all.

Letter from the Provost of Merchants and the Municipal Councilors to the Duke of Normandy

Most redoubted lord, let it please you to remember how you agreed with us that if you received report of anything sinister about us, you would not believe it, but would let us know; and likewise, if we heard anything about you, we would let you know. For this reason, most redoubted lord, we tell the truth in saying that in Paris your people are murmuring a great deal against you and your government for three reasons. First, in the region of Chartres, your enemies and ours, and the kingdom's, are in control and pillaging on all sides, and you who ought to offer a remedy offer none. And also all the soldiers from Dauphiné, Burgundy, and elsewhere, who answered your earlier call to defend the kingdom, have provided neither profit nor honor to you or your people, but have eaten the country bare, and robbed and pillaged the people, despite being well paid. This you well know, for several complaints have been made to you, both by me and by others. Because of this, you ought to have requested that [the soldiers] withdraw to their own lands. And, nevertheless, your people contend that you are keeping them around you, or some of them, whom you have assigned to protect the fortresses of Meaux and Montereau, which control the Seine, Marne, and Yonne rivers, by which means your *bonne ville* Paris must be nourished and maintained, which you hold so dear, as you have always said. The third cause of the murmuring of the people is that you do nothing to fortify the fortresses in the region where your enemies are, but have seized those from which vital supplies can come to us all too well. And what is worse, you have reinforced them with people who wish you no good, as is totally clear to you, as it is to us, because of letters that were found on the gates of Paris, which were shown to you in your great council. Furthermore, you stripped your city of Paris of artillery in order to supply the fortresses of Meaux and Montereau, filled with people who wish you no good, as has been said already, and as is clearly demonstrated by words they spoke to you, which, as we well know, are the following: "Lord, whoever controls this chateau can certainly boast that those *villeins* of Paris are in danger from him, and that very soon they will be biting their nails." Let it please you to know, most redoubted Lord, that the good people of Paris do not take themselves to be *villeins*, but are *prudhommes* and loyal men. So have you found them and so will you find them. Furthermore, they say that *villeins* [by contrast] are those who commit villainies: all these things are causing great displeasure among your people, and not without reason. For first and foremost, you owe them protection and defense, and they owe you honor and obedience. What is lacking on the part of one, will not be held by the other. And it also seems to your people, in the name of truth and reason, that you would have done better to hire people who would fight the enemies of the kingdom, rather than those who take money from it, and rob and pillage its people. And it also seems to them that you, and the men-at-arms who are in your company, would serve your honor better if they were between Paris and Chartres—where the enemy is—rather than where you are, which is peaceful territory and where there is no war. And it is also true that the aforesaid fortresses which you have again seized, were in the hands of very good people who were above suspicion, and they were not on the front lines, nor did it cost you anything to guard them. And it is a truism that whoever has two things to protect and guard should sooner protect and watch over the more valuable, honorable, and profitable one, when it is the one more threatened and more at risk. And you in your new council wanted to strip Paris of artillery in order to supply the aforementioned fortresses, a thing your people would not tolerate, because in this they see the loss and destruction of the kingdom, of you, and of all the people. Therefore, we implore you most humbly, most redoubted Lord, to please return to your *bonne ville* Paris and give it protection and defense, just as you ought to do, and to please remove from your midst all those who do not harbor good will toward your people, whom you can easily recognize by the counsel they give you. Also, please put the fortresses of Meaux and Montereau back in the hands of your faithful and loyal subjects, where they were before, so that your people of Paris have no reason to raise a commotion for lack of food supplies, and so that they stop their murmuring. We also entreat you not to be displeased that we kept the artillery that had already been brought to the Louvre by Jean de Lyons, for, in truth, we did it with all good intention and in order to avoid greater evils and perils. For the people were so upset about this that great ills would have taken place if we had not agreed to keep it.

Most redoubted lord, please know that the people of Paris have a clear memory of the promises that you uttered from your own mouth at Saint-Jacques de l'Ospital, at les Halles, and in your own chambers, in which you promised them that if you were allowed to leave—you, and the thirty or forty who were with you—you would no longer allow things to remain in the state they were in, and—thank God—since then there has been a very slight improvement.

Most redoubted lord, let it please you to arrange each and every one of the things elucidated above, to the praise of God, the honor of the king, our lord [John the Good], of you, and to the profit of the people. . . .

May the Holy Spirit keep you in its holy protection and grant you a good and long life.

Written at Paris, the 18th day of April [1358].

Source: Henri Martin, *Histoire de France depuis les temps les plus reculés jusqu'en 1789* (Paris: Furne, 1864), vol. 5, pp. 565–67. Trans. Deborah A. Fraioli.

DOCUMENT 6
Provisions Needed to Stock a Fortress Prior to Siege

Christine de Pizan

Christine de Pizan was an unlikely person to author The Book of Deeds of Arms and of Chivalry, *a book on military technique, from which the following excerpt is taken. She would have had little experience to write such a work, which was probably commissioned. But her timely treatise amounts to a handbook on how to defend against a siege and how to counter the morale-breaking English tactic of the* chevauchée, *by which civilian populations in isolated and poorly defended towns, villages, and chateaux were being devastated. Christine drew heavily upon the wisdom of Vegetius, a fourth-century Roman military expert, for the best in time-honored strategy and tactics. But one section of practical advice, describing how to supply a fortress in anticipation of a siege, is necessarily medieval rather than classical. Because a fortress, no matter how impregnable, is of no use if the besieged run out of basic necessities, Christine devotes one chapter in particular to enumerating supplies, and the quantities of those supplies, that should be laid in beforehand. She bases her calculations on a hypothetical two hundred men-at-arms, each with two servants, or six hundred men overall. The lists yield details otherwise impossible to imagine about medieval foods and military equipment. The sheer accumulation of items inventoried creates a kaleidoscopic image of* medieval life. *Certain provisions even suggest contemporary cooking techniques, trade activities conducted on the premises (carpentry, masonry, blacksmithing), and what was used in such defensive procedures as countermining (preventing the enemy from digging under fortress walls). Items listed come in an impressive number of different units of measure, from the common Parisian measure (1,872 liters) to pounds, flitches, casks, cartloads, bundles, and hogsheads (barrels). Nothing is overlooked, not even a mill to grind two measures of mustard seed. Fifty pounds of spices undoubtedly aided food preservation, as did salt and wine, in addition to contributing flavor during the months of voluntary incarceration. Calculations suggest that food supplies were meager; defense weapons may have been in greater supply. Per person quantities are instructive but sometimes puzzling. Nowhere else is one likely to learn that 24,000 spinning arrows are deemed sufficient for two hundred men for six months, but that figure provides fewer than one spinning arrow per man per day. The requisitioning of two thousand wooden bowls (three bowls to a man) suggests infrequent dishwashing or the lack of durability of wooden utensils. As a whole, Christine's inventory offers, in miniature, as authentic a picture of life in the Middle Ages as one is likely to find.*

As we have sufficiently discussed in general what is needed for living as well as for defense against enemies, it is useful to complete our work by mentioning in detail the proper estimate, more or less, of what would be sufficient to provide for a certain number of men-at-arms, which could be augmented or diminished according to the number involved. Let us consider then two hundred men-at-arms with their servants . . . two for each man, to be fed for six months. One would need 110 measures of wheat according to the Parisian measure (1872 liters), a third of which would be in prepared bread and ten in flour. Likewise, four measures of dried beans, two measures of peas, one hundred twenty jugs of wine (c. 500 liters each), two measures of vinegar, one measure of sour grape juice, one measure of oil, one measure of salt, fifty pounds of spices (ginger, cumin, and other small spices), two pounds of saffron, two measures of mustard seed, and a mill to grind them to make mustard.

Likewise, salted and fresh meat; one hundred large oxen, both salted and alive, insofar as possible and when there is sufficient space and fodder; one hundred or one hundred twenty flitches [sides] of bacon, eight score of sheep . . . a supply of poultry, as many as can be kept and are wanted.

Likewise, salted fish if it is in Lent, and for the days one does not eat meat, a thousand eels, twenty-five barrels of herring, cod, many hake, a cask of salted butter, eleven pounds of almonds, ten or twelve of rice, the same quantity of oatmeal, rose water and other things thought good for the ill. . . . Ten dozen earthen pots, twelve dozen goblets for drinking, ten leather buckets to hold water, two hundred toises (six-foot lengths) of rope.

Likewise, for the kitchen, if it is in winter, two hundred cartloads of large logs, sixty loads of coal, or thousands of small bundles of wood . . . twenty dozen large earthen pots for making soup and cooking meat, six large cauldrons, two dozen pans—large, medium, and small—four dozen wooden spoons, two thousand wooden bowls, as many trenchers, goblets, and cups, empty caskets, twenty or thirty bellows, and other small necessities. . . .

Now it is time to speak of provisions for the defense of the place. First of all, at least twelve cannons throwing stones, two of which will be larger than the others to break up machines, mantelets [protective shelters], and other coverings, if necessary; two bricoles [catapults] and two other rock-throwing machines, each one provided with slings and ropes and a great stock of stone, and two or three large crossbows on wheels, provided with the necessary arrows.

Likewise, if it is thought that it will not be necessary to fire the cannons too frequently, a thousand pounds of powder should suffice, or fifteen hundred, a third in powder and two-thirds in ingredients, three thousand pounds of lead to make shot for the cannons, six dozen iron-tipped lances, twenty-four good crossbows well equipped, six others on wooden bases, six dozen strings for arrows, with a hundred sheaves of arrows, twelve score crossbows with hooks, twelve machines for bending crossbows plus two other machines for bending them, eighteen leather belts with four dozen strings for them, sixty or eighty large shields, twenty-four thousand spinning arrows, twelve thousand of them for longer distances, two hundred round stones for the cannons and a great many others, enough wood to make four hundred tampons (plugs) and a carpenter to make them and give help where it might be needed; three masons to make stone cannon balls and other things as needed.

Likewise, two horse-operated mills, two ovens, a well-provided forge, four thousand pounds of iron, a half thousand of steel, four hogsheads of coal, twenty-four horseloads of charcoal, four kettles with feet, eight bellows for countermining, two dozen equipped baskets, six dozen wooden shovels, eight dozen stretchers, vats and adequate tubs, as is said.

DOCUMENT 7
The Retaking of Poitiers
August 7, 1372

After confiscating the duchy of Aquitaine in 1369, the French set their sights on retaking it from the Black Prince, in apparent defiance of the Treaty of Brétigny. The English controlled the province of Poitou, where John Chandos, constable of Aquitaine, maintained a strong presence and was greatly admired. But Charles V reinstated Poitou as an apanage of his elder brother, the duke of Berry, and hostilities were renewed. The English suffered two crippling setbacks when Chandos died in a skirmish in 1370 and illness forced the Black Prince to return to England in 1371, where he died five years later. Meanwhile, a plot involving two ecclesiastics from Poitiers with French royalist sympathies was uncovered and the schemers summarily executed. In 1372, the French defeated the English forces at La Rochelle. By early August, as Bertrand du Guesclin approached Poitiers, only a weak garrison held the town.

The following excerpt is from the Song of Bertrand du Guesclin, *an epic poem written in French by a poet known only as Cuvelier. It recounts the surrender of Poitiers to the French, sixteen years after the ignominious French defeat at the battle of Poitiers. The passage addresses a rarely considered question: how townspeople weighed their responsibilities when war arrived at their doorstep. Surprisingly, the English occupation had not been disadvantageous for Poitiers, and loyalty to the occupiers ran deep. The town largely ran its own affairs. The English controlled the castle nearby.*

Cuvelier's description is extraordinary for imparting what seems to be an insider's view of both sides, first, as the French, who were under du Guesclin's command, debate how to take the town and then, on the other side, as the townsmen deliberate a course of action in a closed council. Du Guesclin's tactics incline toward bravado, aggression, and ruse, but he manages to reach consensus with the more moderate princes of the blood despite the awkwardness of their overlapping jurisdictions. The burghers, on the other hand, face a more serious quandary and a gamut of emotions: With whom should their loyalty lie? What would be the repercus-

sions of surrender? Can they turn their backs on Englishmen who have
treated them honorably? Is their first and natural loyalty to the kingdom
of Saint-Denis (France)? Are the English, in fact, the cause of their trou-
bles and best gotten rid of? Initially, the citizens, subjects of the Black
Prince in obedience to the French king's wishes, exhibit little patriotic spirit.
Du Guesclin, however, forcefully summons them to surrender—antici-
pating Joan of Arc's Letter to the English—and rekindles their French
loyalty. The betrayed occupiers watch the French revert to kind.

Stanza 728

"My lords," said Bertrand, "We are going to Poitiers, for my heart assures me that we will hold it by nightfall; whether by force or affection,
we will enter. And if the town is under our command, within a year the
English won't be worth two buttons. If we take the city, we will soon take
the castle." And the barons exclaim: "In the name of God, let us go!"
[. . . .]

And when all our barons had come before Poitiers, they stopped near
some bushes and said to one another: ". . . We see the towers and houses
of Poitiers; if we go up to the gates in too offensive a manner, and harm
women and children, the burghers will find us traitorous." The duke of
Berry declared: "Let us recommend to everyone not to harm a single person . . . we ought to befriend them and [only] if they go against us should
we mount a spectacular assault against the town." [. . . .]

Stanza 729

"My lords," said Bertrand . . . "Let us go forcefully before Poitiers . . .
looking proud, making a clamor, and pretending to mount a brave assault; and for each soldier here, let us say that there are one hundred,
and that the *arrière-ban* will soon be here. Often a case is lost by speaking senselessly; one should speak firmly in matters of war." [. . . .]

Stanza 730

All rallied to Bertrand's will, the dukes and barons, and the princes of
the blood, and set out for Poitiers . . . banners unfurled and pennons
raised . . . helmets on heads . . . swords at their sides, and lances in their
fists. . . .

The people from the countryside headed for Poitiers. Then they shouted: "Betrayed! We are all done for! Here come all the people who conquered Chauvigny and seized the castles and procured oaths of fealty from them."

When the burghers of Poitiers heard this, they closed the gate on that side of the town. . . . Now the leading burghers assembled. There they held council as to whether they should resist our French forces or surrender the noble town. There, if you believe what I say, many views were expressed. There was a burgher named Joseré who told the [other] burghers: "Hear my thoughts. I say that whoever willingly surrenders the town to France commits perjury toward the [Black Prince], since we did homage and swore fealty to the prince at the command of the great crowned king, who handed us over to the prince by a true accord. Think about it; I have given my thoughts."

"Sire," said Foqueré, [another] burgher: "It is very true that we were handed over by the king of France to the prince in whom so much loyalty resides, and were delivered on condition that our prince and King Edward . . . maintain the treaty in good faith, as the peace agreement ordered. And they haven't kept it worth a dime, but instead pillaged and ravaged the entire region. . . . No one owes them faith or loyalty. I advise that all the English be booted out [of France] and that we reach an accord with the duke of Berry." [. . . .]

Stanza 731

Afterwards another spoke whose name was Eli. The noble vassal said: "In the name of the Virgin Mary! I am not against surrendering the town, but there are many English in this fair town, who have lived with us day and night, and they trust us without treacherous design, and we have found them honorable . . . [nor did they require payments from us, or impose fees or the *gabelle* (tax); we lived our lives peacefully under them.][2] In fact, they have improved, enhanced, and reinforced this town. We must not now consider any deceit by which they would be destroyed, or killed, or cut down, for whoever commits treason . . . is reproved by God. . . . If we surrender this city, which is so much better now, the French must pledge their faith that if they find Englishmen in this fair city they will let them go and preserve their lives. But, as for those in the castle, by my faith, I would not disagree if they want . . . to take the castle. . . . "

Then there was a bourgeois of ancient ancestry, of high lineage, with a flowing beard: "Lords . . . we still do not know . . . if the French . . . will ask for sovereignty over our town. I recommend that . . . depending on what they [propose] . . . we answer with love or malice. . . ."

Stanza 732

The bourgeois agreed with this counsel. They came out of the house to which they had withdrawn, and let everything be known to the common people. . . . The English knew well, because it had been told to them, that the duke of Berry was coming with a great many men. . . . All the [English] officers . . . asked the burghers . . . for the keys, in order to protect the city, as they saw fit, against the French who were about to attack them. And the burghers replied: "You could have saved your breath, for you'll never in your lives obtain the keys. We will safeguard them, if Jesus consents. We are strong enough to protect the city." "True," said the English, "but we have been told that for next to nothing you would return to being French [again] and would surrender the castle; and if you relinquish it, that would be a breach of faith. If that happens, you will find [the castle] deserted and in ruins." And the burghers said: "if you are afraid, go seek protection, but we do not even know yet what they will ask of us." "O God," said the English, "Here we are betrayed! Truly those vile people have become French again. If anyone had cut them open like a larded pig, they would have found the *fleur-de-lis* in their hearts!"

Stanza 733

Then the English leadership said . . . that Poitiers had been governed gently and well, without causing the people harm, for many a day and many a week. They see the burghers whom nature returns to honoring the preeminent *fleur-de-lis*. If there were enough Englishmen in the area, they would have already given vigorous battle, but they would not have lasted longer than if you set fire to wool. They head for the castle whose walls are sturdy, and the bourgeois head for the high gate, and they plainly see the insignia of the good duke of Berry . . . and that of Burgundy . . . and many pennons in the wind the color of grain. . . .

Stanza 734

To the gate came Bertrand the young warrior, holding a branch in his hand with the leaves in tact, accompanied by his page, but not many men. He had his page carry his helmet should he have need to put it on his head: "Lords, whom I spy there," said Bertrand, "Hear my thoughts without firing, attacking, or throwing stones. I come on behalf of the king whose responsibility it is to hold [and protect] France. I am his constable, Bertrand is my name. . . . No one wrongs the king you hear me speak of, except when forced to leave in the end after much loss. That applies to the English on either side of the sea who have wanted to harm our king. They were at pains to defeat him, diminish his honor, and disinherit him. . . . And every time we wanted to parley and sign and seal a pact, they just wanted to rule and possess. And the good king of France will not tolerate it, nor will the good duke of Anjou . . . nor the duke of Berry . . . [nor] Burgundy . . . nor the duke of Bourbon. . . . Everyone wants to revolt against the English. . . .

If you do not surrender to the king in short measure, you will see yourselves totally destroyed and cut to pieces. But if you wish to deliver your city to us, we will protect you. . . . Aye! Gentle burghers. . . . [l]ook at those banners blowing in the fields. See the *fleur-de-lis* . . . that comes to warn you to serve him [Charles V]. Consider returning to your rightful nature. . . . How could you have someone in charge of a kingdom whose mother has neither the right nor the ability to possess it? And no one, if he is not a male heir, this you know for certain, can rule France [or] wear its crown. . . .

If you do not soon open up, you will see your city destroyed and set ablaze. And if we can take [the city], I swear by God that we will hang you or cut off your heads. Send me your reply. . . !"

Stanza 735

When Bertrand had spoken to the leading burghers, and they had heard his words, then a burgher, who had been designated, spoke. . . . "Sire," said the honored burgher, "It is very true that in the past we held our fiefs from the king of Saint Denis, and will do so again, if it pleases Jesus Christ! For even though the king ruling Paris agreed to surrender us to the [Black] Prince, [and] we were never English by [our own] intention, we obeyed as would true subjects. They broke covenant with the *fleur-de-lis* [France], and for this reason we will assent to your will. We will be obedient to the *fleur-de-lis*, gentle constable, as long as we are protected night and day by the laws and customs of the good king Saint Louis, without harming us a single bit. And if King Charles is in need of friends, he will find us right at hand, night or day, to go with him against his enemies to live or die under his standard. But we want a concession. Let no one hurt, harm, or outrage any of the good Englishmen whose subjects we are, and whom we have found tried and true friends, and with whom we have for a long time broken bread without incident, whether night or day, provided they are willing to obey you." [. . . .]

Stanza 736

When Bertrand heard the burghers . . . there was joy in his heart. . . . And Bertrand called the [royal] princes who made a solid and generous peace with the burghers . . . the drawbridge was lowered [and] our men went in. . . . The poor simple people knelt down, thanking God and his precious name, saying: "Ah! Welcome, [you who are] men of king Charles! Ah, noble *fleur-de-lis*! You must be held in honor, for you are the flower of consolation. . . . We shall have nothing more to do with the perfidious leopard [the English]. Let him go make his nest elsewhere, we'll have no more to do with him." When the English heard these words, they left at a run . . . shouting loudly: "Ah, false, thieving *villains*! You are traitors, with false opinions." "No," said the burghers, "we are *prudhommes*; but you are traitors, crazed and wicked. For he who fails to keep his word is a traitor."

Stanza 737

In this manner Poitiers surrendered, as I have told you. . . .

Source: La chanson de Bertrand du Guesclin de Cuvelier, ed. Jean-Claude Faucon (Toulouse: Editions Universitaires du Sud, 1990), vol. 1, pp. 440–46. Trans. (slightly modernized) Deborah A. Fraioli.

DOCUMENT 8
Grandferré's Courage

The events described in the following passage by Jean de Venette follow the reconciliation of the duke of Normandy (the future Charles V) and Charles of Navarre. The English looked with particular dismay on the strengthening of French defenses through this union—which lifted the blockade of the Seine through which Charles of Navarre had held Paris in a stranglehold—in view of the new threat that French unity posed to the English campaign launched in northern France that same year. The disastrous English campaign of 1359 was Edward III's last futile blow struck in France. His mission in this venture was as propagandistic as it was military, since Edward's goal was to see himself properly crowned in the French manner at Reims. Among the English defeats in the ill-fated English campaign, which led to the truce at Brétigny, perhaps the best known is a tale of local resistance mounted by a gigantic peasant known as Grandferré. In this passage, chronicler Jean de Venette manages not only to depict vividly the heroism and brave death of Grandferré, but also expresses his sheer delight that for once the much-abused peasantry got the better of the mighty English enemy.

The English grieved at this peace and tried to harass the land still more grievously. They did not succeed in all their enterprises and sometimes, by God's will, had the worst of it in single engagements. I will recount on this page such an instance for the pleasure it gives me, as I heard it at first hand, for it took place near the village where I was born. This affair was valiantly conducted by the peasants, by *Jacques Bonhomme*. In a little village called Longueil, near Compiègne, in the diocese of Beauvais . . . there is a farmhouse, strong and well built, which belongs to the monastery of Saint-Corneille at Compiègne. The peasants dwelling round it realized that it would be dangerous for them if perchance the enemy were to occupy this stronghold. Wherefore, they sought the permission of the regent and the abbot of the monastery and established themselves in it, after they had stocked it suitably with arms and food. . . . They made Guillaume l'Aloue, a tall handsome man, their captain. He had with him his servant, another peasant who took the place of a squire, an incredibly strong and powerful man, exceptionally tall and broad-shouldered and well proportioned, and, in addition, full of energy and daring. This giant, as humble and modest as he was strong, was named

Grandferré. There came to the stronghold about two hundred men, all laborers who supported their humble existence by the work of their hands. The English in Creil castle, on hearing that it was men of this sort who were preparing to resist men of their quality, despised them and regarded them as [worth nothing]. They made ready to attack them, saying, "Let us drive out these peasants and make this well-stocked and well-built fortress our own." Two hundred of them came up before Longueil and, finding the peasants off their guard and the doors open, boldly pushed into the courtyard. The peasants, who were on the second story of the manor house by the windows, caught sight of all these fully armed men and were at first stunned by the unexpectedness of the attack. Their captain, however, descended with a few of his men and began to lay about him on all sides. His courage availed him little, for he was surrounded by the English and mortally wounded. Perceiving this, those of his companions who were still in the upper room, Grandferré among them, said, "Let us go down and sell ourselves dearly. Otherwise they will slay us without mercy." They descended cautiously in small groups and issued from different doors. They struck at the English as if they were engaged in their wonted task of flailing wheat in a barn. They lifted their arms so high and brought them down upon the English with such force that no blow failed to inflict a mortal wound. Grandferré groaned deeply for the grief he felt on seeing his master, the captain, lying close to death. He attacked the English, over whom as well as over his companions he towered head and shoulders, brandishing his ax and redoubling heavy, mortal blows upon them. . . . One of his blows, aimed straight, never failed to cleave a man's helmet and to leave him prostrate, his brain pouring out of his skull. Thus he broke the head of one, the arms of another and dashed a third to the ground. He bore himself so surpassingly well that in a scant hour he had, in this first encounter, killed with his own hands eighteen, in addition to those he had wounded. . . . What more need I say? The English fell in such numbers, especially before Grandferré, that the survivors were forced to turn and flee. Some leaped into the moat and were drowned; some thought to escape by the door and reeled under the blows of the peasants holding the farmhouse. . . . On that day almost all the Englishmen who came to that fight were slain or drowned, or disabled by the aid of God and by Grandferré. [. . . .]

The other Englishmen in France mourned the death and destruction of their men deeply, saying that it was too much that so many of their good fighters had been killed by mere peasants. Wherefore, all the English from the fortresses in the neighborhood assembled and marched against the peasants at Longueil. . . . Yet when the English assailed their farmhouse stoutly, they came forth to battle with good courage. In the front rank was Grandferré, of whom the English had been told. . . . No sooner had they seen him and felt the weight of his ax and the force of his arms than they heartily wished that they had not come to that battle on that day. For, to be brief, all of them were put to flight or mortally wounded or slain. The peasants captured some English noblemen of high rank for whom they would have received all the money they wanted had they been willing to hold them for ransom. But they refused and said that these men should have no chance to do them further harm. . . .

When the English had been defeated and the battle was over, Grandferré, heated by the excessive warmth of the day and by his violent exertion, drew up and drank off great quantities of cold water and was forthwith seized with a burning fever. He took leave of his companions and returned with his wife to his cottage. . . . He went to bed, ill, but not without his ax, which was so heavy that an ordinary man could only with great difficulty lift it from the ground to his shoulders. When the English heard that Grandferré was ill, they rejoiced greatly, for no one had dared attack Longueil so long as he was there. They were afraid that he might recover and, accordingly, sent secretly twelve of their companions to strangle him in his house. His wife saw them coming in the distance, ran to her husband lying on his pallet and said, "Alas! Dearest Ferré, the English are here, looking for you, I verily believe. What can you do?" Unmindful of his fever, he armed himself swiftly and, taking up his heavy ax or *gisarme* with which he had already overwhelmed so many enemies, went forth from his house. As he came out into his little yard, he saw the Englishmen and cried out, "Robbers, you have come to take me in my bed but you have not yet taken me." He stood with his back to the wall so that he could not be surrounded and assailed them violently, wielding his ax with all his old spirit. They pressed him cruelly for they desired with all their hearts to take him or kill him. On seeing himself so extraordinarily hard pressed, he hurled himself mightily upon them with such an access of fury that no one whom he struck escaped an ill death. The mere sight of his blows took from the English almost all desire to defend themselves. In a moment, he had laid five of them prostrate on the ground with mortal wounds. The other seven then left him and turned and fled in confusion. Thus triumphant over them, he went back to bed, and heated by the blows he had delivered, drank abundantly of cold water and so relapsed into a still more violent fever. He grew worse and within a few days he had received the last sacraments and had departed this world. . . . [T]he whole countryside lamented Grandferré's death, for as long as he lived the English dared not come near.

Source: *The Chronicle of Jean de Venette*, trans. Jean Birdsall, ed. Richard A. Newhall (New York: Columbia University Press, 1953), pp. 90–93. Reprinted with permission of the publisher.

DOCUMENT 9
Peasants' Revolt of 1381

This excerpt from the Anonimalle Chronicle *is important in that it details exactly how an actual popular revolution began. In this case it was spurred by indignation at a supplemental levy imposed by Richard II of England after taxes had been duly paid. Taxation and its abuses figured prominently as the immediate cause of numerous rebellions. One of the particular merits of this passage is that it allows us to understand how, after a seemingly isolated and fairly innocuous incident, popular resistance could expand and spread like a contagion. Obviously the author of the chronicle sides with the landed gentry, whom he calls "the good folk of the countryside," but whose possessions opened them, along with the nobility, to popular contempt. The rebels, on the other hand, perceive themselves as supporting their king by ridding him of evil councillors. The king's chief justice, for instance, is deemed a traitor to his royal highness. All royal judicial functionaries are viewed as evil and false. The rebels' moral indignation is aroused and chief justice Robert Belnap is made to forswear on the Bible any future involvement. The chronicler's narrative describes the peasants' almost seamless descent into violence. Their violence is prompted not only by their vision of a new order in which the entire royal bureaucracy will have been slain, but also by the desire to kill those neighbors who refuse to join them. All action is effected in the name of the king. By the end of the passage, a mob of fifty thousand has carried out several beheadings for their exemplary value.*

In the year 1380 . . . because various lords and commons were advised that the subsidies were not duly or loyally levied, but commonly extracted from the poor and not from the rich, to the great profit and advantage of the collectors, and the deception of the king and the commons, the King's council ordained certain commissions to make inquiry in each township how they were levied. One of these commissions was sent to Essex to a certain [John] Bampton. . . . And one day before Witsuntide he held a court . . . to make inquisition. . . . He had summoned before him a hundred of the neighbouring townships and wished to have from them a new subsidy, commanding the people . . . to pay their dues. Amongst these townships all the people of Fobbing gave answer that they would not pay a penny more. . . . On this [John] menaced them strongly . . . and for fear of his wrath the people of Fobbing took counsel with the people of Corringham, and the folks of these two townships made levies and assemblies, and sent messages to the men of Stanford-le-Hope to urge them to rise too, for their common profit. And then the men of the three townships went to [John] Bampton and roundly gave him answer that they would have nothing to do with him nor give him one penny. On this [John] ordered the sergeants at arms to arrest these folks . . . and the commons rose against him and would not be arrested, but tried to kill [John] and the two sergeants . . . and afterwards they went from place to place to stir up other people to rise against the lords. . . . And because of these doings of [John], Sir Robert Belnap, Chief Justice of the Common Pleas of our lord the king . . . was sent to the shire . . . and indictments against various persons were laid before him. . . . Therefore the commons rose against him and came before him and told him that he was a traitor to the king and the realm, and that it was of pure wickedness and malice that he wished to put them in default by means of the false inquests made before him. And because of this evil they caused him to swear on the Bible that he would never again hold such a session nor act as a justice in such inquiries. And they made him tell them the names of all the jurors, and they took all that they could catch, and cut off their heads and cast their houses to the ground. . . . And afterwards the commons assembled together before Witsunday to the number of 50,000 and went to the manors and townships of those who did not wish to rise with them and razed their houses. . . . At this time they caught three clerks of [John] Bampton and cut off their heads, which they carried about with them for several days as an example to others; for it was their purpose to slay all lawyers and all jurors and all the servants of the king whom they could find.

Source: A. R. Myers, ed., *English Historical Documents*, vol. 4, 1327–1485 (London: Eyre & Spottiswoode, 1969), pp. 127–40.

DOCUMENT 10
The Treaty of Troyes

The signing of the Treaty of Troyes on May 21, 1420, brought France as close as it would ever come to rule by England. It was part of Joan of Arc's mission to see that the permanence of that union would never come about. When Joan of Arc promised Charles VII that she would help him recover France, her intention was to restore Charles to the royal inheritance from which he had been explicitly excluded in the transfer of power approved at Troyes. The treaty, signed by the ailing Charles VI, his wife, Queen Isabeau of Bavaria, King Henry V of England, and Duke Philip the Good of Burgundy, was conceived as a diplomatic solution to end the Hundred Years War. Through the provisions of the treaty, Henry was to serve as regent of France until the death of Charles VI, after which he would reign over the dual monarchy of England and France. Peace would be accomplished by placing the warring kingdoms under one ruler. It was anticipated that a marriage, arranged by the treaty, between Catherine of France and Henry V would produce an heir, half-French, half-English, whose descendants would rule the united kingdoms in perpetuity. To avoid the impression that the transfer of power to Catherine's offspring was yielding to the principle of female succession, Henry V was adopted by the French royal couple as their son. The dauphin Charles was not witness to the treaty, although he was removed from the line of succession by its tenets. There was no implication, as many have believed, that the disinheritance was claimed on the grounds of Charles' illegitimacy. By excluding the dauphin from the slightest participation in the monarchy, the French prince was being punished for the murder of Duke John the Fearless of Burgundy in the preceding year. A war party composed of the dauphin's supporters, which would coalesce nine years later under Joan of Arc, strongly opposed the union envisioned in the treaty. The war party advocated instead a military offensive whose goal was to drive the English permanently out of France. A burgeoning sense of French national identity found expression within this group of royalist supporters. Adherents of both the French party and the Burgundian party drafted legal arguments to justify their positions. Legal observers from the French party argued that a royal heir could not be disinherited. Later they would argue that a king of France could not alienate his lands, claiming that during his reign a monarch enjoyed only the fruits of his office (known as a usufruct), not the direct possession of the kingdom. This secular and legal position reinforced Joan of Arc's religious belief that the king of France held his kingdom, in essence, as a vassal of God.

Through the marriage alliance, made for the good of peace, between our son, King Henry [V], and our very dear and most cherished daughter, Catherine, he has become our son and that of our very dear and most cherished companion, the queen, which son will ... honor us ... as his father and mother. . . .

Our son, King Henry, will not disturb, upset, or prevent us from holding and possessing, as long as we live, just as we currently hold and possess them, the crown and royal dignity of France, and its revenues, fruits, and provisions, for the maintenance of our station and the duties of the kingdom. . . .

Immediately after our death and from that time forward, the crown of the kingdom of France, with all its rights and appurtenances ... will belong in perpetuity to our son, King Henry, and his heirs.

Since we are ... impaired most of the time, in such a manner that we cannot, in our person, understand or oversee the management of the affairs of our kingdom, the exercise of governing and legislating for the public good of the kingdom ... will remain, for our entire life, with our son King Henry, with the counsel of the nobles and notable men in our obedience. . . .

Our son will work as hard as he can, at the earliest feasible time, to place under our obedience each and every city, town, chateau, place, province, and person in our realm disobedient and rebellious toward us, belonging to the party ... commonly called the party of the dauphin or the Armagnacs.

The great lords, barons, and nobles ... and also the cities and leading communities, citizens, and bourgeois of the cities of the kingdom who are currently in our obedience will swear. . . . that ... never will they obey anyone but us, as king or regent of the kingdom of France, unless it be our son King Henry and his heirs. . . .

During the course of our life, our son, King Henry, will never call himself or write, or have himself called or described in writing as the king of France, but will completely abstain from the said name as long as we live.

It is agreed that during our life we shall name, call, and designate in writing our son King Henry in the French language in the following manner: "our very dear son, Henry, king of England, heir of France." . . .

So that agreement, peace, and tranquillity between the kingdoms of France and England can be perpetually observed in the future . . . it is agreed . . . that from the time that our son, or any of his heirs, succeeds to the crown of France, the two crowns of France and England will remain together, forever and perpetually, and will belong to a single person, that is, to the person of our son, King Henry, as long as he lives, and from then on, to . . . his heirs, who will succeed one after the other; and that the two kingdoms will be governed . . . not separately by different kings at the same time, but by a single person, who will be, for that period of time, king and sovereign lord of both kingdoms . . . nevertheless, ensuring in every other way, for each kingdom its rights, liberties, customs, practices, and laws, not submitting either kingdom in any manner to the other. . . .

From this moment, and forever more, all dissension, hatred, bitterness, hostility, and war between the kingdoms of France and England will be silenced, appeased, and in all points stopped. . . . and between the aforesaid kingdoms there will be . . . peace, tranquillity, harmony, mutual affection, firm and stable friendships; and the two kingdoms will help one another with their *aides* (subsidies), counsel, and mutual assistance, against all those who try to cause violence, injury, damage, or harm to them, or to one of them; and they will frequent one another and trade with one another. . . .

Considering the horrible and appalling crimes and misdeeds committed against the kingdom of France by Charles, so-called dauphin of Viennois, it is agreed that neither we, nor our son, King Henry, nor our dear son Philip, duke of Burgundy, will negotiate peace by any means . . . with the said Charles, nor will we make or negotiate peace, unless with the advice and agreement of . . . each of the three of us. . . .

Each and every thing written above, we, Charles [VI], the aforementioned king of France, for us and our heirs . . . without ruse, fraud, or trickery, have promised and promise, have sworn and swear in royal words upon the holy gospel of God, corporeally touched by us, to do, accomplish, and observe. . . . Given at Troyes, on the 21st day of the month of May, 1420, and in the fortieth year of our reign.

Source: Eugène Cosneau, *Les Grands Traités de la Guerre de Cent Ans* (Paris: Picard, 1889), pp. 103–7, 110–14. Trans. (slightly modernized) Deborah A. Fraioli.

DOCUMENT 11
Joan of Arc's Letter to the English
March 22, 1429

The following letter, addressed to the young King Henry VI, his regent Bedford, and the English military commanders in France, is the first of the letters dictated by the Maid, and it remains the most famous. It is believed that through this letter, in which Joan of Arc let her mission be known, the English heard of her for the first time. From later documents it appears that the way Joan's presence changed the dynamic of the war was considered "sudden." She sent two shorter versions of the letter before initiating combat, indicating that, among other things, she was adhering to the formality of issuing a war summons. The last message was fired dramatically toward the enemy on a flying arrow.

According to the practice of the times, letters were dictated to a scribe, so it seems reasonable to believe that Joan was being truthful when she told her judges at Rouen that she could neither read nor write. When the Letter to the English *was read aloud to her at Rouen, Joan claimed to have spoken all but three small phrases ("surrender to the Maid," "chieftain of war," and "body for body"), although she admitted that letters were shown to members of her party after she dictated them. For unknown reasons, the* Letter to the English *was not sent until late April from Blois.*

JHESUS MARIA

King of England, and you duke of Bedford, who call yourself regent of the kingdom of France; you, William Pole, count of Suffolk; John

Lord Talbot, and you, Thomas Lord Scales, who call yourselves lieutenants of the said duke of Bedford, make satisfaction to the King of Heaven; surrender to the Maid, who is sent here by God, the King of Heaven, the keys of all the good towns which you have taken and violated in France. She is come here by God's will to reclaim the blood royal. She is very ready to make peace, if you are willing to grant her satisfaction by abandoning France and paying for what you have held. And you, archers, men-at-war, gentlemen and others, who are before the town of Orleans, go away to your own country, in God's name. And if you do not do so, expect tidings from the Maid, who will come to see you shortly, to your very great harm. King of England, if you do not do so, I am chieftain of war, and in whatever place I meet your people in France, I shall make them leave, whether they will it or not. And if they will not obey, I will have them all put to death. I am sent here by God, the King of Heaven, body for body, to drive you out of all France. And if they wish to obey, I will show them mercy. And be not of another opinion, for you will not hold the kingdom of France from God, the King of Heaven, son of Saint Mary; for the king Charles, the true heir, will hold it, as is revealed to him by the Maid, [and] he will enter Paris with a good company. If you do not believe these tidings from God and the Maid, in whatever place we find you, we shall strike therein and make so great a tumult [*hahay*] that none so great has been in France for a thousand years, if you do not yield to right. Know well that the King of Heaven will send greater strength to the Maid and her good men-at-arms than you in all your assaults can overwhelm; and, by the blows it will be seen who has greater right with the God of Heaven. You, duke of Bedford, the Maid prays and requests that you not bring destruction on yourself. If you will grant her right, you may still join her company, where the French will do the fairest deed ever done for Christianity. Answer if you wish to make peace in the town of Orleans; and if you do not, you will be reminded shortly to your very great harm. Written this Tuesday of Holy Week.

Source: Deborah A. Fraioli, *Joan of Arc: The Early Debate* (Woodbridge: Boydell Press, 2000), p. 208. Reprinted with permission.

DOCUMENT 12
The *Song of Joan of Arc* by Christine de Pizan

The Italian-born writer Christine de Pizan is known not only for com-
posing The Book of the Deeds and Good Customs of the Wise King
Charles V *and* The Book of Deeds of Arms and of Chivalry *but also*
for a wide range of works ranging from political tracts to love poetry.
Transformed into a writer when widowhood forced her to seek employ-
ment, Christine was fortunate to have French kings and dukes as patrons.
But she lived through the glorious reign of Charles V only to experience
at first hand the decline of the French monarchy under the mad king
Charles VI—including the dauphin's flight from Paris (and her own) in
1418. In the last years of her life Christine bore witness with a shudder
of joy to the recovery of France, crystallized in the career of Joan of Arc.
The Song of Joan of Arc *captures the personal emotion of the poet—*
then anticipating the liberation of Paris—who finds in Joan's mission the
proof of divine favor for the French.

Stanza 1

I, Christine, who have wept for eleven years in a walled abbey where I
have lived ever since Charles (how strange this is!) the King's son—dare
I say it?—fled in haste from Paris, I who have lived enclosed there on account of the treachery, now, for the first time, begin to laugh. . . .

Stanza 5

The reason is that the rejected child of the rightful King of France, who
has long suffered many a great misfortune . . . now approaches . . . coming as a crowned King in might and majesty, wearing spurs of gold.

Stanza 6

Now let us greet our King! Welcome to him on his return! Overjoyed at
the sight of his noble array, let us all, both great and small, step forward
to greet him joyously—and let no one hold back—praising God, who has
kept him safe, and shouting 'Noël!' in a loud voice. . . .

Stanza 10

Did anyone, then, see anything quite so extraordinary come to pass (something that is well worth noting and remembering in every region), namely, that France (about whom it was said she had been cast down) should see her fortunes change, by divine command, from evil to such great good,

Stanza 11

as the result, indeed, of such a miracle that, if the matter were not so well-known and crystal-clear in every aspect, nobody would ever believe it? It is a fact well worth remembering that God should nevertheless have wished (and this is the truth!) to bestow such great blessings on France, through a young virgin.

Stanza 12

And what honour for the French crown, this proof of divine intervention! For all the blessings which God bestows upon it demonstrate how much He favours it and that He finds more faith in the Royal House than anywhere else; as far as it is concerned, I read (and there is nothing new in this) that the Lilies of France never erred in matters of faith. . . .

Stanza 25

For if God performed such a great number of miracles through Joshua who conquered many a place and cast down many an enemy, he, Joshua, was a strong and powerful *man*. But, after all, a *woman*—a simple shepherdess—braver than any man ever was in Rome! As far as God is concerned, this was easily accomplished. . . .

Stanza 28

I have heard of Esther, Judith and Deborah, who were women of great worth, through whom God delivered His people from oppression, and I have heard of many other worthy women as well, champions every one, through them He performed many miracles, but He has accomplished more through this Maid. . . .

Stanza 34

Oh! What honour for the female sex! It is perfectly obvious that God has special regard for it when all these wretched people who destroyed the whole Kingdom—now recovered and made safe by a woman, something that 5000 *men* could not have done—and the traitors [have been] exterminated. Before the event they would scarcely have believed this possible.

Stanza 35

A little girl of sixteen (isn't this something quite supernatural?) who does not even notice the weight of the arms she bears—indeed her whole upbringing seems to have prepared her for this, so strong and resolute is she! And her enemies go fleeing before her, not one of them can stand up to her. She does all this in full view of everyone. . . .

Stanza 39

And so, you English, draw in your horns for you will never capture any good game! Don't attempt any foolish enterprise in France! You have been check-mated. A short time ago, when you looked so fierce, you had no inkling that this would be so; but you were not yet treading the path upon which God casts down the proud.

Stanza 40

You thought you had already conquered France and that she must remain yours. Things have turned out otherwise, you treacherous lot! Go and beat your drums elsewhere, unless you want to taste death, like your companions, whom wolves may well devour, for their bodies lie dead amidst the furrows!

Stanza 46

And all you base rebels who have joined them, you can see now that it would have been better for you to have gone forwards rather than backwards as you did, thereby becoming the serfs of the English. Beware that more does not befall you (for you have been tolerated long enough!), and remember what the outcome will be!

Stanza 47

Oh, all you blind people, can't you detect God's hand in this? If you can't, you are truly stupid for how else could the Maid who strikes you all down dead have been sent to us?—And you don't have sufficient strength! Do you want to fight against God?

Stanza 53

I don't know if Paris will hold out (for they have not reached there yet) or if the Maid will delay [or if it will resist the Maid]. But if it decides to see her as an enemy, I fear that she will subject it to a fierce attack, as she has done elsewhere. If they offer resistance for an hour, or even half an hour, it's my belief that things will go badly for them,

Stanza 54

for [the King] will enter Paris, no matter who may grumble about it!— The Maid has given her word that he will. Paris, do you think Burgundy will prevent him from entering? By no means, for he does not see himself as an enemy. Nobody has the power to prevent him, and you will be overcome, you and your presumption!

Stanza 55

Oh Paris, how could you be so ill-advised? Foolish inhabitants, you are lacking in trust! Do you prefer to be laid waste, Paris, rather than make peace with your prince? If you are not careful your great opposition will destroy you. It would be far better for you if you were to humbly beg for mercy. You are quite miscalculating!

Stanza 56

It is the evil inhabitants I'm referring to, for there are many good people there, I have no doubt about that; but, take my word for it, these good people, who are no doubt much displeased to see their prince rejected in this way, do not dare speak out. They will not merit the punishment which will fall upon Paris and cost many a person his life. . . .

Stanza 58

And so as to avoid killing and wounding anyone [the King] delays for as long as he can, for the spilling of blood grieves him. But, in the end, if someone does not want to hand over, with good grace, what is rightly his, he is perfectly justified if he does recover it by force and bloodshed. . . .

Stanza 59

. . . Now as loyal Frenchmen submit your hearts and yourselves to him. . . .

Stanza 60

And I pray to God that He will prevail upon you to act in this way, so that the cruel storm of these wars may be erased from memory and that you may live your lives in peace. . . . Amen.

Stanza 61

This poem was completed by Christine, in the above-mentioned year, 1429, on the last day of July. . . .

Source: Christine de Pizan, *Ditié de Jehanne d'Arc*, ed. Angus J. Kennedy and Kenneth Varty (Medium Aevum Monographs, new series, 9) (Oxford: Society for the Study of Mediaeval Languages and Literature, 1977), pp. 41–50. Reprinted with permission.

DOCUMENT 13
Hugh of Lannoy's Memorandum of Advice to Philip the Good

This memorandum was written by Hugh of Lannoy, lord of Santes,
governor of Holland, and high counselor of Philip the Good, in reaction

*to the signing of the Treaty of Arras in September 1435. Lannoy had op-
posed the Arras treaty on the grounds that it resulted in a particular peace
between Charles VII of France and Philip the Good but did not achieve
the conference's chief aim of a general peace among England, France, and
Burgundy. Although the encounter at Arras had reconciled the French and
Burgundian princes sixteen years after the murder of Philip's father at
Montereau, Lannoy believed that the accord raised new dangers of war.
In this letter, Lannoy lays out the risks of a damaging rupture with England, destabilization in Burgundian neighboring states, and rebellion in
Flanders. This unsparing letter from Lannoy to his prince provides an eye-
opening look at internal Burgundian politics, but the letter stands out
equally well for its author's visionary look at the broad scope of European
politics. In dating the onset of the war to the quarrel "between the king of
France and king Edward of England for the crown of France," Lannoy
demonstrates his understanding of the extraordinary duration of the war
(then technically in its ninety-ninth year) and his conviction that its cause
was dynastic. He also understands that war is not an engagement limited
to the main protagonists, but that it breeds chaos and rebellion in neighboring states. The unquestionable purpose of Lannoy's letter is to urge
Philip to pursue the general peace among himself, Charles VII, and Henry
VI, which the encounter at Arras had failed to achieve. The letter ends
with a vision of the prince who Philip might become if he sees to needed
reforms in matters of finance and justice.*

WRITTEN AT GHENT, 10 SEPTEMBER, 1436

Most redoubted lord, I, your obedient subject and servant, who has
more loyalty and goodwill than wisdom and discretion, have been pon-
dering . . . your present situation, day and night, with such wits as God
has given me, to see what can be done. . . . After considering this a great
deal, I have come to the conclusion that you and your affairs are in a
most dangerous situation.

In the first place, I see that you are at war with the king of England
and his kingdom. He is powerful both on land and sea, and you are necessarily forced to maintain powerful garrisons against him on the frontiers of Flanders and Artois. . . . Moreover, wherever war is waged and the
countryside is destroyed and plundered by friend and foe alike and the
populace is restless, little or no money can be raised. Yet this war cannot
be conducted without large sums of money. . . . If the truth be told, you

have no territory whose populace is not hard pressed financially. . . . [Y]ou have seen how agitated your Flemish subjects are; some of them, indeed, are in armed rebellion. Strange and bitter things have been said about yourself, your government, and your leading councillors; and it is very likely that, having got as far as talking in this way, they will soon go further than mere talk. . . . [I]f you pacify them by kindness . . . other towns . . . will rebel in the hopes of getting similar treatment. On the other hand, if you punish and repress them, it is to be feared that they will make disastrous alliances with your enemies. If by chance they start pillaging and robbing, it is possible that every wicked person will start plundering the rich, practising the profession of moving in one hour from poverty to wealth. . . . In this matter, there is much cause for anxiety.

I note that, according to report, the English are planning to keep a large number of ships at sea in order to effect a commercial blockade of your land of Flanders. This is a grave danger, for much harm would result if that country were deprived for any length of time of its cloth industry and commerce. . . .

I note, too, that the king of France can scarcely help you with finance and, if he sends troops, they will be the sort, which you know of, who are as good at destroying the country as defending it. Nor will they serve you at all without payment and, if not paid, they will pillage and plunder those very lands of yours which, as you know, are already devastated. As to the nobility of your lands in Picardy, their estates have already been ravaged and destroyed by the armies that have been assembled there. . . . Moreover, what is worse, hatreds and divisions will probably be stirred up because of this devastation, so that you will get little help from them. It is to be feared that this war will last such a long time that certain people, who secretly harbour feelings of hostility towards you but have hitherto not dared to reveal them, will come out into the open when they see you thus involved. As you know, your lands of Brabant, Holland, Namur and others have some very unfriendly neighbours.

Most redoubted lord, when I examine carefully these perils and dangers, your lack of funds, the divisions which exist among your people . . . and when, on the other hand, I consider ways and means of avoiding them, with my limited understanding I see only one way, in which you can escape once and for all from these difficulties, which would be in your own and the public interest. This is, to find some means of arranging a general peace settlement between the king and kingdom of France, on the one hand, and the king and kingdom of England, on the other. I do not see any way . . . in which you can maintain the lands, peoples, and merchants along the seaboard, who are inclined towards rebellion and disturbance, in peace, justice and obedience towards yourself (as they ought to be), while the war continues between the two above-mentioned kings. For those who are rebelling . . . will gladly ally with one of these two kings or kingdoms, whenever you set out to punish and subdue them as they deserve. I have heard it maintained by old people as a truth that, ever since the wars began between the king of France and king Edward of England for the crown of France, the Flemish have been less obedient to their ruler than they were before.

If anyone wants to argue and maintain that it is out of your power to negotiate a general peace between the two kings, and that, because of the particular peace you made at Arras, you no longer ought to try . . . , it seems to me, subject to correction, that you still can help a great deal towards a general peace . . . if you put your heart into it and follow the advice given here. . . .

To appreciate how such a general peace could be achieved, the internal state of these two kingdoms must be examined. To take France. You can appreciate what sort of prince the king is, who does not himself rule, but is ruled, the great poverty in his situation and throughout the kingdom because of the wars . . . , how little he is obeyed by his captains, the melancholy and displeasure he has suffered from being in such difficulties for so long, and also the longing to be rid of the war which is shared by a good part of the nobles, ecclesiastics and townsmen of France. The probability is, that if they can find a reasonable way to achieve this, they will heartily welcome it.

As regards the king and kingdom of England, the king is young, too young to rule; they have spent excessive sums of money on the French wars for the last twenty years [reference to Henry V's invasion of France in 1415]; they have lost a considerable number of captains, nobility and others in France during these wars; and you, my most redoubted lord, have left their alliance, so that their own English people now have to sustain the whole war and pay for it. . . . Moreover, rumour has it that the common people of England are so tired of the war that they are more or less desperate. It is true that they have experienced important disputes among themselves, for the majority of the people blamed the royal council for not achieving a general peace at the Congress of Arras, and for refusing the offers made to them immediately after it. Besides . . . it is probable that, everything considered, they are tired of war and will gladly embrace a more reasonable policy, the more so now than ever before, since the king will be fifteen on St. Nicholas's day. . . .

[Lannoy then proposes several actions to be initiated by the duke in the name of peace including the release of René of Anjou (brother-in-law of Charles VII); the cancellation of a large mortgage owed Philip the Good by the king of France for Amiens, the county of Ponthieu, and the Somme towns; and the brokering of the release of the duke of Orleans from prison in England.]

My most redoubted lord, if it seems to you that the abandonment of the above-mentioned mortgage . . . would mean too great a financial loss . . . if you took careful stock of your own situation and the government of your lands; if you took your affairs to heart in an effort to adjust your way of life and the duchess's, to moderate the liberality in which you have been somewhat excessive . . . and remove the superfluities and duplications that exist in many ways . . . you would find that you would recover each year as much, or almost as much, revenue as the mortgage you hold from the king brings in to you. . . .

And, if you and your lands remain in peace with the two above-mentioned kings and kingdoms and your domain has been redeemed and relieved of debt, if you govern reasonably and spare your people excessive taxes . . . , undertaking no wars except by permission of the Estates of your lands, and taking advice from people who are experienced, rather than those inspired by flattery or greed . . . you will find yourself among the richest princes in the world, feared and loved by all your subjects. . . .

My most redoubted lord, to sum up my advice . . . you must ensure that peace is made between the two kings and kingdoms as soon as you possibly can . . . , and you must reform your government in matters of finance and justice so that you win more popularity than you currently enjoy.

Source: Richard Vaughan, *Philip the Good: The Apogee of Burgundy*, repr. (Woodbridge: Boydell Press, 2002), pp. 102–7. Reprinted with permission.

DOCUMENT 14
The *Fifteen Joys of Marriage*

Despite the survival from the era of the Hundred Years War of exten-
sive documentation on the social, economic, and political institutions of
the time, it is unusual to find traces, as we find in the Fifteen Joys of
Marriage *of individuals, in this instance married couples, reacting to those*
institutions. The work is cast as an antimatrimonial satire in the mold of
numerous works in the antifeminist literary tradition, where women are
portrayed as shrewish, unfaithful, and spoiled, to the disadvantage of their
husbands. A prominent model for medieval antimatrimonial satirists was
the fourth-century tract against marriage by Saint Jerome, called Against
Jovinian. *But the* Fifteen Joys of Marriage, *more specifically, parodies*
a well-known devotional work of the late Middle Ages, the Fifteen Joys
of Notre Dame. *In the passages excerpted below, the anonymous author*
intends that the word "joy" be understood ironically. From the perspec-
tive of the downtrodden male, the author recounts humorous episodes of
wives wreaking havoc on the lives, reputations, and livelihood of their
spouses. But the antimatrimonial stance is often a means of introducing
social commentary. The friction between a man's duty to his lord and his
obligations to his family, the protection of one's fief, the disruption and
displacement caused by war, the contradictory impulses of personal
courage and providing for the safety of one's family, the injustice of the
judicial duel, and the degeneracy of the nobility in the late Middle Ages
are topics boldly aired in the Fifteen Joys of Marriage *under cover of*
satire. The husband's servitude to his wife stands as a token of the greater
servitude imposed on him by the oppressive institutions of medieval life,
whether marriage, justice, chivalry, war, or feudalism.

The Twelfth Joy

The twelfth joy of marriage is when . . . the young man finally . . . finds
just the woman he was seeking. . . . To his mind, there's none like her. . . .
And perhaps the young man tends to jump to her beck and call, acting
only on her advice, so that whenever anyone has dealings with him, he
says, "I'll discuss it with my wife." . . . If she wants something done, it's
done . . . for the good fellow is so henpecked, he's as docile as a plow
ox. . . . If he's a nobleman and the prince requires his service, then he'll
serve if his wife so desires. Perhaps he'll say, "My dear, I must go off."

"Go off? And whatever for? You'll spend a fortune, get yourself killed, and then the children and I will be in a fine predicament!"

In short, if she's against it, he won't go; he'll have to save face and defend his honor [the] best he can!

As if this weren't enough already, now a new tribulation descends: his country goes to war, and the entire population must withdraw to the cities and castles. But the good fellow can neither leave his home nor abandon his wife; then, too, perhaps he's captured, led off ignominiously, beaten, and forced to pay a huge ransom. Now he really has problems! And to avoid certain recapture he retires . . . but first he must zigzag through the woods and grope through hedges and thickets, so that he emerges ragged and bruised. Screaming and scolding, his wife welcomes him home; she blames him for all the troubles and turmoil, as if he could arrange a truce between the two warring kings. To make matters worse, she refuses to remain at home, so the good fellow has to scurry to cart the family to the city or castle, and God knows the grief he has loading and unloading wife and children, packing and loading trunks, finding an inn and unpacking when at last they arrive safely within the fortress walls—there's not a man alive who could say! You can imagine, too, what distress he endures, how he slaves, and how he's bombarded with endless chatter, for his wife can only vent her frustration on him. The husband braves wind and rain, trotting off now by day, now by night on foot or on horseback, according to his means, first here, now there, always searching for food and other essentials. In brief, he'll never rest his weary bones; rather he'll know only the tribulation and trouble to which he was born. And if it happens that he gets so fed up with his wife's nagging that he tries to retort . . . then he'll have double trouble, for surely he'll be humiliated and vanquished in the end. . . . Then when the war is over, the whole cartload has to be hauled back home, where the torture begins anew.

The Thirteenth Joy

The thirteenth joy of marriage is when the bachelor has entered the snare [of marriage] and lived with his wife for five or six years. . . . Now perhaps he's a nobleman who, in order to win honor and prestige, feels pressed to leave home for a while. He breaks the news to his wife, who kisses and caresses him, saying . . . "Alas sweetheart! Would you leave your wife and children not knowing if we'll ever see you again?" Thus she strives night and day to make him stay.

"My dear," he says, "I must go for my honor and in obedience to my king, otherwise I stand to forfeit the fief I hold from him. God willing . . . I'll see you again soon."

Perhaps he goes abroad to win honor and distinction in a strange land, for perhaps there are yet certain noble, stout-hearted men whom not even devotion to wife or children can hinder from constantly performing noble deeds. . . . Then again, there are many others who, even for defense of life and property, can't leave their wives for a ten- or twelve-league campaign unless forced and driven with a goad. Surely this lot is a great disgrace to the nobility; such men are cowards and should be stripped of the good company, privileges, and all the titles of aristocracy. I dare say no one with any knowledge in this matter could call such people truly noble, albeit their fathers might have been. . . .

Sometimes, too, it happens that, provoked by his wife, the brave and noble-hearted husband goes to fight on the dueling ground; depending on Lady Fortune's whim, perhaps he's even overpowered and mercilessly slain—such a pity! It happens quite frequently that the just one loses while the offender carries the day . . .

Now you see how such folk are lured into the net of matrimony. They thought they would find comfort; instead they've discovered just the opposite, though you won't convince them of it. Thus they spin out their lives in pain, their constant companion, till the end of their miserable days.

Source: The Fifteen Joys of Marriage, trans. Brent A. Pitts (New York: Peter Lang, 1985), pp. 104–12. Reprinted with permission.

NOTES

1. Alison Weir, *Eleanor of Aquitaine* (London: Jonathan Cape, 1999), p. 20.

2. Only four manuscripts of the *Song of Bertrand du Guesclin* contain the passage in brackets.

GLOSSARY

Aid: Term in feudal law referring to monetary assistance owed by a feudal vassal to his lord. Also duties or indirect taxes.

Alienation: The act of transferring property from one owner to another. By the latter part of the fourteenth century, the kings of France took a coronation oath not to alienate lands from the royal kingdom.

Ancient liberties: Any special privileges, often in the form of tax exemptions, enjoyed by a municipality or region, frequently guaranteed by ancient charter and zealously protected by local populations.

Angevin Empire: Vast territory ruled by the Plantagenet (or Angevin) dynasty, which came to encompass most of western France (and all of England) in the twelfth century, after Henry II, duke of Normandy and count of Anjou, married Eleanor of Aquitaine in 1152 and ascended the throne of England in 1154. Subsequently, the disintegration of English holdings in France led to a fierce contest over the duchy of Aquitaine, a root cause of the Hundred Years War.

Anoint: From the Latin *inungere*, to smear. To apply oil or unguent, especially in the performance of a sacred rite such as consecration.

Apanage: Generally refers to land granted by a sovereign that reverted to the crown on the death of the holder.

Aquitaine: Plantagenet possession in southwestern France whose southwestern portion is called Gascony. Also called Guyenne or Guienne from the French.

Archer: During the time of Charlemagne, an infantryman who used the simple short bow as a weapon. By the eleventh century, unmounted archers formed a distinct unit of the French army. By the thirteenth century, the short bow was replaced by the crossbow, which was in turn replaced by the longbow.

Armagnacs: Name of the French party, originally the Orleanist party, that opposed the Burgundian faction during the civil war (1407–1435). Party named after Bernard VII, count of Armagnac, and properly called the French or dauphinist party after Bernard's death in May 1418.

Arrière-ban: From the Latin *retrobannum* or "rear" summons. Technically, the term referred to a royal military summons directed at vassals who owed fealty to an intermediate lord other than the king. Used to call up able-bodied soldiers in an emergency or raise funds from those who did not serve.

Artillery: From the Old French *artiller*, to equip or fortify. Prior to the fourteenth century, the term referred to missile-throwing engines such as the catapult, French *trébuchet*, or battering ram. After the advent of cannons and other gunpowder-operated weaponry during the Hundred Years War, artillery became indispensable to the practice of warfare and required compensatory changes in the art of fortification.

Bastide: Name given to a type of fortified community characterized by streets laid out in grid formation with a large marketplace.

Brigand: A professional foot-soldier, so named because of the protective metal rings (*brigandine*) on his jacket that substituted for chain mail. From the mid-fourteenth century, the term was used pejoratively to refer to unruly soldiers who pillaged and looted for supplies and booty.

Capetian dynasty: Named after Hugh Capet, this long-running dynasty of French kings ruled from 987 to 1328. It followed the Merovingian and Carolingian dynasties as the "third race" of French kings.

Chanson de geste: A category of epic poem praising the great deeds (Latin *gesta*) of national heroes. The noble exploits described in the *Chanson de Roland* (Song of Roland), for instance, had a lasting impact on the development and continuance of chivalry.

Chevauchée: A raid conducted on horseback characterized by the ruthless devastation of enemy lands, designed to subdue the enemy by terrorizing the population.

Chivalry: Most commonly refers to a set of military and moral values, described in manuals of chivalry and in literature, to which medieval mounted knighthood aspired. Scholars dispute whether the ideals were achieved in fact or not. The chivalric virtue most admired was prowess. Chivalry, as a code of conduct in which warriors were trained, proved valuable to rulers as a mechanism for acquiring an elite fighting force.

Chivalry (Orders of): Secular fraternities of knighthood created by potentates to instill the principles of chivalric conduct in their own military. Examples include the Order of the Golden Fleece, the Order of the Garter, and the Order of the Star.

Chrism: Consecrated oil, often mixed with plant resin and spices, for performing sacred rites.

Commune: Also commons, *communitas*. Terms designating coalitions, organized as political corporations, functioning as self-governing units.

Consecrate: To render sacred or to dedicate for a sacred or holy purpose.

Constable: Originally meant "count of the stable," a household officer. During the Hundred Years War, the commander-in-chief of the French royal army.

Coronation: A royal crowning ceremony, distinct from, but generally performed in conjunction with, the anointing of a monarch.

Crossbow: A medieval, arrow- or stone-throwing weapon, consisting of a bow set crosswise on a shaft. Slower to reload than the longbow.

Dauphin: From 1349 the title bestowed on French heirs, as lords of the province of Dauphiné. Title preferred by Joan of Arc until Charles VII was anointed at Reims.

Defiance: From the French *défi*. A challenge representing the cessation of a personal, usually feudal, loyalty whereby a vassal, faced with injustice on the part of his lord, refused further homage to his overlord.

Demesne: Legal term for land held by a lord for his own use, typically rented to a tenant for profit. Leases were viewed by landlords as a short-term solution to increase income during economic downturns.

Dignitas: An almost inexpressible quality of French kingship—royal dignity—that women were said to lack. Used as grounds to exclude women from the crown.

Double or dual monarchy: Refers to the ambition of English monarchs, from Edward III to Henry VI, to rule simultaneously as kings of England and France.

Estates General: French representative body convoked by the king for the first time in 1343. Generally less influential than English Parliament.

Fealty (Oath of): Publicly pronounced sworn statement by which a vassal pledged to observe all obligations to a feudal overlord.

Feudalism: Term referring to a highly variable system of political and social organization during the medieval period in Europe, now considered less prevalent than previously thought, and whose usefulness is questioned. Under the name vassal, princes administered territories for the king, known as fiefs (Latin, *feodum*), in return for military service. The overlord of the vassal was called the suzerain, who secured a pledge of faithfulness in a ceremony known as homage. Fiefs, in turn, were often leased to serfs or villains who worked the land. Feudalism should be distinguished from its component parts, the manorial system and vassalage.

Fief: Land unit furnishing basis for feudalism, granted by suzerain to his vassal, although without outright ownership, in exchange for service, fidelity, and support.

Flanders: Name derived from word meaning lowland or flooded land. Strategic territory north of France and across the channel from England. A fief of the French crown whose counts were vassals of the king of France.

Fleur-de-lis: French for "flower of the lily." A stylized flower resembling the iris, adopted by France as its coat of arms in the twelfth century. Gradually developed its own sacred mythology heightening the cult of French kingship.

Francia: Land of the Franks, an early Germanic people, from which the word France derives.

Gaul: Roman name for present-day France and Belgium, as well as parts of several other western European countries.

Great Company: Name of the most significant of the "free companies," or bands of undisciplined, independent soldiers, who lived off the land and fought for booty.

Holy Ampulla: (*Saint Ampoule*) The term refers to the holy flask, or ampulla, of French legend, said to have descended from heaven in the beak of a dove, bearing oil exclusively for the consecration of French kings.

Homage: Term ultimately derived from the Latin for man (*homo*), referring to a public ceremony by which a man vowed to become the man of a lord, particularly upon entering into vassalage. Homage as an institution predated the oath of fealty often coupled with it.

Jacquerie: Any peasant rebellion, derived from the name of the most significant peasant uprising in France during the Hundred Years War.

Jacques Bonhomme: Symbolic name for the peasantry thought to derive from a cloth or leather jacket (*jacque*) worn by peasants.

Klauwaert: From the Dutch word *klauw* meaning claw, from the lion's claw on the Flemish coat of arms. Anti-French party in Flanders, opposed to *Leliaerts*.

Knight: Translates French term *chevalier*, cavalier or horseman. A mounted warrior, whose exploits were judged according to the high-minded principles of the code of chivalry.

Lancaster: Name of ruling English dynasty from Henry IV to Henry VI.

Leliaert: Flemish supporters of the king of France, suzerain of Flanders. The party adopted the French *fleur-de-lis* as its symbol, hence *Leliaert* (*lelie* in Dutch).

Liege homage: Exclusive homage by which a vassal pledged to serve one suzerain, called a liege lord, above all others.

Longbow: A wooden bow, most likely introduced in Wales, sometimes over six feet in length, with firing speed superior to that of the crossbow.

Manorial system: Social and economic system based on the manor (district), administered by a feudal overlord, and for which peasants furnished the agricultural labor.

Mercenary: A soldier willing to serve any master for pay or profit.

Minute: Original French transcript of the condemnation trial of Joan of Arc, thought to be the only text accurately representing her words.

Considered more accurate than the official Latin translation of 1435.

Montjoye Saint-Denis: Medieval battle cry of France.

Nullification trial: More accurate term than "Rehabilitation trial" for the 1456 retrial of Joan of Arc, since it did not rehabilitate her but rendered nul and void the verdict of the condemnation trial of 1431.

Ordo: (Latin, pl. *ordines*) The script of the liturgy, or public rites, of a given coronation ritual.

Oriflamme: From the Latin *aurea flamma*, golden flame. A narrow banner of red silk entrusted to medieval French kings by the abbot of Saint-Denis upon leaving for battle. A symbol of all-out warfare.

Peer: From the Old French *pair* meaning "equal." One of superior noble rank selected by the king for special dignity. According to legend, there were twelve peers at the court of Charlemagne.

Provost of the merchants: Senior municipal official in Paris, equivalent to mayor.

Prudhomme: A man of probity or moral virtue; one possessed of prowess (French, *preux*).

Rehabilitation trial: *See* Nullification trial.

Religion of the monarchy: A systematic belief in the divine virtues and powers of kings and, by extension, their realms. The cult of sacred kingship was particularly strong in France during the medieval period. Although imitated by English monarchs, sacred kingship never gained the same stature in England.

Routier: A member of a class of undisciplined adventurers, often unemployed soldiers, who lived by plunder or pillage during the Hundred Years War.

Salic Law: A law code of ancient Germanic tribes, including the Salian Franks, who were Merovingians, one paragraph of which states: "Of Salic land no portion shall come to a woman." Although used to exclude women from succession to the throne, the clause was apparently meant communally and did not refer to kingdoms as a whole.

Seneschal: From the Old French meaning "senior servant." An official representing a lord who administered estates, a district, or a province. Especially common in southwestern France, the seneschal managed financial, judicial, and military affairs for his lord's fief.

Serf: From the Latin for slave (*servus*). Refers to the lowest class in the medieval social hierarchy. A serf was bound to the soil of a landowner but could be freed.

Sovereign: Person or body in whom ultimate, independent authority resides, such as a monarch.

Sovereignty: The state of being in supreme command or authority, as in the case of a monarch.

Suzerain: An overlord or feudal lord to whom a vassal has pledged fidelity.

Taxation: Taxes during the Hundred Years War were levied irregularly and bore many different names such as aid, *taille*, *maltôte*, poll tax, and *gabelle* (salt tax), depending on how they were levied.

Tenure: The act of holding (French, *tenir*) from a superior, especially as with land from an overlord, whether he be a simple lord, a king, or, in the case of the French sacred kingship so well publicized by Joan of Arc, God.

Valois: Region northeast of Paris that gave its name to the dynasty of French kings—beginning with Philip VI—that ruled from 1328 to 1589.

Vassal: Term (from Celtic word for "servant") referring to someone who performed service to an overlord under the system of vassalage. The vassal, whether an aristocrat or a simple lord, performed homage and swore fidelity to his suzerain.

Vassalage: Originally a system based on a personal bond whereby a vassal owed allegiance to a lord for protection. Later, vassals were awarded fiefs, which they held in tenure from overlords, or suzerains, in exchange for service.

Villain (villein): Someone of low birth, especially of serf or peasant status, and subsequently a base, vulgar, boorish, or evil person. After the thirteenth century, villain and serf were more or less synonymous terms whereas, previously, French villains in particular had technically been free.

ANNOTATED BIBLIOGRAPHY

Allmand, C.T. *Henry V*. Reprint, Berkeley: University of California Press, 1992. Au-thoritative modern biography. Clearly written but sophisticated.

————. *The Hundred Years War: England and France at War c. 1300–c. 1450.* Cambridge, England: Cambridge University Press, 1988. First thirty pages narrate the Hundred Years War. Remainder is thematic, including approaches to war, recruitment, and taxation. Scholarly.

Barber, Richard W. *Edward, Prince of Wales and Aquitaine: A Biography of the Black Prince*. London: Allen Lane, 1978.

————, ed. and trans. *The Life and Campaigns of the Black Prince, from Contemporary Letters, Diaries and Chronicles, including Chandos Herald's* Life of the Black Prince. London: Folio Society, 1979.

Barrett, W[ilfred] P[hilip], ed. and trans. *The Trial of Jeanne d'Arc: Translated into English from the Original Latin and French Documents*. With Pierre Champion "Dramatis personae," trans. Coley Taylor and Ruth H. Kerr. New York: Gotham House, 1932. The standard English translation of the Latin translation of Joan's condemnation trial, prepared from the French minutes by men unsympathetic to Joan in 1435. Fascinating, often poignant, testimony. Captures the spirit of Joan and demonstrates the great imbalance of power between Joan and her accusers.

Beaune, Colette. *The Birth of an Ideology: Myths and Symbols of Nation in Late-Medieval France*. Translated by Susan Ross Huston. Fredric L. Cheyette, ed. Berkeley: University of California Press, 1991. Interesting work pertinent to sacred kingship, origins of nationalism, and building of nation-states.

Bloch, Marc. *The Royal Touch.* Translated by J. E. Anderson. New York: Dorset Press, 1989. Original title: *Les rois thaumaturges.* Treats much more than reputed healing power of French (and English) kings for the disease of scrofula. Crucial work for understanding the power rituals and symbolism of French and English kings and their differences. Extracts from Jean Golein's important *Treatise on Consecration.*

Christine de Pizan. *The Book of Deeds of Arms and of Chivalry.* Translated by Sumner Willard. Charity Cannon Willard, ed. University Park: Pennsylvania State University Press, 1999. Not well known before this translation. Draws on Vegetius and Honoré Bouvet for war theory, but adds much original material as well.

————. *Ditié de Jehanne d'Arc.* Angus J. Kennedy and Kenneth Varty, eds. Medium Aevum Monographs, new series, 9. Oxford: Society for the Study of Mediaeval Languages and Literature, 1977.

The Chronicle of Jean de Venette. Translated by Jean Birdsall. Richard A. Newhall, ed. New York: Columbia University Press, 1953. Fascinating account of life in the region of Compiègne prior to the Treaty of Brétigny. Includes the memorable story of the peasant Grandferré and vivid description of the desolation of France due to the Hundred Years War.

Contamine, Philip. *La guerre de cent ans* (Que sais-je?) Paris: Presses universitaires de France, 1968. Strongly recommended for readers of French. Brief but satisfying account of the Hundred Years War. Contains important details not generally found in overviews and efficient analysis.

————. *War in the Middle Ages.* Translated by M.C.E. Jones. Oxford: Blackwell, 1984. First published as *La guerre au moyen âge* in 1980. An essential work by the leading French military historian of the Hundred Years War.

Curry, Anne. *The Hundred Years War.* Houndmills, Basingstoke: MacMillan Press, 1993. Valuable book that synthesizes much research into a compact overview of the war. Opens with a beneficial examination of the historiography of the Hundred Years War, showing methodologically rigorous study of the war as relatively recent. Alludes to topics of debate among historians. Joan of Arc mentioned only incidentally.

————. *The Hundred Years War: 1337–1453.* New York: Routledge, 2003. A shorter treatment. Numerous photographs, maps, and color reproductions. Does not replace the excellent grounding furnished by Curry's 1993 volume. Only incidental references to Joan of Arc.

DeVries, Kelly. *Joan of Arc: A Military Leader*. Stroud, Gloucestershire: Sutton, 1999. Author sees Joan's renown as due to her military ability. One of a handful of military studies in English.

Dobson, R. B., ed. *The Peasants' Revolt of 1381*. 2nd ed. London: Macmillan, 1983. Basic work by respected authority.

The Fifteen Joys of Marriage. Translated by Brent A. Pitts. New York: Peter Lang, 1985.

Fowler, Kenneth A. *The Age of Plantagenet and Valois: The Struggle for Supremacy, 1328–1498*. London: Elek Press, 1967. Large format with many color reproductions. Still a good choice for understanding the period.

Fraioli, Deborah. *Joan of Arc: The Early Debate*. Woodbridge: Boydell Press, 2000. Inquiry into the meaning of Joan's claim to a divine mission for her contemporaries. English translations of five pertinent Latin and French texts.

———. "Why Joan of Arc Never Became an Amazon." In *Fresh Verdicts on Joan of Arc*. Eds. Bonnie Wheeler and Charles T. Wood. New York: Garland, 1996, 180–204.

Froissart, Jean. *Chronicles*. Ed. G. Brereton. Baltimore: Penguin Books, 1968. Excerpts from this well-known writer of memorable prose from Valenciennes. Emphasis on institution of chivalry whose decline is indirectly perceived by author. Froissart occasionally embellishes the facts, but there are few who would not forgive him for the panoramic view he crafts of an entire age. Excerpts can be found online.

Hooper, Nicholas, and Matthew Bennett. *Cambridge Illustrated Atlas of Warfare: The Middle Ages, 768–1487*. Cambridge, England: Cambridge University Press, 1996. Rich, reliable source.

Keen, Maurice. *Chivalry*. New Haven: Yale University Press, 1984. Fundamental work on the subject. Main topics: secular origins of chivalry, chivalry and the church, knighthood, the tournament, literature, heraldry, nobility, secular orders, pageantry, and chivalry and war.

Kibler, William W., and Grover A. Zinn, eds. *Medieval France: An Encyclopedia*. New York: Garland, 1995. Richly informative reference work. More pertinent to the Hundred Years War than the companion volume, *Medieval England: An Encyclopedia*. Length of entries sometimes misleading (more space allotted to Froissart, for instance, than to Hundred Years War). Excellent article on Flanders. Useful genealogies. Bibliography can be quite specialized.

Kilgour, Raymond Lincoln. *The Decline of Chivalry as Shown in the French Literature of the Late Middle Ages.* Cambridge, MA: Harvard University Press, 1937. Main contribution to fascinating debate on chivalry as reality or ideal. Usefully links late medieval literature to history.

Le Patourel, John. "Edward III and the Kingdom of France." *History* 43(1958), 173–89. Author entertains idea that Edward III was serious about his claim to the French throne. Therefore an important article.

Lightbody, Charles Wayland. *The Judgements of Joan: Joan of Arc, a Study in Cultural History.* Cambridge, MA: Harvard University Press, 1961. First three chapters important for description of Armagnac, Burgundian, and foreign chronicle sources on Joan of Arc.

Margolis, Nadia. *Joan of Arc in History, Literature, and Film: A Select, Annotated Bibliography.* New York: Garland, 1990. Informed selection of 1516 entries. Extends and replaces, for modern use, the monumental French bibliography by Pierre Lanéry d'Arc, *Le Livre d'Or de Jeanne d'Arc*, Paris: Techener, 1894, reprint, 1970. Margolis has keen insights and a forthright, often witty style. Includes sections on chronicle sources, special topics such as bastardy theory and witchcraft, literature, and cinema.

Mollat, Michel, and Philippe Wolff. *The Popular Revolutions of the Late Middle Ages.* Translated by A. L. Lytton-Sells. London: Allen & Unwin, 1973. Authors sometimes underestimate the programs of the rebels by favoring old-fashioned Froissardian view of rebels as operating incoherently. Argument made that these were mostly *not* revolutionary movements, since they replaced men rather than changed institutions. Still, a treasure trove of information on the revolts.

Neillands, Robin. *The Hundred Years War.* Revised edition. London: Routledge, 2001. Better on English history than French.

Nicolle, David. *French Armies of the Hundred Years War, 1337–1453.* Men-at-Arms Series, no. 337. Oxford: Osprey Military, 2000. A glossy picture book paperback. Uncluttered narrative with clear explanations of technical French and Latin terms. Black-and-white manuscript illuminations and color drawings.

A Parisian Journal, 1405–1449. Translated by Janet Shirley. Oxford: Clarendon Press, 1968. Very interesting anonymous journal by Anglo-Burgundian sympathizer in Paris. Hostile to Joan of Arc.

Pernoud, Régine. *Joan of Arc: By Herself and Her Witnesses.* Translated by Edward Hyams. New York: Stein & Day, 1966. Remains the finest introduction to Joan of Arc. Composed of contemporary sources. Technical without being daunting. Author's commentary follows each chapter. Flags important issues. Pertinent (French) bibliography.

Pernoud, Régine, and Marie Véronique Clin. *Joan of Arc: Her Story*. Revised and translated by Jeremy duQuesnay Adams. Bonnie Wheeler, ed. New York: St. Martin's, 1998. English translation of last serious scholarship on the Maid by Pernoud (Régine Pernoud and Marie Véronique Clin, *Jeanne d'Arc*. Paris: Fayard, 1986). Welcome translation of rich volume with appended documents, letters, and biographies (some of imperfectly known historical players). Additions by Adams not distinguished from original work. Should be viewed as Pernoud's addendum to her earlier works.

Perroy, Edouard. *The Hundred Years War*. Translated by W. B. Wells. Reprint, New York: Capricorn Books, 1965. First published as *La Guerre de Cent Ans* in Paris in 1945. A true classic. Engagingly written by very clear and persuasive writer. Part of the flavor comes from caustic thumbnail sketches of the principal players and their actions.

Rogers, Clifford J., ed. *The Wars of Edward III: Sources and Interpretations*. Woodbridge: Boydell Press, 1999.

Schramm, Percy E. *A History of the English Coronation*. Translated by Leopold G. W. Legg. Oxford: Clarendon Press, 1937.

Scott, W. S., trans. *The Trial of Joan of Arc*. Reprint, London: Folio Society, 1968. English translation of French *Minute*.

Seward, Desmond. *The Hundred Years War: The English in France, 1337–1453*. Reprint, New York: Penguin Books, 1999. Interesting book, with special emphasis on military history, written from English perspective. Delightful details such as Christmas presents exchanged between Lord Suffolk (figs) and Dunois (a fur coat) during siege of Orleans. Not a good source for Joan of Arc.

Shakespeare, William. *Henry V*. Gary Taylor, ed. Oxford World's Classics. New York: Oxford University Press, 1982. Accessible play that brings Henry V (and his French bride) to life.

Speed, Peter, ed. *Those Who Worked: An Anthology of Medieval Sources*. New York: Italica Press, 1996. One of three volumes representing the divisions of medieval life: knights, clerics, and peasants. Short selections, in highly readable translations, create a true sense of what it meant to live in medieval times. Full of gems.

Strayer, Joseph R. "France: The Holy Land, the Chosen People, and the Most Christian King." In *Medieval Statecraft and the Perspectives of History: Essays by Joseph R. Strayer*. Princeton: Princeton University Press, 1971, 300–314. Seminal article on sacred kingship, crucial for understanding Joan of Arc era. Scholarly.

Sumption, Jonathan. *The Hundred Years War I: Trial by Battle*. Reprint, Philadelphia: University of Pennsylvania Press, 1999. A 600-page account of the war from 1328 to 1346. The author's strength lies in the wealth of information offered, written in prose that remains enjoyable and interesting. More factual than analytical.

———. *The Hundred Years War II: Trial by Fire*. Reprint, Philadelphia: University of Pennsylvania Press, 2001. Continues the narrative from 1347 to 1369 in another 600 pages. Extensive, but technical, bibliography.

Szarmach, Paul E., M. Teresa Tavormina, and Joel T. Rosenthal, eds. *Medieval England: An Encyclopedia*. New York: Garland, 1998.

Vale, Malcolm G. A. *Charles VII*. London: Eyre Methuen, 1974. A rare study in English on the king to whom Joan of Arc lent her support.

———. *The Origins of the Hundred Years War: The Angevin Legacy, 1250–1340*. Oxford: Clarendon Press, 1996. Examines conditions leading up to Hundred Years War. Author renowned for his work on Gascony and Hundred Years War. Scholarly.

Vaughan, Richard. *John the Fearless: The Growth of Burgundian Power*. Reprint, Woodbridge: Boydell Press, 2002. First published 1966.

———. *Philip the Good: The Apogee of Burgundy*. Reprint, Woodbridge: Boydell Press, 2002. First published 1970. One of four excellent biographies on the four great Burgundian princes. Based on archival sources, these detailed volumes can be challenging but remain nonetheless fascinating.

Warner, Marina. *Joan of Arc: The Image of Female Heroism*. New York: Knopf, 1981. First modern feminist reading of the Maid. Highly readable and always interesting, a cascade of intriguing facts and thoughts. Divided into chapters by theme. A popularization of much of the scholarly research of previous decades. Some notes inaccurate.

Audio and Video

Dreyer, Carl-Theodor, director. *The Passion of Joan of Arc.* With [Renée] Fal-
conetti. Janus Films. Gaumont. Société Générale de Films, 1928. Silent film
on Joan's trial. Arguably the best film ever made on Joan of Arc. VHS video
from Home Vision Cinema: Public Media, Inc., 1999, features Richard Einhorn's *Voices of Light.* DVD available from Criterion Collection.

Einhorn, Richard. *Voices of Light.* Sony Classical. Audio-CD ROM, 1995.
Oratorio inspired by Carl Dreyer's film *The Passion of Joan of Arc.*

Ruiz, Teofilo F. *Medieval Europe: Crisis and Renewal.* Sound recording on audio-
cassette. Springfield, VA: The Teaching Company, 1996. The set contains
eight cassettes on such topics as urban society, hunger, popular rebellions,
politics, and war. Ruiz's engaging style effortlessly draws the listener into the
medieval world. Complicated aspects of the Hundred Years War are reduced
to their simplest terms without sacrificing accuracy. *The Teaching Company*
records the lectures of the most acclaimed American university professors.

Secrets of the Lost Empires II: Medieval Siege. VHS format video. Released 2000.
One of a series of *Nova* videos on ancient science and technology. Focuses
on the modern construction of a medieval siege weapon, the trébuchet.
This war machine launched projectiles that could inflict devastating blows
on castles or fortified towns. [Not seen.]

Wheeler, Bonnie. *Medieval Heroines in History and Legend.* Sound recording on
audio-cassette. Springfield, VA. The Teaching Company, 2002. Lectures
on Joan of Arc, Eleanor of Aquitaine, Heloise, and Hildegard of Bingen.
Wheeler's enthusiasm for Joan and wealth of insights provide an excellent
introduction to the Maid.

Web Sites

General

The Age of King Charles V (1338–1380). Wonderful manuscript illuminations
from the Bibliothèque nationale in Paris: www.bnf.fr/enluminures/accueil.
htm.

CNRS (*Centre National de la Recherche Scientifique, Institut de Recherche et d'Histoire des Textes*). Manuscript illumination site. Click on "visites virtuelles"
to open series of illuminations including kings of France (*Les rois de France*)
and war (*La guerre*): www.enluminures.culture.fr.

De Re Militari: The Society for Medieval Military History. Web site includes extracts from primary sources translated into English. Also extensive bibliography, some articles and book reviews. Site has no visuals: www.deremilitari.org.

The *Internet Medieval Sourcebook* by Paul Halsall, ORB Sources Editor, Fordham University Center for Medieval Studies. Links to electronic texts, film, music, and maps: www.fordham.edu/halsall.

The Labyrinth at Georgetown University. Extensive web site for medieval studies: www.georgetown.edu/labyrinth/.

The Middle Ages Trust Medieval Web Site Locator. An alphabetical index of medieval sites. Contains an array of useful sites not otherwise easy to find: members.aol.com/tmatrust/websites.html.

Netserf: The Internet Connection for Medieval Resources. Visually appealing site with multiple resources: www.netserf.org including impressive *Hypertext Medieval Glossary* with links to related terms in the glossary and sites for further information: www.netserf.org/Glossary.

ORB On-line Reference Book for Medieval Studies at College of Staten Island, CUNY: the-orb.net.

The *Société de l'oriflamme* (a web site in English). Contains excellent links where photographs are plentiful. Useful items: Final phase of the Hundred Years War, nongunpowder and gunpowder artillery, map of Angevin Empire, and site for Battle of Bouvines with organ music (*Les Amis de Bouvines*). xenophongroup.com/montjoie/oriflam.htm. For war chronology: www.xenophongroup.com/montjoie/hywchron.htm.

Joan of Arc

Centre Jeanne d'Arc. Founded in Orleans, France, by Régine Pernoud in 1974. Central clearing house for research on Joan of Arc: www.orleans.fr/jeannedarc/.

The International Joan of Arc Society web site: www.smu.edu/ijas/.

Joan of Arc Online Archive by Allen Williamson: members.aol.com/nywwebsite/private/joanofarc.html.

Saint Joan of Arc Center, Albuquerque, NM, by Virginia Frohlick: www.stjoan-center.com.

INDEX

About the Author

DEBORAH A. FRAIOLI is Professor of Foreign Languages and Literatures at Simmons College, Boston. She is the author of *Joan of Arc: The Early Debate*.